Good Practice with Vulnerable Adults

Good Practice Series

Edited by Jacki Pritchard

This series explores topics of current concern to professionals working in social work, health care and the probation service. Contributors are drawn from a wide variety of settings, in both the voluntary and statutory sectors.

Good Practice Series 9

Good Practice with Vulnerable Adults

Edited by Jacki Pritchard

Jessica Kingsley Publishers
London and Philadelphia

First published in the United Kingdom in 2001 by
Jessica Kingsley Publishers Ltd,
116 Pentonville Road,
London N1 9JB, England
and
325 Chestnut Street,
Philadelphia, PA 19106, USA.

www.jkp.com

Copyright © 2001 Jessica Kingsley Publishers

Library of Congress Cataloging in Publication Data
A CIP catalog record for this book is available from the Library of Congress

British Library Cataloguing in Publication Data
A CIP catalogue record for this book is available from the British Library

ISBN 1 85302 982 3

Printed and Bound in Great Britain by
Athenaeum Press, Gateshead, Tyne and Wear

CONTENTS

For my Mum, June Pritchard, who became very vulnerable recently and was surrounded by abuse and neglect. Also for my grandmother, Dorothy Kendall.

INTRODUCTION

JACKI PRITCHARD

Every human being becomes vulnerable during their lifetime for any number of reasons; they all respond differently to events that happen to them because of who they are and the support (or lack of it) that they have around them. The term 'vulnerable adult' is now used more widely in the social care field than it ever was, but it may be open to interpretation. Being vulnerable means different things to different people. The Collins English Dictionary defines it as: 'capable of being physically or emotionally wounded or hurt; exposed to attack'.

My objective in editing this book was not to consider every aspect of vulnerability, which would be an impossible task for anyone. This book covers issues that I consider to be important currently to practitioners working in a variety of settings across the sectors. Before explaining this further, it is important to define the term 'vulnerable adult'.

A decade ago a vulnerable adult was defined by the Association of Directors of Social Services (ADSS) by client group:

- the elderly and very frail
- those who suffer from mental illness including dementia
- those who have a sensory or physical disability
- those who have a learning disability
- those who suffer from severe physical illness.

(ADSS 1991)

More recently, the Department of Health included the following definition in its new guidance *No Secrets: Guidance on Developing and*

Implementing Multi-Agency Policies and Procedures to Protect Vulnerable Adults from Abuse:

> The broad definition of a 'vulnerable adult' referred to in the 1997 Consultation Paper *Who decides?*, issued by the Lord Chancellor's Department, is a person:
>
>> 'who is or may be in need of community care services by reason of mental or other disability, age or illness; and who is or may be unable to take care of him or herself, or unable to protect him or herself against significant harm or exploitation'

(DOH 2000, Section 2.3)

Since adult abuse has gained a higher profile, there has been much debate about whether a welfare model or a criminal justice model should be adopted. Some practitioners and policy-makers feel that too many mistakes have been made in the child protection field and that we should not adopt the same framework. After the recent death of Victoria Climbié (also known as Anna Climbié and Anna Kouao), child protection systems are likely to come under close scrutiny. I personally disagree with the view that child protection systems are unhelpful in relation to adult abuse. I think many positive lessons can be learnt from the child protection field, but fully acknowledge that there *are* differences between child abuse work and adult abuse work. No decision to date has been made about whether statutory protection will be introduced for mentally incapacitated adults and in the meantime practitioners have to carry on working with vulnerable adults who are being abused or who may be abused in the future. So this is why I wanted to edit this particular book. I felt there was a need to consider current practices rather than regurgitate what has already been written about theory and policy development.

For years I have seen practitioners in all sectors struggling with the practical and ethical dilemmas of working with vulnerable adults. When I began my career in social work in the early 1980s, there was no guidance at all on what to do if an adult was being abused. We have moved on a long way since then. Slowly but surely, work with vulnerable adults is being recognized as an important issue, but it is still not as emotive to society at large as child abuse. The advent of *No Secrets* in March 2000 was a major step forward, in that John Hutton and John Denham, Ministers of State for Health, joined with Charles Clarke, Minister of State for the Home Office, to state:

> Action
>
> The co-ordinating role falls to social services departments and this circular is guidance under Section 7 of the Local Authority Social Services Act 1970.
>
> All agencies will need to collaborate closely on developing their local code of practice so that they can deal effectively with incidents of adult abuse. In doing so they should whenever possible endeavour to _prevent_ abuse from occurring in the first place. The attached guidance explains how to develop the local codes of practice.
>
> Directors of Social Services will be expected to ensure that the local multi-agency codes of practice are developed and implemented by 31st October 2001. The Social Services Inspectorate will be monitoring these arrangements.
>
> (DOH Circular HSC 2000/007)

I welcome the emphasis on preventative work, because it seems that, at the current time, many practitioners only undertake crisis intervention. It is important that all agencies are proactive in taking steps to prevent abuse.

The development of policy and procedures is welcome, but other things need to be put in place at the same time – for example, funding for training of all workers and resources to work effectively with both victims and abusers in the long term.

The literature on adult abuse has increased greatly in recent years and much has been written about policy development and theoretical issues. My objective in editing this book was to address _some_ of the key issues practitioners struggle with; this book could not include _all_ issues related to vulnerable adults who are abused. When I was thinking about editing this book, I first pondered on the dilemmas and issues I work with myself and hear about on a daily basis from other practitioners. I then approached people who I felt had something constructive to say and who would be able to share their views about how to promote good practice. One of my main criteria in commissioning contributors to this book was that they have to be in touch with the real world and understand the difficulties that face practitioners in working with adult abuse.

My hope is that there is something in this book for everyone. The early chapters focus on procedural issues relating to the introduction of *No Secrets* and the Home Office's implementation of *Action for Justice* (Home Office 1999). I am pleased that I have been able to include contributions from a range of professionals to give different perspectives – e.g. police, medical. For a long time I have been concerned that in this country, people who are working in different specialisms (child abuse, domestic violence, adult/elder abuse) do not liaise as much as they could. I believe that they could learn so much from each other, and that it would be advantageous to share experiences and knowledge rather than be precious about having expertise in one particular field. This is why I wanted to give attention to child abuse and domestic violence in this book. I also feel that institutional abuse has been swept under the carpet for far too long. Another hobby horse of mine is that people with mental health problems are not given enough attention when considering adult abuse issues. Very little has been written in relation to their being victims of adult abuse; society often sees them rather as perpetrators. Other issues to which attention is given attention include neglect, alcohol abuse and advocacy.

The implementation of *No Secrets* and *Action for Justice* should promote good practice across the agencies that are involved with vulnerable adults. It will be some time before we see how practice does in fact improve and perhaps alter. In the meantime I hope this volume will be a contribution to encouraging practitioners to take the issue of adult abuse seriously. The chapters will illustrate that effective work can be undertaken to prevent abuse but also that there can be positive outcomes for victims if work is undertaken with them in the long term.

REFERENCES

Association of Directors of Social Services (1991) *Adults at Risk*. Lancaster: ADSS.

Department of Health (2000) *No Secrets: Guidance on Developing and Implementing Multi-Agency Policies and Procedures to Protect Vulnerable Adults from Abuse*. OH Circular HSC 2000/007.

Home Office (1999) *Action for Justice*. London: HMSO.

Lord Chancellor's Department (1997) *Who Decides?: Making Decisions on Behalf of Mentally Incapacitated Adults*. Cm 3803. London: The Stationery Office.

CHAPTER 1

COMMENT ON *NO SECRETS*

GUIDANCE ON DEVELOPING MULTI-AGENCY POLICIES AND PROCEDURES TO PROTECT VULNERABLE ADULTS FROM ABUSE

ADRIAN HUGHES

INTRODUCTION

For some years now many of those working directly with vulnerable adults have stressed the need for specific legislation to protect and, where necessary, take action against perpetrators of abuse. The current range of legislation fails to offer adequate protection and often can only be used when abuse has already occurred or is suspected.

Legislation that applies to crimes against the person and would ordinarily be applicable is often not pursued, either because the victim is a vulnerable adult and therefore considered not to be a credible witness or other witnesses are not available. Understandably the police are often reluctant to become involved and to make things more difficult the Crown Prosecution Service may be unlikely to take a case forward. It may be that with some pressure from social workers or advocates to support the victim in demanding access to the criminal justice system, any obstacles placed by either the police or the Crown Prosecution Service could be overcome. Practitioners should examine their own agendas and determine if the perceived reluctance of the police is in some cases an excuse to avoid themselves or the service user becoming involved in the criminal justice model.

In implementing the *Speaking up for Justice Report* (Home Office 1998), the government has recognized that the present arrangements are failing to protect vulnerable victims. Many court proceedings involving vulnerable victims have been abandoned or have failed to get off the starting block because the witness has been unable or considered to be unable to give his or her account reliably. Furthermore, other witnesses may be reluctant to come forward for fear of reprisal, and this lack of corroboration compounds the problem further. The full implementation of *Action for Justice* (Home Office 1999) should address some of the obstacles that may have discouraged practitioners from supporting service users to access the criminal justice system. This clearly is a positive step in the right direction and is to be commended. In the meantime there is other legislation such as section 127(2) of the Mental Health Act 1983, which sets out clearly the offence of wilful neglect or ill treatment of a mentally disordered person, but this is neither well known nor widely used.

The Law Commission published a report in 1995 on mental incapacity which identified these concerns, stating at the time that the current legislation detailing powers to protect vulnerable adults must be overhauled. Despite a draft bill prepared by the Commission the matter was not taken forward. Following the Labour election victory in 1997 the Junior Minister of Health, Paul Boateng, published a Green Paper entitled *Who Decides?* (Lord Chancellor's Department 1997). This consultation document set out a number of proposals that promoted genuine protection for vulnerable adults but, disappointingly, to date implementation of the key recommendations has not been initiated.

In late 1998 the Department of Health embarked on producing a policy framework to offer greater protection to adults at risk. This culminated in the publication and launch of *No Secrets: Guidance on Developing Multi-Agency Policies and Procedures to Protect Vulnerable Adults from Abuse* by the Health Minister in March 2000 (DOH 2000).

The Minister stated:

> Abuse of people in any setting is unacceptable. The government is taking strong measures to ensure that this cannot and does not happen in the future. We must treat vulnerable citizens with the respect that they deserve. (Department of Health press release, 20 March 2000)

Later in the year the Welsh Office issued an equivalent document, *In Safe Hands* (The National Assembly for Wales 2000), and in broad terms it mirrors a similar policy direction as *No Secrets*. This chapter is specifically concerned with *No Secrets* but many of the comments will apply equally to *In Safe Hands*, and will reflect on the guidance, identifying some of the strengths of the initiative together with some of the weaknesses.

DEFINITIONS

It is recognized that in establishing a legal framework for the protection of adults there will be tensions. The legislation must apply to those who are at risk and perhaps do not have the capacity to protect themselves thus increasing the risk of exploitation. However, at the same time it must not inadvertently bring within the framework those citizens who are not seen as vulnerable adults. Some adults choose to be in relationships that others would consider to be abusive but have made informed choices about doing so. The right to autonomy and self-determination must be protected for all citizens, and any decision to become involved in the detail of the lives of individuals must be undertaken with some caution.

It is therefore helpful that the government has accepted the broad definition of a vulnerable adult, as set out in *Who Decides?*, as a person:

> who is or may be in need of community care services by reason of mental or other disability, age or illness; and

> who is or may be unable to take care of him or herself, or unable to protect him or herself against significant harm or exploitation.

(Lord Chancellor's Department 1997, paragraph 8,7)

This is sufficiently broad to enable practitioners to work effectively with a range of individuals who would be generally described as vulnerable adults. However, it would have enabled practitioners and services to respond more appropriately to a wider range of clients if, rather than one overall definition, 'and/or' was used to link the two components.

Nonetheless, this definition is a useful starting point and should deal with some of the difficulties of the past. There have been incidents in which workers have been reluctant to become involved in specific incidents of abuse because they are not sure that they have a remit. The following case study is an example of this.

CASE STUDY

Pauline is a 24-year-old woman with a learning disability, who has lived with her older brother Steve since the death of their mother. She is not in receipt of any care or support from statutory agencies and has a part-time job in a local supermarket. There is some gossip in the local neighbourhood about the relationship between Pauline and Steve, with suggestions that they may be involved in a sexual relationship although there is no hard evidence of this, only local gossip. A care manager is tasked with arranging to meet Pauline to discuss any support she may require and to attempt to determine if Pauline is at risk. In discussion with Pauline she confirmed that she has a close and supportive relationship with her brother who cares for her, and she would not want their arrangements to be changed. In discussion with key professionals it is decided that as Pauline is not making any allegations of abuse, there is no evidence to prove that abuse is taking place and as she is considered to be making informed choices about her lifestyle, the matter need not be pursued further.

In this example workers did not feel that they had the right to intervene, believing it would compromise the right of the individual to self-determination. The guidance set out in *No Secrets* challenges this notion, demonstrating ways in which multi-agency working and shared values can explore concerns in a more open forum, agreeing ways to offer help and support. It is vital for practitioners working with vulnerable adults to remember that any allegation or concern regarding abuse that may amount to a criminal offence would override the service user's rights to self-determination. If in this example the care manager had any uncertainty as to whether a sexual relationship was taking place she/he would have a duty to report this to the police.

It is important that the response to an incident of alleged abuse is not delayed in respect of people who live in one area but for whom some responsibility remains with the area from which they originated. It will be vital that consideration be given to these situations as part of the locally devised procedures. There may be confusion in respect of service users who are either self-funding or in receipt of preserved rights where workers assume that social services departments do not have any duty to intervene.

Clearly the implementation of *No Secrets* is not the panacea for all suspected incidents of abuse, but it should provide a framework for practitioners and others to work in partnerships with service users, enabling them to maximize protection and safety. A purist interpretation of the definition may result in Pauline in the case study not being considered to be within the scope of the framework as she was not in receipt of community care services but nonetheless as falling within the second element of the definition. Any concern regarding a framework inappropriately intruding into the lives of citizens is unfounded, as it will be integral to any protocol or policy derived from *No Secrets* that refusal of help or input would be respected. It may be the fact that the lead body for the implementation of the framework rests with social services greatly influences the importance of the 'vulnerable adult' definition.

THE CO-ORDINATING ROLE

The guidance document sets out that the development of codes of practice should be co-ordinated locally by each local authority social services department, stating that legal responsibility rests with that agency. It is important to have a body or service to take the lead, but it is of concern that this is assigned to social services. In doing so the government may have inadvertently laid down a marker that abuse of vulnerable adults is a social issue rather than a criminal one. Other forms of abuse may all be criminal acts and therefore the protection offered to the majority of citizens should be extended to ensure that, in the words of the Minister, 'we treat vulnerable citizens with the respect that they deserve' (John Hutton, Department of Health press release, 20 March 2000). Treating with respect must include ensuring that the same level of protection to prevent abuse and adequate redress is available to the vulnerable adult when abuse occurs as to others. The protection of citizens against assault, theft and sexual crimes is not co-ordinated by the social services department in respect of society at large, and therefore the aim to treat vulnerable adults with respect may not be realized. In order to ensure equal treatment the lead might have been given to the police, as this may have fitted more easily with crime and disorder initiatives. In addition it would have given a clear and unequivocal message that the protection of vulnerable adults was higher on the priority list rather than being viewed solely as a social issue. At the risk of labouring the point we cannot and should not underplay the fact that most abuse is of a criminal nature and the fact that the law is not applied to confirm this is a disservice to vulnerable adults.

If *No Secrets* had been implemented under the Crime and Disorder Act 1998 and it was decided that a key strategy was for the prevention and investigation of the abuse of vulnerable adults as part of a overall objective to reduce crime it would have been clear to 'whistle-blowers' and others who witness abuse to report it. This would also result in the categorization of the victim of abuse as a vulnerable adult being less important, and would place the focus on the act of abuse itself, as in crimes against other citizens as 'a violation of an individual's human and civil rights by any other person or persons' (DOH 2000, page 9).

The introduction to the guidance document refers to the Human Rights Act 1998, and any person who is suspected of being abused would be covered by the principles of the guidance. It would still be important for a multi-agency partnership to consider the development and implementation of a policy but the lead role would be with the police. Locating the responsibility for the implementation of *No Secrets* as part of a crime and disorder initiative would fit with the general policy objective, which is set out in Section 6 as the reduction of crime and disorder in the area. In situations of identified abuse in this context the partnerships would be able to set up ways to encourage a more accurate reporting of all incidents of abuse whilst at the same time seeking to reduce the actual number of incidents. In working with the perpetrators of abuse the police would give out a powerful message as to the view of a civilized society. Whilst action against abusers will not necessarily help, or make amends to the victim, it would send out a message that abuse is not acceptable, will not be tolerated and the weight of the law will be brought against perpetrators.

MAKING A DIFFERENCE

If *No Secrets* is to make a difference to the lives of vulnerable adults and offer protection from abuse three key questions must be answered:

1. Is the initiative adequately resourced?
2. Is there a statutory requirement to implement it?
3. Is it robust?

Clearly there is no new money to develop the local framework, so creating new dedicated posts where they do not already exist will be difficult in a climate of budget cuts, overspending and competing priorities. This is a very different scenario to the implementation of the Children Act 1989, as this was heavily funded from central government. The financial investment would suggest that the government was fully committed to the success of the proposals whereas the legislative weakness of *No Secrets* must imply that the same commitment is not present. There is no suggestion on my part that funding to protect children should be reduced but rather that the funding available to promote adequate protection for vulnerable adults should be ratcheted up. This lack of funding will therefore require directors of social services in the main to consider ways in which it can be funded at a local level. This will require that the issue of protecting vulnerable adults is pushed up the policy agenda if it is to compete with the other demands placed on local authority budgets. The Minister in launching the policy was clear that directors of social services will be expected to co-ordinate the development and implementation of local multi-agency procedures, which must be in place by 31 October 2001. The Social Services Inspectorate (SSI) will monitor the multi-agency approach procedures, assessing the way in which they work in practice.

Clearly the message from central government is that there is a duty to implement this policy initiative, which is issued under Section 7 of the Local Authority Social Services Act 1970. This requires local authorities in discharging their social services functions to act under the general guidance of the Secretary of State. In practice this means that the document does not have the full force of statute, but should be complied with unless local circumstances indicate exceptional reasons that justify a variation. The inclusion of *No Secrets* in a performance assessment framework for social services departments and the proposed monitoring by the SSI should demonstrate whether local inter-agency procedures are developed, but only time will tell if there is any demonstrable change in practice.

There will be costs associated with implementation, as the only way to let the public know that abuse of adults is an issue will be through publicity campaigns. However, in reality I fear that the main thrust will be a reactive one focusing on the investigation of abuse rather than the prevention. Avoiding harm and hurt for individuals must be a key objective shared by all those involved in the lives of vulnerable people. It is likely in the present climate that the funding of *No Secrets* at a local level will not be sufficient to respond to both the preventative and investigatory roles.

In assessing the potential robustness of the policy initiative the measurement will be in part the development and implementation of local inter-agency policies and whether they are developed in ways that seek to increase protection rather than focus on the investigative practice when abuse has occurred. The robustness of the policy will be evident if the bulk of investment of time, resources and energy is devoted to educative and preventive measures.

It is important to recognize the importance of the investigation into allegations of abuse, which in the main is to determine who did what, to whom, where and when, and to learn from the experience. However, as I have previously stated, for those who are abused and therefore damaged by the process it may have little if no consequence that the matter is looked into; this neither reduces the pain or the harm caused.

Paragraph 1.2 states:

> The agencies' primary aim should be to prevent abuse where possible but, if the preventive strategy fails, agencies should ensure that robust procedures are in place for dealing with incidents of abuse. (DOH 2000)

Therefore an important and essential role for the new partnerships must be to encourage greater reporting of incidences of abuse whilst at the same time considering ways in which the actual incidents of abuse can be reduced. The new adult protection procedures must have at the heart an educative role to ensure that staff in care settings develop a greater understanding of what constitutes abuse. Staff and managers must understand that which is acceptable and that which is not. However, the plethora of definitions and especially the different ones used in *No Secrets* and *In Safe Hands* could work against this. One strength of *No Secrets* in this regard is that as a guidance document it sets out a framework to support the development of local inter-agency protocols. These could be owned and identified with at a local level ensuring shared and understood protocols across partnerships within a set geographic area. The downside is of course that protection of vulnerable adults could become a postcode lottery, with less importance and therefore fewer resources allocated in some areas. It is vital through publicity to heighten general awareness that adult abuse exists and is unacceptable in the same way as the National Society for Prevention of Cruelty Against Children (NSPCC) Full Stop campaign made statements about children.

TRAINING

The guidance document reminds agencies of the importance of training for staff and volunteers and this is a policy objective with which no one could disagree. It is regrettable that the guidance does not give any indication as to where the financing of such training will rest. As part of the role of regulation or implicit within contracting there could be a requirement for staff to receive training to the level as set out in paragraph 5.2. It is accepted that most care and nursing homes do not have the resources and nor for some the inclination to purchase good quality training. In chapter 6, on the role of the registration and inspection officer, it is noted that staff do not always have an appreciation of what constitutes abuse and within institutions abuse is often denied. In order to ensure that training is provided and is to a required standard it will be essential that a legal requirement specifies the type and quality of training. Under the present arrangements those who are committed to protecting vulnerable adults will continue to do so whilst it is likely that abuse will continue in settings where it is part of the established patterns of behaviour or as a consequence of poor quality care.

In order to make awareness and identification part of the lifeblood of professionals involved with vulnerable adults it will be essential that resources are made available to provide initial and ongoing training for staff at all levels across all agencies. It is essential that working partnerships with shared values, priorities and mutual understanding are fostered and developed. Shared training opportunities are a key way in which to achieve these goals. Without central funding the bureaucracy of pooled budgets is likely to result in each agency only training its own staff.

It would be helpful if the training that is currently being provided for staff in the criminal justice system including the police as part of the implementation of *Action for Justice* (Home Office 1999) was extended to other agencies. This could include all those who work with and respond to vulnerable adults who are the victims of abuse.

The recommendations in *Action for Justice* include the development of extensive guidance for practitioners including a memorandum of good practice for interviewing vulnerable adults. Practitioners at all levels will need opportunities to explore the memorandum and practise new skills in safe settings prior to having to utilize the skills and learning in the real environment. It will be a disservice to victims of abuse to be used as 'guinea pigs' for untrained workers to learn on the job.

In order to fully support vulnerable adults without unnecessarily intruding into their lives practitioners will need to understand the importance of risk assessment and what it means in practice. They will require detailed and proper training to explore and understand how risk assessment is balanced with the rights to self-determination and autonomy without compromising either the individual's safety or the agency's duty of care. *No Secrets* reminds us:

> assessment of the environment, or context, is relevant, because exploitation, deception, misuse of authority, intimidation or coercion may render a vulnerable adult incapable of making his or her own decisions. Thus, it may be important for the vulnerable adult to be away from the sphere of influ-

ence of the abusive person or the setting in order to be able to make a free choice about how to proceed. (DOH 2000, p.11)

Practitioners may not instinctively be able to work through these complex issues and dilemmas, and with proper training and opportunities to explore and discuss them with other key professionals these skills can be developed.

It is worthy of note that the first chapter of *No Secrets* includes a credible and informative overview of abuse issues including definitions, problems responding to and dealing with abuse and some action that can be taken. This opening chapter is recommended to any manager or training officer to facilitate practitioners in further understanding the nature and pathology of abuse. It is helpful that in the document the definitions of the six categories of abuse are included:

- **physical abuse**, including hitting, slapping, pushing, kicking, misuse of medication, restraint, or inappropriate sanctions;

- **sexual abuse**, including rape and sexual assault or sexual acts to which the vulnerable adult has not consented, or could not consent or was pressured into consenting;

- **psychological abuse**, including emotional abuse, threats of harm or abandonment, deprivation of contact, humiliation, blaming, controlling, intimidation, coercion, harassment, verbal abuse, isolation or withdrawal from services or supportive networks;

- **financial or material abuse**, including theft, fraud, exploitation, pressure in connection with wills, property or inheritance or financial transactions, or the misuse or misappropriation of property, possessions or benefits;

- **neglect and acts of omission**, including ignoring medical or physical care needs, failure to provide access to appropriate health, social care or educational services, the withholding of the necessities of life, such as medication, adequate nutrition and heating; and

- **discriminatory abuse**, including racist, sexist, that based on a person's disability, and other forms of harassment, slurs or similar treatment.

(DOH 2000, p.9)

However, whilst the remainder of the guidance is perhaps not written in a way that is so easily accessible to practitioners, being geared more to managers and planners to devise the procedures, it could be used as part of a training course to explain the overall objectives and underlining principles. In addition there are some useful reminders for practitioners with quotes such as: 'an initial rejection of help should not always be taken at face value' (p.11).

> 'harm' should be taken to include not only ill treatment (including sexual abuse and forms of ill treatment which are not physical), but also the impairment of, or an avoidable deterioration in, physical or mental health; and the impairment of physical, intellectual, emotional, social or behavioural development. (p.12)

These may appear obvious but serve as useful reminders that dealing with and responding to abuse has no easy answers or blueprint for action.

INVESTIGATION

As previously indicated the investigation is important but it must not be at the expense of good preventative work. The guidance document is littered with terms concerned with prevention but it is light on any definitive statements as to what action is expected or could be taken in this regard. The guidance suggests that the framework could mirror that of area child protection teams but does not go as far as making this a requirement. One of the main difficulties in allocating staff to respond to allegations of abuse is that the role is often a bolt-on to existing posts, and therefore urgent work has to be fitted in or worked around the main roles and responsibilities of the worker.

The procedures set out in the guidance document with regard to the framework for reporting and investigating are essentially sound but would in my view require designated staff to pick up the referral and co-ordinate a response. By developing referral teams it would be possible to ensure consistency of approach, with all those involved rapidly learning the standards of behaviour and conduct below which no one should fall. The provision of intensive training similar to that provided by area child protection committees would be invaluable. Any ad hoc arrangement coupled with a lack of adequate financial resources will inevitably lead to inconsistency and individuals making judgement about what constitutes abuse and what does not.

No Secrets has sought to address some of the shortfalls as identified in the Longcare inquiry (Bergner 1989). A private company comprising primarily a husband-and-wife team provided the Longcare homes in Buckinghamshire. Despite concerns regarding the suitability of the individuals providing the care, the way in which the homes operated and a number of inconclusive investigations, the abuse of clients went undetected in the homes for a number of years. The report, detailing the findings of the investigation into the two homes following the conviction of the owners, identified that in the early stages of the abuse investigation the main activity was undertaken by the police. The police mounted a criminal investigation that involved collecting evidence, interviewing witnesses, identifying other witnesses, collecting and analysing records. In the meantime the homes continued to operate and clients continued to live there. The subsequent report was critical of this, stating that the involvement of the police does not suspend the legitimate role of other agencies.

It is important that in reading and interpreting the guidance practitioners do not take the statement 'Criminal investigation by the police takes priority over all other lines of inquiry' (DOH 2000, p.10) to mean that their role is suspended. This is clarified by the later comment that 'police investigations should proceed alongside those dealing with the health and social care issues' (DOH 2000, p.28). The guidance places the primary duty for the protection of vulnerable adults with social services whilst the police would focus on the investigation with a possibility of criminal prosecution. This is in accordance with the lessons of Longcare.

The importance of reporting concerns regarding abuse to the relevant authority cannot be overstated. As with Longcare the abuse of vulnerable adults was undetected but apparently known about for some time. In chapter 6 on the role of the registration and inspection officer I refer to the fear staff sometimes have in reporting abuse. There is a fear of personal reprisals, that they will not be believed, listened to, that the alleged perpetrator is too powerful or that the staff have been threatened with dismissal if they breach confidentiality with a third party. The implementation of the Public Interest Disclosure Act 1998 has in part addressed this. Whilst it is often referred to disparagingly as the 'whistleblower's charter' it does provide a safe way for individuals to raise concerns. Any suspicion of abuse could be reported in line with Section 43B(d) Public Interest Disclosure Act 1998 which provides for workers to report suspicion that the health or safety of any individual has been, is being or is likely to be endangered. In reporting the concerns in line with the legislation the worker would be freed from the threat of detriment such as the termination of employment.

THE GUIDANCE

The document contains further chapters giving advice on:

- setting up an inter-agency framework
- developing inter-agency policy
- the main elements of a strategy
- procedures for responding in individual cases
- getting the message across.

The main thrust of the guidance is the focus on developing inter-agency working, which must be at the heart of protection.

There is evidence to demonstrate the positive working partnerships between social services, the health service and the police, but it is also recognized that these partnerships have not always been easy journeys. The lessons from child protection legislation have shown that the greatest investment of time and resources are targeted to the investigation. Clearly there is work in protection issues such as the guidance to child care providers regarding safe recruitment practice and the various lists maintained by the Department of Health. However the bulk of work is reactive rather than proactive.

In developing the partnerships to ensure the implementation of *No Secrets* it is important that some of the lessons from child protection legislation are learned. An emphasis on investigative practice means that someone is 'hurt or harmed' before any action is taken. In order to avoid this it will be essential to ensure that the key professional disciplines involved not only recognize and understand the respective roles and responsibilities of other partner agencies but also explore a shared value base and language. One example of this is the word 'abuse', which does not in itself describe any crime. A report made to the police of alleged or suspected financial abuse does not alert them to allocate officer time to look into the possibility of theft or fraud. The term 'abuse' in this example tends to reduce the potential crime to the status of a welfare issue, which is the traditional remit of social services. Whilst recognizing that time and resources for social services are stretched it must also be noted that the police and health service colleagues have the same pressures, and the police will at times have to prioritize competing demands.

CONCLUSION

There are disappointments and concerns with the content of *No Secrets*, which audits by the Department of Health over the coming years may address. It is important to note the many positives arising from this initiative which will not in themselves prevent abuse. It will require imagination and creativity on the part of key players to make sure that the intention of the government is realized in practice. This is not to damn the guidance with faint praise but to recognize that staff working with vulnerable adults have had to be imaginative in the absence of robust legislation. It is often as a result of the commitment, creativity and imagination of individuals that the rights of vulnerable adults to be citizens free from abuse and harm, and with access to justice are not compromised.

The National Assembly for Wales in publishing *In Safe Hands* has reminded practitioners of the context in which adult protection policies should operate. Policies should not be seen as separate to or as a substitute for good care practice. The creation and maintenance of safe services must have clear standards, particularly in respect of difficult and sensitive matters such as challenging behaviour, sexuality and restraint. Adult protection policies must be part of an overall package that sets the tone for safe services, including policies on issues such as medication, handling clients' money, whistleblowing etc. The organizations in which staff work must have open and effective human resource management policies in place. Extremes of isolation must be avoided as research has shown these lead to abuse occurring and remaining unchallenged over time. Staff must be monitored, supervised and accountable. These ideas are equally applicable to the work of practitioners in England, and it is unfortunate that it was not spelled out in the same detail in *No Secrets*.

I am generally confident that in this context there will be positive outcomes for vulnerable adults but I cannot and do not underestimate the uphill struggle in some parts to make the guidance work. Perhaps the reviews and monitoring by the Department of Health coupled with lessons learned following implementation will result in revisions to the guidance. This will mean that locally agreed procedures are developed and refined to ensure positive work towards good preventative approaches. Where it is necessary for investigative action this should be free from unnecessary bureaucracy and artificial demarcation in the roles and responsibilities of the agencies involved.

REFERENCES

Bergner, T. (1989) Independent inquiry, Department of Health. London: HMSO.

Children Act 1989. London: HMSO.

Crime and Disorder Act 1998. London: HMSO.

Department of Health (2000) *No Secrets: Guidance on Developing Multi-Agency Policies and Procedures to Protect Vulnerable Adults from Abuse*. London: HMSO.

Eliot, T. S. (1945) *The Hollow Men. Poems Of Our Time*. London: J. M. Dent and Sons.

Home Office (1998) *Speaking up for Justice Report on Vulnerable or Intimidated Witnesses in the Criminal Justice System in England and Wales*. London: HMSO.

Home Office (1999) *Action for Justice*. London: HMSO.

Human Rights Act 1998. London: HMSO.

Law Commission (1995) *Mental Incapacity* (Report Number 231). London: HMSO.

Local Authority Social Services Act 1970. London: HMSO.

Lord Chancellor's Department (1997) *Who Decides? Making Decisions on Behalf of Mentally Incapacitated Adults*. London: The Stationery Office.

Mental Health Act 1983. London: HMSO.

Public Interest Disclosure Act 1998. London: HMSO.

The National Assembly for Wales (2000) *In Safe Hands*. Wales: Social Services Inspectorate.

CHAPTER 2

HARD CARE

THE ROLE OF AN ADULT PROTECTION UNIT AND CO-ORDINATOR

MIKE LINNETT

BACKGROUND AND DEVELOPMENT

In 1989 Gloucestershire, like all other local authorities, was attempting to prepare itself for the advent of NHS and Community Care Act 1990. In the midst of these preparations an event occurred that precipitated later formation of the Adults at Risk Unit (to become the Adult Protection Unit). The event in question was the death of Beverley Lewis – a 23-year-old black girl with severe physical and learning disabilities. Beverley was found dead in squalid conditions in the front room of her mother's house on an estate in Gloucester. She appeared to have been starved and neglected to death while in the care of her mother – later found to be suffering from mental illness herself.

Beverley was well known to both health and social services, who had over the years attempted to provide care and support for her both informally and formally. There was intense local and national media coverage of the case at the time and an inquest was conducted. The coroner, after an extensive hearing, found that no individual member of staff involved had acted improperly and that they had performed their care tasks within their role. However, concern was expressed that the information that staff from individual agencies held was not shared and that co-ordinated working did not appear to have taken place. It was soon after this finding that the Social Services Inspectorate visited the county and instructed the authority to look at ways of preventing such a tragedy in future.

The response was predictable and traditional – a multi-agency working party was convened to develop procedural guidelines. The working party was made up of executive managerial representatives from the LMC (Local Medical Council – general practitioners), social services, registration and inspection, the two health service Trusts in the County (representatives from Learning Disability, Mental Health, Older People and Physical Disability Services), the health authority, County Legal Services, Gloucestershire Police, Gloucestershire branches of the National Schizophrenia Association, MENCAP, Royal National Association for the Blind and Royal National Institute for the Deaf, health and social service fieldwork representatives from relevant disciplines.

It was recognized early on that, although Beverley was the trigger, other groups of adults were vulnerable and because of this vulnerability, could be at risk of abuse, exploitation or neglect. Hence the target group was defined as vulnerable adults consistent with the NHS and Community Care Act – i.e. frail elderly, learning disabled, mentally ill, physically disabled and the sensorily impaired who are at risk of abuse, exploitation or neglect. The working party took Child Protection Procedures as their reference point and produced *The Gloucestershire Multi Agency Procedural Guidelines for Adults at Risk* in late 1989. These guidelines were accepted by the Social Services Inspectorate (SSI) and adapted and adopted by the Association of Directors of Social Services (ADSS). The working party felt that their brief had been fulfilled.

However, two years later (1991 – the year of transitional grants) the SSI returned to the county to examine the effectiveness of the procedures. Their conclusion was that the implementation of the procedures had been limited in effect and usage, so asked the county to look again. It was as a result of this request that the social services department created the Adults at Risk Unit and the post of assistant principal officer, Adults At Risk (see Appendix 1 for job description) to head it up – the initial task being to review and then to implement the procedures.

The timing and direction of the SSI intervention was a big factor in creating the response achieved and in directing attention to the plight of vulnerable adults in the community, but in view of the political climate and direction of governmental thinking at the time, political needs as well as those of individual vulnerable adults possibly had a bearing on the thoroughness of the SSI.

On creation of the Adults at Risk Unit, a new multi-agency working party, with representatives from statutory and voluntary agencies in the county, was convened under the chairmanship of the assistant principal officer. Its purpose was to review the procedures with a view to increasing their usage and effectiveness. The review was completed in late 1991, published and implemented in February 1992.

UNIT OPERATION

The working party concluded that it was necessary for the assistant principal officer to take a lead hands-on role in delivering the service and the postholder became responsible for the implementation and delivery of the service. This included the convening and chairing of all case conferences in the county – invitations and minutes delivered by the unit. The assistant principal officer was to offer a central consultation, advice and co-ordination point to all agencies and others involved in working with vulnerable adults at risk of abuse, exploitation and neglect. The unit was to develop and deliver multi-agency training, collect data on the incidence and nature of referrals, compile and monitor statistics. Annual reports were to be produced outlining the operation of the unit and including year-on-year statistics. The unit was also responsible for the promotion and development of the service. Plus a few other bits and pieces! An independent user satisfaction survey was commissioned and published in 1996 (Payne 1996). The assistant principal officer became the co-ordinator in 1996 and a further co-ordinator was appointed in June 1999.

How the service operates is shown in Figure 1.1. Throughout this process, a number of cases 'drop out' at each stage either because enquiries show the vulnerable adult is safe, or because advice and assistance that control the risk is accepted. In the year 1999/2000 approximately one in eight referrals went to conference.

A vulnerable adult is suffering abuse, exploitation or neglect

★

Someone recognizes or suspects this abuse, exploitation
or neglect

★

A referral is made to the social services duty officer or the police
(notify Adult Protection Unit)

★

Enquiries are made and investigation begins –
results discussed with Adult Protection Unit

★

If, after discussion between the investigating officer and the
adult protection co-ordinator, it is considered that
the vulnerable adult has been abused or is at significant
risk, an Adults at Risk conference is held.
(convened and chaired and minuted by Adult Protection Unit)

★

If the conference decides the vulnerable adult remains at risk,
his/her name is placed on the Adults at Risk register, a care plan
and actions are agreed and a key worker appointed.

★

The situation and registration are reviewed regularly
at conference (maximum six monthly)

★

When it is deemed at review that the vulnerable adult is no
longer considered to be 'at risk' or the risk is being managed,
the name is removed from the register.

Figure 1.1: Adult Protection Service

Although there is no formal list of conference attenders – adults may not be involved with any service – as a matter of course those always invited are:

1.   the individual

2.   the individual's informal carer (if the individual wishes)

3.   the individual's general practitioner

4.   County Legal Services

5.   Adult Protection Secretary

6.   Adult Protection Co-ordinator

7.   the investigating officer

8.   Team/line manager – social services

9.   Service manager – health

Other potential attenders to be invited may include formal and informal carers, relatives, advocates, interpreters, home care, agency carers, police, psychiatrist, community psychiatric nurse, district nurse, health visitor, day care and persons in a position to provide care and support or provide information on the risk. The prime thrust of the unit is to try to provide a platform from which to offer a response to ensure the safety and care of the individual.

The following chart gives a snapshot of attenders at 30 case conferences:

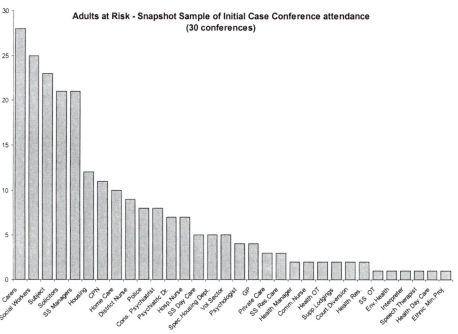

Adults at Risk - Snapshot Sample of Initial Case Conference attendance (30 conferences)

The full impact of the Human Rights Act 1998 on the registration process is yet to be fully clarified. However, the issue has been raised in the past and the advice has been that, if an individual is considered to be at risk, the local authority should recognize this under its duty to care and take whatever steps possible, with due regard to individual rights and choice, to attempt to minimize this risk. Registration can be seen as a tool enabling formal multi-agency recognition of risk.

I would go further and suggest that the disabling and disempowering effects of abuse need positive intervention and recognition of the seriousness of the problem allied to the importance of the abused individual. Formally registering this concern can be a way of demonstrating respect for the individual and a step on the way to the accessing of rights through enablement.

DAY-TO-DAY ACTIVITIES

The time of the co-ordinator(s) is primarily dedicated to five main areas of work:

- consultation/advice
- convening and chairing case discussions
- convening and chairing case conferences
- monitoring service/statistic gathering
- development and delivery of training.

Consultation/advice

All cases perceived to be at risk are referred to the unit, usually after the referrer has discussed it with their line manager. Referrals from the public can be made directly to the unit or to the social services duty officer. The case will be discussed to ascertain whether or not the criteria are met, and appropriate responses and means of managing the risk will be considered. The philosophy of the service is consistent with sensitive and proper consideration of civil rights, and respects the principles of self-determination and 'least disruptive alternative'. It is frequently possible at this stage to devise and implement actions and plans that are acceptable to the individual and minimize the risk. This process may well be maximized by the fact that the co-ordinator(s) are the central point of referral for the whole county and a pool of expertise and knowledge has developed with experience. In 1999/2000, 397 referrals of Adults at Risk were made to the unit, 305 of which were managed at the consultation stage. All referrals to the unit are recorded along with actions taken, thus sharing responsibility with those directly involved in service delivery. This, according to feedback, is reassuring to those providers, hopefully supporting them in working confidently and in concert with their service users without considering restrictive action to 'cover their backs'.

A number of these consultations are with workers who have assessed the situation, and have developed a response but wish to ensure they have considered all the options and alternatives – a full professional and totally valid use of the service. The consultation/advice aspect of the work is the main consumer of the time of the unit.

Convening and chairing case discussions

In the early stages of the implementation of the service, it was recognized that some referrals of concern were not resolvable at the level of advice and consultation, nor was a case conference appropriate. These referrals took a variety of forms – perhaps the criteria were not fully met or the condition of the vulnerable adult indicated that, although risks were managed at present, predictable changes could precipitate unmanageable risk. At times it was indicated that, in order to devise a risk management strategy, a formal meeting of those involved in providing care was necessary to devise a risk response strategy. The service responded to this need on a pragmatic basis but a further need was highlighted by the 'coal face' workers. As the word 'risk' was part of the description of the service, those involved in care and service delivery began to refer individuals they felt to be at risk as a result of their behaviour, i.e. the manager of a residential unit for people with learning disabilities referred a resident he was extremely concerned about. It was felt that the resident was at risk of harm from others and/or arrest. The reason for this was that the resident had been observed watching children from the local school and apparently masturbating in a covert way. He had also occasionally gone missing on his way back to the unit from his day centre and there had been reports that he had made sexual approaches to children when this happened. The members of the public who reported this were threatening to 'take the law into their own hands'.

The manager felt that this presented a risk to the resident of physical injury as a result of his behaviour. However, it seemed that the people really 'at risk' were children. Equally, the staff of the unit also felt a high degree of stress in exercising their responsibility to care for a resident who presented a danger to the public – a dilemma for all involved, with no apparent means of formally addressing the situation.

In view of the fact that no other forum appeared to exist, the unit pragmatically agreed to convene a multi-disciplinary/agency case discussion with a view to discussing and developing a risk management plan and address the issues raised by this case which appeared to be both fish and fowl – the potential perpetrator and victims both being 'vulnerable'.

A 'case discussion' was duly convened by the unit. Those invited were clinical psychologist, Learning Disabilities; residential unit manager; day centre manager; specialist social worker, Learning Disabilities; county legal services; general practitioner; community policeman; and the consultant psychiatrist, Learning Disabilities. The resident was invited to attend the meeting after an initial discussion between the professionals to devise a strategy and response.

During the discussion information regarding the resident's previous sexual behaviour, unknown to the residential unit or day centre, came to light. This new information and the previous responses assisted in the formulation of a risk management plan that was then discussed with the resident. It comprised a series of actions:

1.   It was made clear to the resident that if he persisted in inappropriate sexual behaviour towards children, he would not be able to remain at the home.

2.   The consequences of his behaviour could result in prosecution.

3.   A full reassessment by the Learning Disabilities Team would be undertaken with a view to therapeutic intervention.

4.   Sexual counselling would be undertaken by the clinical psychologist.

5.   National Association for the Protection from Sexual Abuse of Adults and Children with Learning Disabilties (NAPSAC) [now the Ann Craft Trust (ACT)] and RESPOND to be contacted for advice to inform counselling and assessment.

6.   Resident to take the (escorted) transport to and from day centre.

7.   Residential home to maintain vigilance and offer one-to-one support to the resident until therapeutic interventions implemented and assessed.

8.   Key worker – specialist social worker – to be appointed

9.   The issue of people with learning disabilities who present a risk to others to be brought to the attention of the Departmental Management Team.

10. Review to be held in three months.

The above were all discussed with the resident and accepted by him. It did appear that he was aware of the consequences of his behaviour and was keen to avoid prosecution. He responded well to the input over time and seems to have learned ways to manage his behaviour – over the last four and a half years. Oddly enough he also appeared to look forward to the reviews – possibly to demonstrate his achievements.

This case was the first to highlight an ongoing problem whereby vulnerable adults presented a risk of harm to others, but it did not remain isolated – cases of this nature cropped up at the rate of one or two a month. It was as a result of referrals and requests from the 'front line' for assistance in this difficult area that the unit developed another aspect to its work – the Multi-Agency Risk Assessment and Management Project (MARMAP) in 1998 with the help of Mental Illness Specific Grant (MISG) funding.

Cases of this nature are now dealt with in this forum. In the year 1999/2000, 75 'Adults at Risk' case discussions were held and 24 under the MARMAP umbrella. Case conference convention takes approximately 1½ hours including invitations, the discussions themselves, with extra time for travelling.

Convening and chairing case conferences

In the year 1999/2000, 57 initial case conferences were held and 61 review conferences. The purpose of the conference is to identify the risk and its causes as far as is possible, registration of the individual as being at risk and the devising of a care plan to manage the risk, and the appointment of a key worker. The conference platform also has to recognize that the vulnerable individual may not wish to accept all or any aspect of the care offered and may, as a result, continue to live in a risky situation. The individual has the right to do this, unless it is proper to consider formal intervention (i.e. under the Mental Health Act 1983), but it is incumbent on the conference to fully inform the vulnerable adult of the perceived risk and its potential consequences to enable choice to be as fully informed as possible. This respects the rights of the individual but also recognizes that with rights go responsibilities. In these particular circumstances, it is important that the care remains on offer and that any aspect that is agreed to continues to be delivered. The conference process can therefore be supportive in these cases to the workers whose role is accepted, allowing them to work with the individual on their self-determining terms.

The conference is constructed to be as 'user friendly' as possible but it must be acknowledged that formal meetings can be inhibiting. To try to inform and demystify as much as possible, the referring officer outlines the reason for and the purpose of the conference. An explanatory leaflet (see Appendix 2) is sent to the subject and carer(s) with the invitation to attend – this may be delivered personally by an involved worker. There is always an attempt to arrange the venue with the agreement of the subject – the meeting can be held in the home if this is the most comfortable and convenient arrangement for the vulnerable adult.

The chairperson always offers to see the vulnerable adult for a few minutes before the conference in order to give the individual a chance to meet the chair and ask any questions regarding the process or their concerns. The conference runs, as far as is possible, to a written agenda and is minuted by the Adult Protection Unit. A copy of the minutes is sent to all who attend.

The process itself involves, after introductions, presentation and discussion of the factors and evidence of risk, consideration of registration, care/risk management plan and identification of providers, appointment of key worker and date of review. Whilst the role of most attenders is apparent, the solicitor from County Legal Services is there to provide advice regarding registration and any legal interventions or actions that may be appropriate for either conference or the vulnerable adult to consider.

To follow the issue of involving the vulnerable adult in formal meetings and the feeling that this may be a disabling experience suggests that, although conference participants are frequently nervous, the fact that the meeting is for and about them has the potential to empower – this is particularly important for people who may have been disenfranchised by virtue of vulnerability amplified by abuse. I would also add that, to make plans about individuals without involving them fully in the process, could be considered patronizing, possibly in contravention of their rights and likely to be unsuccessful as the best laid plans can only work with the agreement of the subject of those plans.

Doubts have also been expressed regarding the question of registration, but it is worth remembering that Adult Protection Conferences are not about victims and perpetrators, they are about risk reduction/management. If a criminal offence has occurred and action is sought by the vulnerable adult, the police will follow this up at the request of the individual or conference. The conference is an attempt to exercise the duty to care, and recognition and registration of concern is part of this. I would suggest that, when conferences are held (with or without the vulnerable adult), conclusions are reached as to whether or not there is a risk. Do conference participants not then record this on their files and if they do is this a form of undercover registration? Dare I also suggest that registration is also a formal statement to the vulnerable adult that the effects of abuse, exploitation and neglect are being taken seriously, and so are they. The effects of long-term abuse on self-esteem are well known and best countered by empowering the subject of the abuse.

A case that illustrates the process and perhaps some of the points above involved a 53-year-old blind physically disabled woman, Mrs C, who lived with her 15-year-old son. A social worker for the blind and a mobility officer were working with the woman to try to maximize her living skills. Their efforts were somewhat hampered by Mrs C frequently not being able to see them when arranged or not able to work with the mobility officer as she had hurt herself. These injuries were, she said, as a result of not being able to see and being unsteady on her feet, bumping into things or falling. The social worker attempted to set up regular day care as part of the care plan and also attempted to get clearer details about the falls with a view initially to an occupational therapist (OT) assessment. Mrs C became increasingly reluctant to talk to the social worker, and increasingly unavailable when the social worker called, and rejected OT input.

The concerns were discussed with the Adults at Risk Unit and it was agreed that it was necessary to monitor the situation via the mobility officer. She frequently noticed marks on Mrs C. Polite questions of concern as to how they were caused were again met with vague explanations. The mobility officer kept the social worker informed but was unable to gain any real understanding of why the injuries were happening until calling and finding Mrs C in great distress with a large (six-inch long) deep cut on her face. She blurted out that she had had a row with her son and he had struck out at her with a stick. After attempting to get Mrs C to see her doctor or attend A & E, which she adamantly refused, the mobility officer, after settling Mrs C, told her that she had to report the incident, under the Adults at Risk procedures, to the social worker. The social worker duly called to investigate the situation and Mrs C still upset and apparently a little fearful said that it was 'one of those things that happens in the heat of the moment' and it had never happened before or would again. The social worker asked if Mrs C wished to take any action about what had happened but she was vehement that she did not want to. She did not wish to see the doctor, nor would she let the social worker see her son.

The social worker explained that she had a duty to report the incident to the Adults at Risk Unit and on return to the office, did so. It was agreed that the incident certainly fell within the criteria for physical injury and warranted a case conference.

The conference was duly convened and Mrs C did reluctantly attend. However, she retracted all she had said about her son hitting her, saying she had made it up. She refused to consider any legal action or contact with her son, insisting there was nothing to worry about, but was tearful and nervous.

After discussion, conference felt that there was a risk that warranted registration and did so, although Mrs C was not keen. She was also advised of her rights to make a statement to the police, of support available for her son (he had been known in the past to child care) and of her rights under civil law. None of these courses of action were acceptable to her and she insisted there was no need as things were all right. Supports were also offered to Mrs C in an attempt to encourage her to spend time away from the house at a day centre and a weekend drop-in centre. The mobility officer would continue to offer a service, and home care could call to assist with some of her personal care tasks. Mrs C accepted the offer of the day centre and the mobility officer but nothing else. In view of Mrs C's vulnerability, the severity of the injury and past observations there was a high level of concern at the limited nature of the protection acceptable to Mrs C. A review was therefore set for one month's time.

At this review it transpired that further bruising had been noted at the day centre and Mrs C had admitted that they had been caused by her son 'but he doesn't mean it'. This and the previous incident were discussed and Mrs C did confirm that the previous injury and bruises had been caused by her son as well as the most recent ones. She insisted that he did not do it intentionally and that it was just teenage behaviour. She denied that she was in fear and did not want any action to be taken, nor did she think her son would want to see anyone as he would think they were trying to make him go to school! It transpired that he had been school refusing for the past six months.

Conference maintained Mrs C's name on the register and yet again went through the legal and civil options open to her, stressing their concerns for her safety. She was offered respite care in addition to the services already available and social work input for her son. Mrs C accepted all these offers but with the condition that she would not make her son see the social worker.

Conference still felt a high degree of concern and because of the uncertainties and the recent incident, arranged a further review in four weeks' time. A further incident of injury (a black eye) occurred shortly before the review. Attempts had been made by the child care social worker to see Mrs C's son but were unsuccessful – the boy locking himself in his room and yelling obscenities at the social worker from behind the door. It was noted that his yelling had a rather bizarre content.

At this review, Mrs C volunteered that she was afraid of her son and had been for a long time. However, she felt that 'he can't help it – he is very mixed up'. Despite this she was beginning to feel that she dare not stay in the house with him any longer. After thorough discussion of his behaviour and actions, it was felt that her son may have some mental illness. Mrs C herself felt this but did not want him 'taken away and locked up' but felt he needed help. Mental Health Act interventions and her rights as nearest relative were explained and she, as a result, requested an assessment under the Mental Health Act. This was duly carried out and her son was found to have an acute psychosis warranting admission. He was assessed and treated and later placed, with his agreement, in properly supported accommodation. Mrs C and her son see each other regularly but no longer live together. There have been no further incidents of assault and Mrs C works as a volunteer two days a week in a local charity shop.

As an aside, to effect the Mental Health Assessment, it was necessary to involve the police, as the son became threatening and violent, again locking himself in his room. When access was gained, he threatened the police with a long-bladed knife – nine other weapons were found in his room, including a crossbow.

The above case history is obviously summarized but gives, I hope, the flavour of the case. It was very noticeable that the insistence of the conference that what happened to Mrs C was of grave concern and importance had an effect on her perception of her self, enabling her to take action to protect herself.

Mrs C later was a major contributor in the compilation of the Adults at Risk user/carer leaflet (see Appendix 2).

Monitoring service/statistic gathering

The unit provides a service for the whole of the county and all contacts are recorded with a view to monitoring need and incidence. One advantage of being a central reference point is that, when compiling information, trends and needs are sometimes indicated by the nature of referrals – different areas and agencies may feel that they have a 'few' cases of difficulty or concern but are not necessarily aware that similar problems are emerging in other areas or disciplines. The unit, in having an overall picture, can sometimes identify areas for action that otherwise may be plugged away at on an individual basis. The aforementioned MARMAP project is one instance, but equally a small but insistent number of cases of victims of abuse who were not able to provide sufficient evidence to enable court action led to the unit setting up a working party to devise a protocol with all agencies and the police, to maximize access to justice for the learning disabled – also used for other vulnerable groups. It was also noted that many referrals of cases of self-neglect in older people involved alcohol, which led to the unit doing research on alcohol and older people. The results of this research are now the basis of an intended education and response programme.

In the five years 1994/5 – 1999/2000 the unit has processed 1755 consultations comprising:

957 Elderly

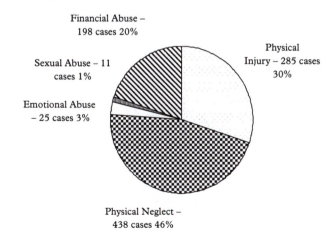

Financial Abuse – 198 cases 20%

Sexual Abuse – 11 cases 1%

Emotional Abuse – 25 cases 3%

Physical Injury – 285 cases 30%

Physical Neglect – 438 cases 46%

279 Learning Disabled

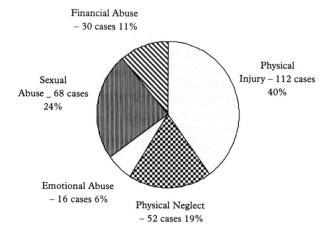

Financial Abuse
– 30 cases 11%

Physical
Injury – 112 cases
40%

Sexual
Abuse _ 68 cases
24%

Emotional Abuse
– 16 cases 6%

Physical Neglect
– 52 cases 19%

213 Physically Disabled

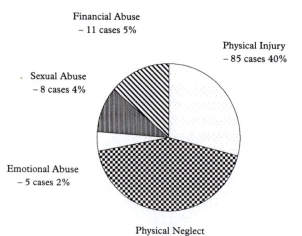

Financial Abuse
– 11 cases 5%

Physical Injury
– 85 cases 40%

Sexual Abuse
– 8 cases 4%

Emotional Abuse
– 5 cases 2%

Physical Neglect
– 104 cases 49%

214 Mentally Ill

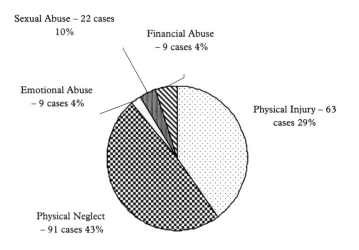

Sexual Abuse – 22 cases 10%

Financial Abuse – 9 cases 4%

Emotional Abuse – 9 cases 4%

Physical Injury – 63 cases 29%

Physical Neglect – 91 cases 43%

33 Sensory Impairment

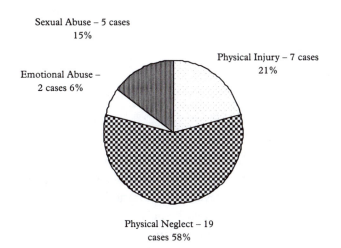

Sexual Abuse – 5 cases 15%

Physical Injury – 7 cases 21%

Emotional Abuse – 2 cases 6%

Physical Neglect – 19 cases 58%

Referrals of Adults at Risk to the unit have increased by 83 per cent in the past five years. In the same period 216 initial case conferences were held, 275 review conferences and 259 case discussions. Statistics are contained in annual reports (copies available at Adult Protection Unit, Gloucestershire Social Services, Shire Hall, Gloucester GL1 2TR. Tel. 01452 425109).

Development and delivery of training
In the process of creating the procedures and the unit, it was recognized that, to make the service responsive and effective, it was necessary to educate and train people in the nature of the problem and responses to it. The unit was accordingly charged with responsibility for delivering and developing appropriate training. At the time, there was little expertise and little money and so the unit developed a basic awareness programme, more intensely combining this with investigation and response and use of procedures. Initially, the training was delivered to professional staff in health and social services but it has moved on to include the voluntary, statutory and private sectors.

As time has gone on, customized courses have been delivered in response to individual establishments in relation to their need. Additionally, events and circumstance have thrown up areas of uncertainty related to vulnerable adults and so training has been developed in an effort to respond – i.e.
- capacity and related issues
- use of Section 47
- vulnerability and abuse in learning disabilities
- alcohol and older people
- awareness for advocates, amongst others.

Last year the unit delivered training to a cross spectrum of caring staff – 584 people in all. Alongside this, since the advent of MARMAP, the unit has developed training in risk assessment and management in conjunction with social service and health training sections and probation. Thirty courses have been run in the year 1999/2000, ranging from two full-day multi-agency courses through to half-day and evening sessions for assorted voluntary and user groups. The unit also inputs into a variety of multi-agency reference and steering groups.

CONCLUSION

Since the publication of *No Secrets* (DOH 2000) in March 2000 there has been a surge in requests to the unit for information about the work it does coinciding with a large number of co-ordinator posts being advertised nationally. It is perhaps therefore a time for reflection on the changes in my role since its inception. Definitely the biggest change has been in the workload (a vast increase). The reasons for this must be many and varied – awareness that there is a service, training and publicity etc., but resource issues must also play a part. Social services' department budgets, which have become increasingly stretched, have been rationalized, amplifying the burden of carers, both formal and informal. The staff of caring agencies are also feeling vulnerable and looking to 'cover their backs', particularly in the light of the growth of the potential for litigation and the need to balance budgets. As a result, the 'defensible decision' aspect of conference has assumed greater importance. The aspect of staff support has over time asserted itself as a vital part of the job – staff who are feeling insecure may well look to take the most obvious (and possibly restrictive) course of action, i.e. residential care. To find real solutions it is necessary to work *with* the vulnerable adult; trust, honesty and an unbiased approach are vital in this process.

There has also been a persistent increase in the development of the role of the unit in providing the co-ordination of initial investigations at the request of those involved – the provision of a central point of reference has provided unforeseen benefits in communication and development of services – the 'Access to Justice Protocol' being an example of this.

As for the future, the growth in the number of Adult at Risk co-ordinators will hopefully begin to provide compatible services across the country. However, in looking at the job descriptions and the few contacts I have made, the role of co-ordinator varies widely from the 'enabling' hands-off to a dedicated team of investigators with all shades in between. It seems unlikely that there will be consistency of service around the UK by October 2001 as outlined in *No Secrets*, but hopefully the increased numbers will offer new perspectives, ideas and responses.

Locally, the main thrust of work has been directed towards response to and management of risk. However, it is now time to consider means of prevention, that is, with financial abuse, the education and training of the staff of financial institutions (banks, building societies, post offices etc.) and in recognition of indicators of financial abuse and means of response, education of the public generally in the nature of abuse of adults. Education of the public and professionals in proactive responses to alcohol abuse in older people can be achieved using leaflets easily and readily available on shop counters etc. Further accent on the rights and responsibilities of all adults (which includes the vulnerable) using the awareness of the Human Rights Act – empowerment is the best protective tool.

Finally, I am unable to judge the comparative effectiveness of the Gloucestershire procedures in relation to others as there are few similar approaches and data is limited. However, risks over the years have been addressed and managed and I would like to think that if these procedures were in place at the time perhaps Beverley Lewis may have benefited from the following statement: 'Everyone has the right to live in freedom and safe from harm' (Article 1 of the National Council of Civil Liberties (NCCL) summary of The Universal Declaration of Human Rights).

Appendix 1

GLOUCESTERSHIRE COUNTY COUNCIL
JOB DESCRIPTION

Department SOCIAL SERVICES	Section	
Job Title ASSISTANT PRINCIPAL OFFICER (ADULTS AT RISK)	Grade PO 38 – 41	
Work Location SHIRE HALL	Post No.	

JOB PURPOSE

To promote the implementation of the Adults at Risk Procedures within the Social Services Department and all other appropriate agencies.

To convene and chair all conferences called under the Adults at Risk Procedures.

MAIN DUTIES AND RESPONSIBILITIES

1. To convene and chair all conferences called under the Adults at Risk Procedures.

2. To promote the implementation of the Adults at Risk Procedures across all appropriate agencies.

3. To work with other statutory and voluntary agencies to ensure and promote multi agency working with Adults at Risk.

4. To assist in the design and delivery of multi agency training in respect of work with Adults at Risk.

5. To provide a resource of expertise in respect of work with Adults at Risk and the implementation of the Adults at Risk Procedures.

6. From time to time to lead a multi agency review of the Adults at Risk procedures, under the guidance of the Principal Officer.

7. To be a member of the Child Protection and Adults at Risk Unit.

8. To undertake specific work and projects concerned with Adults at Risk as directed by the Principal Officer.

Appendix 2

Care Services in Gloucestershire
Information Sheet

AI

Adults at risk

A service for vulnerable adults

Information for service users and carers

This information sheet tells you what the Gloucestershire "Adults at Risk" procedures are, why they have been developed, how they work and how they apply to you. It has been written in consultation with service users and people looking after them (carers).

Recently it has become clear that there are adults who are particularly vulnerable due to age, physical disability, mental illness, learning disability or sight and hearing disabilities. Sometimes this can create special risk of neglect or abuse for these people. The care they need can be stretched to breaking point, creating such a risk.

At the moment there is no special legislation to protect and help vulnerable people, except in extreme circumstances. It is usually thought that adults are able to protect and care for themselves.

However, Gloucestershire County Council Social Services Department now feels that it must give special support to adults who are at risk to help them to keep themselves from harm. The "Adults at Risk" procedures are an attempt to do this.

The procedures

If a vulnerable adult is found to be living in a situation where they are at risk (of physical injury, neglect, financial abuse, or sexual abuse) a professional worker will call to investigate the situation, taking into account the feelings and wishes of the individual and/or carer.

The situation may be resolved at this point but if not, a conference (meeting) will be called. It will decide whether the person is at risk and, if so, whether they should be 'registered' with Social Services. The meeting will also develop a 'care plan' to try to reduce the risk.

A written record of the meeting is sent to everyone involved.

The registration and care plan will be looked at again after a suitable time - never longer than six months.

Questions

Do the procedures have legal standing?
No, they are an attempt to co-ordinate help and ensure good practice.

Can I refuse to participate?
Yes, there is no wish to impose on your civil rights.

What about confidentiality?
The procedures are strictly confidential and only the people involved in the conference will know any of the information. If someone else requests information, they must get permission from the conference.

Can I ask someone to represent/support me?

Yes, you can ask a friend or advocate to help you or a Solicitor if you wish. If you have a communication difficulty or English is not your first language, we can provide an interpreter. Ask your Social Worker of Care Manager about this.

What help can I get to enable me to attend the meeting?

If you prefer, the meeting can be held at your home or at a venue of your choice. We can provide transport if you have difficulty attending. If you need it, we can arrange a sitting service whilst you attend.

Who is involved in a conference?

You and your carer (if you wish) a chairperson, a note taker, a solicitor (for legal advice to all), your G.P. (if possible), a social worker, a social worker manager, a health service manager and any other person who is providing direct care or support. Advocates, interpreters and relatives may also attend.

What can the conference do?

It can make a recommendation to register the risk and suggest legal action if appropriate. The meeting will make a 'care plan' with you and your carer (if you wish) to try answers to problems and minimise risk.

Can the conference force me to take action, legal or otherwise?

No, it can only advise or recommend - it takes away none of your rights.

Is the conference looking to blame someone for the risk?

No, it is not a court and is not making judgements. It is there to give help to people at risk and the people looking after them.

What is put on the register?

Your name, address, age, the name and address of your carer, the name and address of your GP and Social Worker, the nature of the risk and the arrangements for your care and any special needs you may have (communication, for instance).

What is it for?

To make sure that you get appropriate help in an emergency. The register is held centrally and it is confidential.

Do I have to be registered?

In most cases, no. But, if the conference members are very concerned about the risk to you, the Conference may register without your agreement. You can make an appeal against this.

Will I have a record of the meeting?

Yes, you will get a copy of the minutes (notes) and recommendations in a form which you will be able to read and understand (your own language, large print or Braille, for instance). If you cannot read, someone will read them to you and answer any questions you may have.

We hope that this information sheet will answer some of the questions you may have but more information is available from your local Social Services Office and the 'Adults at Risk' Unit. A copy of the procedural guide is also available at your local library.

Useful addresses

Social Services

Social Services Area Offices
(see the panel on page 52)

Adults at Risk Unit
Social Services Department, Shire Hall. Gloucester GL1 2TR. Tel: (01452) 425109/425157

Interpreting and Translation

Black and Ethnic Minorities Mental Health Project
Tel: (01452) 387744

Tapestry
(for Gloucester City) Contact Mr. Suleman Patel. Tel: (01452) 396909.

Language Line
11-21 Northdown Street, London N1 9BN. Tel: (0171) 520 1430
Advice on access to interpreters is also available from:

The Institute of Linguists
Saxon House, 48 Suffolk Street, SE1 1UN Tel: (0171) 940 3100 (between 9.00 and 5.00)

The London Interpreting Project
20 Compton Terrace, London N1 2UN. Tel: (0171) 359 6798

Hard of Hearing and Deaf People

Gloucestershire Deaf Association
Tel: (01452) 372999.

Royal National Institute for the Deaf (RNID)
South West, 13b Church Farm, Gorston, Bath BA2 9AP. Tel: (01225) 874460

Independent Service
Wessex Interpreting Unit. Tel: (01225) 874460

Advocacy

Contact your social worker or care manager for advice/referral or:
Quality in Advocacy Scheme (QuAd), c/o Gloucestershire Advocacy Trust, 9 Russell Street, Stroud, Glos., GL5 3AB
Some Citizen's Advice Bureaux also offer advocacy.

How to get in touch

Social Services

Bourton-on-the-Water Office
(Home Care & Care Management) Salmonsbury House, Station Road, Bourton, GL54 2EP. Phone: (01451) 821015

Cheltenham Office
Sandford Park House, 39/41 London Road, Cheltenham, GL52 6XJ. Phone: (01242) 532500

Cheltenham Office (Hesters Way)
(Housing & Social Services) Edinburgh House, Coronation Square, Cheltenham, GL51 7SA. Phone: (01242) 532500

Cotswold Office
The Old School, 47 Lewis Lane, Cirencester. Phone, 01285 881000/Fax: 01285 881059

Dursley Office
Boulton Lane, Dursley, GL11 4LJ. Phone: (01453) 760500

Forest Office
Dean House, Station Street, Cinderford, GL14 2JF. Phone: (01594) 820500

Gloucester Office
Quayside House, Quayside Wing, Gloucester. Phone, 01452 426000/Fax: 01452 425148

Stow-on-the-Wold Office
Victoria House, Sheep Street, Stow-on-the-Wold, GL54 1AA. Phone: (01451) 832272

Stroud Office
Health Centre, Beeches Green, Stroud, GL5 4BH. Phone: (01453) 760500

Tewkesbury Office
Church Street, Tewkesbury, GL20 5SW. Phone: (01684) 275852

South Tewkesbury Office
Elmbridge Court, Gloucester GL3 1AG. Phone: (01452) 410345

Cheltenham General Hospital (Social Work Team)
Sandford Road, GL53 7AN. Phone: (01242) 273052

Gloucestershire Royal Hospital (Social Work Team)
Great Western Road, Gloucester, GL1 3NN. Phone: (01452) 528555

*You can use **Language Line** telephone interpreting service in all main Gloucestershire County Council Offices Housing Services*

Housing Services

Cheltenham Borough Council
Municipal Offices, The Promenade, Cheltenham, GL50 IPP. Phone: (01242) 262626

Cotswold District Council
Trinity Road, Cirencester. Phone: (01285) 643643

Forest of Dean District Council
The Council Offices, The Directorate of Housing and Environmental Services, High Street, Coleford, GL16 8HG. Phone: (01594) 810000

Gloucester City Council
Herbert Warehouse, The Docks, Gloucester. Phone: (01452) 522232

Stroud District Council
Ebley Mill, Westward Road, Stroud. Phone: (01453) 766321

Tewkesbury Borough Council
Council Offices, Gloucester Road, Tewkesbury. Phone: (01684) 295010

Health Services

For general enquiries about health services, please contact:

Gloucestershire Health
Victoria Warehouse, Gloucester GL1 2EL Phone: 01452 300222

Severn NHS Trust
Rikenel, Montpelier, Gloucester GL1 1LY. Phone: 01452 891000

East Gloucestershire NHS Trust
1 College Lawn, Cheltenham GL55 7AG. Phone: 01242 222222

Gloucestershire Royal Hospital
Great Western Road, Gloucester GL1 3NN. Phone: 01452 528555

Gloucestershire Ambulance Service Ambulance Trust
Horton Road, Gloucester, GL1 3PX. Phone: 01452 395050

The numbers for Hospitals, Health Centres etc. are listed in the Business Section of the telephone directory under "H" for Hospitals. Doctors are listed by name.

If you need urgent medical care that cannot wait until normal surgery hours, you can get emergency treatment at any time from your GP, the ambulance service or the Accident and Emergency department nearest to your home.

This information sheet is available in Braille, large print and on computer disc and audio tape. Phone GUiDE Information Service on (01452) 331131 for details.

A complete list of these information sheets is available in the booklet "Community Services in Gloucestershire" from GUiDE.

Gloucestershire Social Services, Gloucestershire Health Authority and District Councils. June 2000. The information in this leaflet is correct at the time of printing.

01452 331131

http://www.gloscc.gov.uk/socialservices

REFERENCES

Department of Health (2000) *No Secrets: Guidance on Developing and Implementing Multi-Agency Policies and Procedures to Protect Vulnerable Adults From Abuse.* London: HMSO.

Gloucestershire County Council (1992) *The Gloucestershire Multi Agency Procedural Guidelines for Adults at Risk.* Gloucestershire: Social Services Department.

Gloucestershire County Council (1993/4 to 1999/2000) *Adults at Risk Unit Annual Reports.* Gloucester: Social Services Department.

Human Rights Act 1998. London: HMSO.

Mental Health Act 1983. London: HMSO.

NHS and Community Care Act 1990. London: HMSO.

Payne, J. (1996) *Gloucestershire Adults at Risk Procedure: Its Effectiveness for Users and Carers.* Gloucester: Gloucester Social Services Department (available from the Adult Protection Unit, Social Services, Shire Hall, Gloucester, GL1 2TR).

CHAPTER 3

What Is Good Interviewing in Adult Abuse Work?

A Police View

Steve Kirkpatrick

INTRODUCTION

I have been a police officer for 25 years. For the last ten years I have
worked as a detective inspector; to begin with as crime manager of a
busy police area, then in charge of three police Family Protection
Units, and now currently as a deputy senior investigating officer with
the Thames Valley Police Major Crime Unit, Loddon Valley,
Reading, predominantly investigating murder. Throughout my
service I have been on numerous courses with officers from all
around England and Wales, but during the last two years in
particular, I have attended many courses and modules to develop in
the role of senior investigating officer. On all of these courses there
has been a good mix of course participants from all around the
country. I have also been involved in the training of police, social
services, education, health, crown prosecutors and other
professionals at various times.

It is an everyday occurrence for me to have to develop interview
strategies and advise officers on the best approach to any interview
they are about to carry out. On occasions I am still required by my
line managers to interview significant suspects or witnesses, and
these interviews have been critiqued by them.

I therefore believe that I have a good idea of what good
interviewing is, but I stress that what I write in this chapter can only
ever be my opinion. I set out good principles of how I believe the best
evidence can be obtained during interviews, and my comments

should be read in conjunction with the codes of practice and advice set out in *Speaking Up For Justice* (Home Office 1998), *Action for Justice* (Home Office 1999) and *No Secrets* (DOH 2000). There will no doubt be other publications issued during the next few years, some being advisory and some being legislative.

The role of the police will change as the recommendations are phased in over the next few years. The police will be required to video record interviews of more witnesses and victims, particularly those who are considered vulnerable or intimidated. This will have an impact on police resourcing and training.

It is not yet known to what extent these interviews will be carried out on a joint basis but *No Secrets* recommends 'a properly co-ordinated joint investigation will achieve more than a series of separate investigations' (Para 6.10). Unfortunately, there will inevitably be different local practices when deciding whether to investigate an allegation jointly with social services or whether to carry out a single agency investigation. Likewise, the decision whether to mount a prosecution or not may differ from area to area with each Crown Prosecution Service. Much work is done to standardize good working practices by organizations such as the Association of Chief Police Officers, but decisions reached in an individual case are bound to reflect the individuals involved and the dynamics of the agencies working together in partnership.

The main strategies for professionals should be:

- to build up good working relationships with local police
- to discover the thresholds of local crown prosecutors before a caution or a prosecution will be undertaken.

KEY SKILLS OF A GOOD INTERVIEWER

Whether an interviewer is a police officer or not, the skills of a good interviewer will always remain the same, whatever the context of the interview.

Good interviewing involves:

- *Discovering the truth about a given situation or set of circumstances.* An interviewer will have a certain task in mind, which will generally be to establish what a person has to say about a situation or an event. It might be that the person being interviewed is not able to provide any information or will not wish to provide the information. Impartiality is crucial. If the interviewer is not open to the possibility that the circumstances may be different to what is understood, the truth will not be established.

CASE STUDY 1

I interviewed a man on suspicion of abduction and rape of a woman. Witnesses had made statements that they had seen the man drive off in his car accompanied by a woman. She had been abducted from a women's refuge. The woman was seen to be screaming and shouting. The other people had been unable to stop him, despite having tried to smash the windows of the car as the man drove off. This occurred at 1.30 in the morning. The woman later telephoned the police and informed them that she had been raped in a lay-by out of town, and then abandoned.

The man had previously been interviewed by police for several similar incidents with other women. He had so far escaped charge.

During the interview he pleaded his innocence. I asked him for his version of the events. He stated that the woman had gone willingly with him. She had only screamed and shouted because she was not meant to be seeing him and she might have lost her place at the refuge. He said that they had gone for coffee at a local hospital restaurant, normally reserved for hospital staff, where he and the woman had sexual intercourse together. According to the man she was very willing. The man was charged with rape and abduction due to the overwhelming evidence and was remanded in custody.

My mind was open to the possibility that the man was telling the truth and made further inquiries. The man's story was verified. Not only did the man know the correct security code to gain access to the hospital restaurant but two night porters were traced who had watched the sexual act out of voyeurism. The account they provided to the police was the witnessing of an intimate and consensual act and not a rape. The rape had not, therefore, taken place in a lay-by in the countryside. The man was released from custody.[1]

---

1   This is the only false rape claim I have come across in my working life, so it is not intended to be a representative sample of this type of crime investigation – rather it is used here to emphasize the importance of not having preconceptions in interviews with clients.

- *Being non-leading.* The interviewer should phrase the questions so as to not suggest an answer. This is because some subjects will provide answers that they believe the interviewer wants to hear in order to pacify them, or provide an easy response. Questions that promote an answer of 'Yes' or 'No' should be avoided, as should questions that provide alternative responses for the subject to choose – for example 'Did she hit you on the arm, or the body or leg or somewhere else?' As a general rule, leading questions will produce unreliable answers, even if the subject is strong-willed, highly educated and intelligent.

- *Having empathy.* The interviewer needs to show an understanding and sympathetic approach to the subject who is being interviewed. It is not necessary for the interviewer to like the subject but if the subject detects that s/he is not liked then this will produce difficulties for the interviewer in establishing the truth. The more the interviewer is able to display that he is interested in the subject, the more successful the interview will be, and the more likely that the subject will speak freely.

- *Positive non-verbal communication.* If the interviewer uses inappropriate body language whilst interviewing, this will produce unnecessary barriers to the interview. The interviewer should be conscious that they project interest in what the subject is saying by the open way they are sitting and responding with other parts of their body. For example, the interviewer's arms should never be folded, nor should the interviewer yawn or look at their watch or clock.

- *Active/reflective listening.* This method involves repeating a key word used by the subject to encourage more information and it shows that the interviewer is listening. For example the subject might say, 'she stopped me going outside' and the interviewer might simply mirror, 'Outside?'. This sometimes produces more explanation of how the subject was prevented from going outside.

- *Being non-confrontational.* Use of P.E.A.C.E. (discussed in detail below).

- *Detailed knowledge of a suspect's rights as contained in the Codes of Practice and the Police and Criminal Evidence Act 1984.* If a person is a suspect, then any infringement of these rights by *any* person in authority could prevent a later admission to police being allowed in evidence. This infringement could be where a suspect is not cautioned, or offered an inducement or incentive to tell the truth, or denied direct access to a solicitor. If the police are likely to become involved it is imperative that any questioning is left to them.

- *Good working knowledge of the criminal law in relation to criminal offences and points to prove* (see Appendix 1).

- *Knowledge of the rules of disclosure of material as contained in the Criminal Procedure and Investigations Act 1976 and 1996.* All material coming into possession of the police or viewed by the police may have to be disclosed to the defence at a future trial. The police have to prepare a schedule of all material, sensitive or otherwise, and bring to the attention of the prosecutor any material that might undermine a prosecution case.

THE APPROACH TO THE INTERVIEW

Gathering evidence from vulnerable adults by interview is one of the more difficult tasks for the police investigator. If the vulnerable adult is unable to communicate properly because of dementia or because of severe learning disabilities, some would say that such a task is impossible.

If a crime has been committed against a vulnerable adult and there are no outward signs, it is imperative that they are able to communicate clearly and convincingly to a jury as to what has happened. Without this the criminal case cannot proceed. At the present time the criminal justice system does not allow the Crown to call psychological or psychiatric evidence to support the reliability of a witness's evidence, or to interpret what the witness is really saying.

Before interviewing a vulnerable adult the police and the social services need to make some hard decisions. The key test is whether it is believed that the vulnerable adult will make a credible witness before a jury. If this is not so, and, the vulnerable adult has no clear and unequivocal way of communicating, it is probably best that an investigative interview is not conducted. There are other ways in which evidence of a crime can be gathered without the need to call the evidence of the vulnerable adult. The investigative interview only really works for a vulnerable adult who has some level of communicative ability and can state verbally what has happened to them.

Action for Justice, in the next few years will implement the recommendations from *Speaking up for Justice.* Definitions of those who may be vulnerable are contained in the Youth Justice and Criminal Evidence Act 1999. Special Measures may be used for those who are vulnerable and this includes being able to video record their interview and present it to the court as their 'evidence in chief'. *Action for Justice* recommends a phased approach to the interview which is similar to the way a child or young person is interviewed in accordance with the current *Memorandum of Good Practice on Video Recorded Interviews with Child Witnesses for Criminal Proceedings* (DOH/HO 1992).

In some circumstances the police can decide whether to mount a prosecution or not. If the police decide to prosecute then the decision must be reviewed and endorsed by the Crown Prosecution Service at the earliest opportunity. They will examine all the evidence contained in the case papers. The way in which the decision is reached is contained in detail in *The Code For Crown Prosecutors* (CPS 1994; also Appendix D in Archbold 2000). The decision-making process, known as the evidential test, is quite involved. The crown prosecutors must first be satisfied that there is enough evidence to provide a 'realistic prospect of conviction'. In reaching this decision they must decide whether the evidence is reliable and can be used in the courts. Finally, the crown prosecutors should consider whether it is in the interest of the public to prosecute. The more serious a case, the more likely it is that a prosecution will be needed in the public's interest.

The aim of any interview is to obtain an account in an uninterrupted and non-leading manner which should then be gently tested by an open style of questioning (National Crime Faculty 1996). Any inconsistencies in the account should be carefully investigated in other ways and not by any aggressive interviewing of the vulnerable adult. This approach will apply whether the crime committed is a theft, or one of neglect, or a physical assault, but more so if the crime is of a sexual nature.

In any investigation it is best to allow the person interviewed to explain what has happened first of all without any questions being asked. Questions at an early stage can distract the subject from providing vital evidence and take them off on a different tack. Experience has also shown that interruptions can contaminate the evidence and confuse the subject about what has happened to them. This is obviously even more likely if the subject is an adult with learning disabilities or dementia.

If the vulnerable adult is unable to communicate in a way which would be clear to a jury, it may be decided that the vulnerable adult should be interviewed using communication tools or interview aids. No such communication tools should be used if they will produce an interview that involves closed or leading styles of questioning. Graphic diagrams depicting sexual acts are leading interview aids. They will not be accepted in a criminal trial and may result in the case being discharged, even if there is other supportive evidence. (For further discussion of styles of questioning, see below.)

If there are a number of possible victims of sexual abuse in a residential establishment or a day care centre, then it is important that the victims are first approached in an open and impartial manner. The following have been held to be good sound principles to follow by the criminal courts and by police investigators:

- Agree joint strategies with social services as to how the investigation is to be conducted.
- Clearly document in policy, and repeat to investigators at verbal briefings and in writing, that the intention is to thoroughly de-brief the subject concerning their time spent at the residential home or day centre, and their relationship with all members of staff. (If a victim is questioned about a particular member of staff it is likely that this will be held to be suggestive and leading.)
- Build up confidence and trust between the joint team and the subject, thereby providing them with an opportunity to disclose abuse if it has taken place.
- Ensure that the approach to all possible victims is co-ordinated to take place at the same time so that no one has an opportunity to discuss matters with anyone else.

CASE STUDY 2

R v C 1999

C had been convicted of serious sexual offences and the man-slaughter of a 14-year-old male.

He was known to have been step-father to four children in the 1970s. When previously interviewed by police in 1991, he refused to provide their surnames making it impossible to trace them.

A new investigation was set up in 1998 as a result of a television programme and information came into police possession providing the details of a surname. The current addresses of the four step-children were located. Strategies were put into place to make a co-ordinated approach to all four victims at 3.00 pm on 24 November 1998.

The police inquiry teams were given a full briefing and issued with an operation order clearly stating the following:

1. The aims – to de-brief the subjects concerning their activities, antecedents and associations with C and to build up their confidence and trust, providing them with an opportunity to speak about possible abuse if they wished.

2. The police were not to make any suggestion that the subjects may have been abused.

3. Each inquiry team was issued with a flow chart as to the type of questions that could be asked. This was prepared together with a chief crown prosecutor.

4. The police were to use the P.E.A.C.E. model style of interviewing.

5. The police were not to discuss criminal injuries compensation at any time.

6. Everything was to be clearly documented and timed.

Two of the men approached disclosed serious persistent sexual abuse over a number of years. C later pleaded guilty to these offences at the Crown Court and received two life sentences of imprisonment. The careful and considered approach to the victims by the police was one of the reasons why the prosecution case succeeded.

- On no account should the question of criminal injuries compensation be mentioned or discussed at any time until after the case has been dealt with at court.

STYLES OF QUESTIONING

Open style

This is the best form of questioning and consists of questions of the type, 'Who?', 'What?', 'Where?', 'When?' and 'How?'. The questioning should never interrupt the flow of the free narrative of the subject. Questions such as 'How did he do this?', and 'What happened next?', are the best type of questions to use in order to keep the subject talking freely. Questions such as, 'What colour was the car?', and 'What time did this happen?', will interrupt the subject's flow and may cause the subject to lose their train of thought. Questions that tend to do this should, therefore, be avoided and not used until absolutely necessary.

Leading style

This is the worst kind of questioning and should never be used in an investigative interview. It will produce evidence which cannot be relied upon, or facts which will always be questionable because of the way they have been obtained.

Examples of such questions are:

'Did he take your wallet?'

'Did she hit you in the face?'

These type of questions would be better phrased in the following way:

'How was your wallet taken?'

'Please tell me, how did you get that bruise on your face?'

Video interviews

Where an interview is video recorded for court purposes there is a different type of leading questioning that should not be used. Such video interviews are currently used in a case involving violence, or threats of violence against a person under the age of 14 years, and in cases of sexual assault against a person under the age of 17 years. In the future, legislation is expected to cater for such an interview, in certain circumstances, with a vulnerable or intimidated witness, and with all children under the age of 17 years, no matter what the crime is under investigation.

Action for Justice states:

Criteria for video recording an interview

Section 21 of the Youth Justice and Criminal Evidence Act creates three categories of child witnesses:

(i) Children giving evidence in sexual offence cases;

(ii) Children giving evidence in cases involving an offence of violence, abduction or neglect; and

(iii) Children giving evidence in all other cases.

(Home Office 1999, p.15)

Vulnerable or Intimidated Adults

(i) ... It is imperative therefore that investigators establish at an early stage whether the adult witness is likely to qualify for Special Measures direction under the 1999 Act (Youth Justice and Criminal Evidence Act) and if so, of what particular Measures, if any will assist the witness to maximise the quality of their evidence. This will need to be discussed with the witness to ascertain their views.

(Home Office 1999, p.3)

These Special Measures include being able to video interview the witness but this should only be carried out if it is believed the video will be allowed by the court as the witness's *evidence-in-chief*. In my opinion, even if there is doubt, it is likely to become good practice to video interview a vulnerable witness. If the video is not allowed the consideration will then be whether the witness can give evidence in person in court. This is not the best way forward as the witness will then have to remember and repeat the evidence which they have already given during the video interview. An impossible task for some vulnerable witnesses, you may think.

A video interview undertaken in such circumstances and which is accepted by the court will be played at the court hearing as the *evidence-in-chief* of the witness. The video itself is then accepted by the court as a 'document'.

In Crown Court a barrister is not allowed to 'lead' the witness, who is giving their *evidence-in-chief*, to any facts that have not already been proved in court. These Crown Court rules apply to all video interviews, and the interviewer must therefore be careful not to mention any facts unless the witness brings these facts into the interview. For example, it might be known to the interviewer that the subject was locked in his room, but the question, 'Tell me about the time you were locked in your room?' is a leading question unless the subject mentions it first.

Most police forces have special adapted interview suites where children can be video interviewed. Some of these are currently used to video interview vulnerable adults. These suites are normally a house or set of rooms away from a police station. They are normally decorated and equipped with soft furnishings to create a user-friendly and relaxed environment for the witness. There is normally a lounge area to interview witnesses. This room or a separate room will be equipped with clearly visible video cameras to record the interview. One of the cameras will be capable of panning, tilting, zooming and focusing by remote control; the other will be fixed with a wide angle lens to show the whole room.

In an adjoining room there will be the monitoring equipment consisting of a twin deck video tape recorder, a television monitor and remote control. The person carrying out the monitoring will be capable of communicating with the interviewer via a radio-controlled ear-piece. (N.B. These facilities and the way interviews are carried out and monitored do vary between different areas in England and Wales.)

A video interview will greatly assist the Crown Prosecution Service in assessing the credibility of a vulnerable witness. It is my experience that more cases have gone to court as a result of the witness's testimony being recorded on video.

THE NATIONAL P.E.A.C.E. MODEL

The stages of the police investigative interview are almost the same whether for a suspect or for a witness, and they follow what is known nationally as the P.E.A.C.E. model. All police officers undergo training in how to interview using the P.E.A.C.E. model. Of the investigations in which I have been involved we actively remind detectives to interview both witnesses and suspects according to this model. P.E.A.C.E. is a mnemonic for:

1.   **P**lanning and Preparation

2.   **E**ngage and Explain

3.   **A**ccount Clarification and Challenge

4.   **C**losure

5.   **E**valuation.

1. Planning and Preparation

Planning and Preparation for the interview is vital. It helps to know the background of the person being interviewed, but care should be taken not to form any conclusions beforehand. The interview should take place where it is best for the subject and not where it is best for the interviewer. The venue can be chosen in conjunction with those who know best, such as the social worker or family.

The police will carry out as much research as possible on the person who is to be interviewed. This is the case whether the subject is a witness or a suspect. The following will therefore be considered:

- The age, gender and domestic circumstances; cultural background; educational background and intellectual ability; physical and mental health; previous contact with police; any recent experiences with the police.
- Legal requirements: how and where to interview if the subject is a suspect; the use of appropriate adults to act in the best interests of the subject; non-contamination of evidence – could the interviewer be said by the courts to have a vested interest and therefore make the interview unreliable in the view of the courts? If the interview is to be undertaken on a joint basis, perhaps with social services, it is best not to use the subject's social worker for the joint questioning, although it is all right for this social worker to be present to act as a supporter or to act in the interests of the subject.

- Points to prove or disprove: if there appears already to be an allegation amounting to a criminal offence: whether the subject is a witness, victim or an offender the interviewer should know about how to prove, from the knowledge the subject has, the *mens rea* (the intent), the *actus rea* (the act), and the *modus operandi* (the method). If the right questions are not asked the evidence can be ruined or the evidence the subject has will not be brought out.

- Disclosure of evidence: if the subject is a suspect, the police have to decide what evidence should be disclosed to the solicitor. Some of the facts in police possession might be withheld in order to test the veracity of the information held by the interviewer without influencing the subject, but generally a solicitor is given as much information as possible so that the subject can be best represented.

- Practical arrangements: deciding the location of the interview, making the room conducive to the interview; deciding which role each interviewer will have; checking the equipment; planning the time of the interview, its duration, breaks or deciding whether to conduct the interview over several days. If it is practicable the interviewer should be familiar with the place where the events occurred in order to bring out the best explanation and clarification from the subject. The interviewer should bear in mind that the jury will not know the place although it is possible for photographs and plans to be produced for the court. Once the subject has said what has happened it might be best to show a photograph of the room, building or area to assist with clarification, depending on the level of communication of the subject.

- Making a written plan: formulating questions and phrases is invaluable, especially if the subject is suffering from dementia, or has a lack of understanding of some types of questions. Consultation is important here, perhaps with members of the family or with the subject's care worker. If an interview is to be conducted on a joint basis then it is imperative to have discussed these things beforehand together.

2. Engage and Explain

- This is about creating the right atmosphere and includes how to address the subject; establishing their immediate needs and concerns; showing an interest in them and their individual circumstances.

- Explaining the interview procedure, the reasons for the interview and providing a broad outline of what is going to happen in the interview.

- Establishing the truth: if the subject is a child or a vulnerable adult, it is best practice to try to establish that they know what truth is and to obtain their agreement that they will tell the truth in the interview. It is also best to ask the subject to provide as much detail of their account as possible in their own words.

- Explaining their rights. Witnesses and victims have rights as well as suspects. This is the best place in the interview to thank the subject (when not being interviewed as a suspect) for their time and to explain that the interview is voluntary.

3. Account, Clarification and Challenge

- Obtaining the account in as much detail as possible, in the subject's own words and without interruption.

- Expanding and clarifying the account where necessary but only after the subject has finished. The questions should be open as detailed above.

- Breaking down the questioning and making notes about any questions not prepared for.

- How to challenge: inconsistencies need to be ironed out in a non-leading and careful manner. The problem-solving approach can be used, in which the subject's help is requested to clarify things where they do not make sense or are inconsistent. On no account should a direct confrontation be made with suggestions of falsehoods. This will act as a barrier to obtaining any more information.

4. Closure

- Information to suspects and witnesses/victims about what to do next. Any practical advice can be given here, such as dealing with the subject's fears or anxieties about a repeat crime.

- Preparing future ground. Further interviews may be required and so communications should be left open for this to take place.

- Summary of the facts provided by the subject to check the correct assimilation of the information by the interviewer.

5. Evaluation

- This is vital if the interviewers are to work again on a joint basis and build up a good interviewing style.

- Evaluate the evidence. Do the facts amount to a crime? Do the facts tend to suggest that a crime has not occurred?

- Evaluate the performance of the interview. Did you do well? What could you have done better? What areas can you develop? How do you acquire these skills?

VULNERABLE ADULT VICTIMS WHO ARE ALSO ABUSERS

It is a general rule that a person cannot be dealt with as a victim of abuse if they are also suspected of being an abuser themselves. It is best that they are first dealt with as an offender and a decision is reached as to whether they should be prosecuted, officially cautioned or no further action taken. The interview will normally take place at a police station and according to the Codes of Practice contained in the Police and Criminal Evidence Act 1984. These interviews will invariably be after the arrest of the vulnerable adult.

However, it is not always practical to treat a vulnerable adult as an offender, depending on the seriousness of the crime of which they are accused. The same difficulties that make it difficult for them to be a witness, apply even more when trying to deal with them as a suspect. If the allegation is one involving sexual intercourse, or indecent assault or physical assault, and it is against another vulnerable adult, then all kinds of issues will come into play for the police or Crown decision-makers to consider. Lack of consent is difficult to prove if neither party has an understanding of what consent is, or if either party does not understand their actions. The difficulty here would be in proving *mens rea*, or the intent to commit the crime. These difficulties would probably not be an issue if the offence was one of forcible rape or involved the use of violence and manipulation. It would be difficult to proceed if the allegation was that a vulnerable adult with learning disabilities 'groomed' another vulnerable adult with learning disabilities to commit indecent assaults and buggery. Every case would need to be considered on its merits.

I have not known of any cases of a vulnerable adult with learning disabilities being prosecuted for rape, buggery or indecent assaults unless they have also involved force. Therefore, although vulnerable adults with learning disabilities or dementia who are themselves abusers would need to be dealt with as suspects first, it is unlikely that they would be unless the offence was extremely serious and there was other independent evidence.

HOW NOT TO CORRUPT THE EVIDENCE

1. Immediate report to police

There has been considerable recent advancement in DNA (Deoxyribonucleic acid) profiling, in particular with a process known as SGM+ (Second Generation Multiplex) and with 'Low Copy Number' (ability to obtain DNA profile from dandruff and from surfaces merely touched by an offender). Because these processes rely upon minute traces of body fluids, which are quickly lost or contaminated, any delay in reporting crimes to the police will result in the loss of valuable evidence.

2. Keeping accurate records

If a vulnerable adult reports a crime to a professional, it is important to record, as soon as possible, the exact words spoken. This becomes more imperative if the crime is one of sexual assault. The vulnerable adult should not be directly questioned about the incident but it may be difficult not to ask some questions, particularly if the vulnerable adult wants to tell a professional what has happened to them. In these circumstances it is important to listen carefully and not to ask any questions. Clarification questions are OK if it is with a view to avoid a misunderstanding. A vulnerable adult might say of a parent, 'she took my nightie off and tickled me'. In this case it is OK to ask,

'How did she tickle you?' (N.B. not 'Where did she tickle you?') as this may produce an innocent explanation such as the parent tickled his feet. Remember, no matter how good you may be at interviewing, if you interview the vulnerable adult before the joint team, the case may be discharged by the Crown Court Judge due to a perceived contamination of the evidence.

3. How to record information

The following information should be recorded as soon as practicable after the conversation:

(a)   Time and date.

(b)   Where the conversation took place.

(c)   The wording of any questions asked.

(d)   The words spoken by the vulnerable adult. Words recording the general gist of the conversation are OK but any words spoken in relation to a sexual assault should be exact and unambiguous. Therefore, if the vulnerable adult said, 'He touched me you know where', under no circumstances should you record, 'She said that she had been sexually abused'. Cases have been lost at court due to the inappropriate questioning of victims by well meaning but misguided professionals.

It is good practice that other agencies, such as social services, health and education, do not carry out any investigation or interviews without first contacting the police. In my experience I have found that the criminal courts tend to be quick in finding fault with interviews that are conducted by professionals other than the police. This is particularly true for interviews of suspects, as there are many considerations in relation to safeguarding a suspect's rights that are contained in the Codes of Practice and the Police and Criminal Evidence Act 1984. For example, interviews need to be tape recorded using special equipment and the suspect should be afforded the rights of having a solicitor's advice and presence.

INTERVIEWING IN CASES OF NEGLECT

Section 1 of the Children and Young Persons Act 1933 creates an offence for a person over the age of 16 years, who has responsibility for a child under that age, to wilfully assault, ill-treat, neglect, abandon, or expose the child in a manner likely to cause unnecessary suffering or injury to health. There is no such legislation for vulnerable adults.

There is limited legislation and this is found under the Mental Health Act 1983 and applies to those who ill-treat or wilfully neglect a patient in their care or under their guardianship. Fuller details of these offences are given in Appendix 1. They are difficult to prove but if investigators are thorough then there is no reason why successful prosecutions cannot be obtained. The old adage that investigators should not be afraid to 'grasp the nettle' is key so long as the investigators remember to wear an old pair of gardening gloves when conducting their enquiries. There is one stated case that provides guidance, R v Sheppard [1981], which outlines that the neglect can be a failure to act but the 'wilful' element means that the failure to act must be deliberate. There is an example given by Lord Keith, where a parent who knows that his/her child needs medical care and deliberately, by conscious decision, refrains from calling a doctor would be guilty of an offence.

In 1994 the Thames Valley Police investigated Longcare Ltd residential homes for adults with learning disabilities. Successful prosecutions were mounted for ill-treatment under the Mental Health Act 1983 but this was only because current legislation was inadequate to bring more serious charges. During the Longcare Investigation by the Thames Valley Police it became clear the only offences which the perpetrators might be prosecuted for were under section 127(2) Mental Health Act 1983. This section creates an offence for any person to ill-treat or wilfully neglect a 'mentally disordered patient' who is for the time being subject to his/her guardianship or is otherwise in his/her custody or care (whether by virtue of any legal or moral obligation or otherwise).

These cases are extremely difficult to prove and, without other eyewitnesses or medical evidence, may hinge on the amount of detail an interviewer can obtain from the subject. It is important that the interviewer is able to establish what happened whilst they were in the suspected person's everyday care and how they were treated. Again, there is a need to emphasize that this should be done, not only in a non-leading style, but also in an impartial way without the interviewer having formed any preconceived ideas. After all, asking general questions about how the subject was treated by the suspect might produce a positive response.

INTERVIEWING IN CASES OF FINANCIAL ABUSE

In order to prove an offence of obtaining property by deception or the obtaining of property dishonestly from a vulnerable adult, it is necessary to establish that the vulnerable adult did not give the person permission to take the property or was deceived into parting with the property. This again is an area where the facts can be difficult to prove. For example, the offender talks his/her way into the home of an older person who may be suffering with senility, and persuades them to let them clean their kitchen floor for the payment of £350. The older person agrees to this and pays the money. The floor is spotlessly cleaned. Once the offender sees where the elderly person keeps their money, s/he also takes another £50 when they are not looking. In this example, the older person has agreed a price and may not realize that another £50 is also missing. Again, it is vital that the older person is carefully questioned, and is asked to relay the facts in a non-leading style. The interview should not be hurried and it may be best for the older person to be given assurances that they have not been foolish or done anything wrong. It will be helpful to the investigation if it can be established how much cash the older person had before the visit of the offender. Relatives may be able to help here, but you the interviewer will then need to ascertain that no other monies were paid out to anyone else or stolen by another offender because doors were insecure. Other factual information can then be gathered by the police investigators. However, if the offender denies conning the older person then it is ultimately for a jury to decide whether a deceit was practised.

CONCLUSIONS

Much headway has been made during the last ten years gathering evidence from witnesses who are vulnerable. At one time it was quite difficult to bring a case to court when the only evidence was that of a child or young person. Now with the everyday use of video interviews the quality of a child's evidence has improved and it can be gathered whilst it is still fresh in the child's mind and before it is contaminated by any other source. This increases the confidence of the legal professionals and enhances the credibility of the child's evidence. In my experience they have produced many more safe convictions as the video interview can be properly assessed by professionals and experts before it is decided whether to prosecute. I am sure over the next few years that this will happen with vulnerable witnesses. For those who are unable to communicate verbally, there is no reason why other methods should not be found to help them communicate in a non-leading and effective manner. No police officer can ever be trained to understand how to communicate with the wide range of vulnerable witnesses who all have their individual special needs. It is therefore vital that if we are to succeed in the future the police must work closely with those professionals who do understand and who are trained and experienced, and who can advise their police colleagues on appropriate ways to communicate with vulnerable adults.

FURTHER CASE STUDIES

CASE STUDY 3

Field View Nursing Home

In 1995, Mr M, aged 84 years, was found dead in his bed. The attending GP noticed that the deceased's bed and some of the other beds were soaked in urine. The two night staff were dismissed for their lack of care. The matter was reported to the Head of Nursing who carried out an investigation. It was not reported to police.

In October 1998, two members of staff were witnessed, independently by another member of staff, slapping one of the residents, an 87-year-old woman. The member of staff did nothing until he resigned in November 1998, when he wrote a letter to the Head of Nursing, detailing what he had seen, and giving some details of the death of Mr M in 1995. He also alleged that there were other people who died under mysterious circumstances two years previously. The two members of staff were suspended, then reinstated in January 1999, then suspended again whilst the Nursing Unit carried out its own investigation. In February 1999 it was eventually reported to the Police Family Protection Unit. A strategy meeting was held and the details were submitted to the

Detective Chief Inspector of the police area. The investigation was given low priority due to a number of serious incidents that had been reported, and because the allegations were now old and there had been a delay in reporting it to the police. In April 1999, it was investigated but the police found no evidence to be able to prosecute anyone. The elderly resident who had been slapped could not remember anything happening to her. All doctors who had certified the deaths of the elderly residents mentioned by the complainant were satisfied that the deaths were of natural causes. There had been no post-mortems and the bodies were cremated.

1.   Would there have been a different outcome if all these matters were reported to the police at the time of first coming to notice?

2.   What valuable evidence do you think may have been lost as a result of these matters not being reported immediately?

CASE STUDY 4

Case of 'T' 1998

'T' was charged with rape of and indecent assault upon four women, all with learning disabilities, who were resident in a home run by T and his wife. Before police involvement, social services had carried out their own questioning. When it was reported to the police, the police had interviewed all four women without recording the interviews on video and had interviewed them each on separate occasions. The accounts the women gave were quite 'matter of fact' in relation to the assaults, and the lack of consent was not brought out properly in their statements.

T's wife and two other members of staff made witness statements disputing the allegations and stating that T never slept on the premises, thereby making the sexual assaults unlikely.

Senior Prosecution Counsel, in consultation with the police, discharged the case against T. He believed that the case was beset with the following weaknesses:

•   Before the police interviewed the complainants, social services had done their own questioning. The complainants' subsequent witness statements were, therefore, valueless.

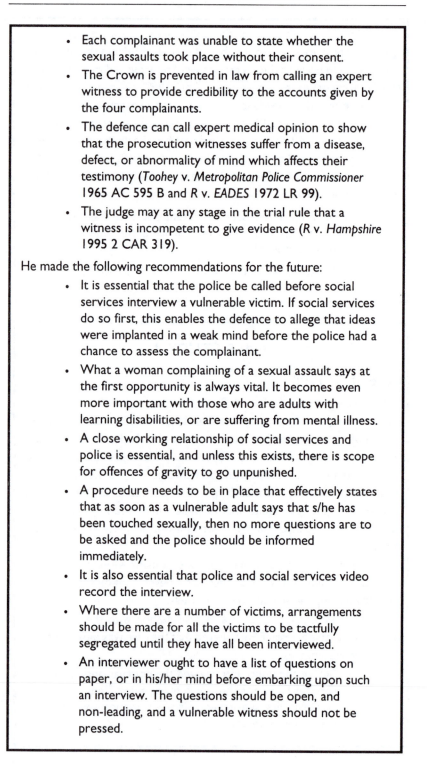

- Each complainant was unable to state whether the sexual assaults took place without their consent.
- The Crown is prevented in law from calling an expert witness to provide credibility to the accounts given by the four complainants.
- The defence can call expert medical opinion to show that the prosecution witnesses suffer from a disease, defect, or abnormality of mind which affects their testimony (*Toohey* v. *Metropolitan Police Commissioner* 1965 AC 595 B and *R* v. *EADES* 1972 LR 99).
- The judge may at any stage in the trial rule that a witness is incompetent to give evidence (*R* v. *Hampshire* 1995 2 CAR 319).

He made the following recommendations for the future:

- It is essential that the police be called before social services interview a vulnerable victim. If social services do so first, this enables the defence to allege that ideas were implanted in a weak mind before the police had a chance to assess the complainant.
- What a woman complaining of a sexual assault says at the first opportunity is always vital. It becomes even more important with those who are adults with learning disabilities, or are suffering from mental illness.
- A close working relationship of social services and police is essential, and unless this exists, there is scope for offences of gravity to go unpunished.
- A procedure needs to be in place that effectively states that as soon as a vulnerable adult says that s/he has been touched sexually, then no more questions are to be asked and the police should be informed immediately.
- It is also essential that police and social services video record the interview.
- Where there are a number of victims, arrangements should be made for all the victims to be tactfully segregated until they have all been interviewed.
- An interviewer ought to have a list of questions on paper, or in his/her mind before embarking upon such an interview. The questions should be open, and non-leading, and a vulnerable witness should not be pressed.

Appendix 1

LIST OF THE MORE COMMON CRIMINAL OFFENCES TO CONSIDER DURING AN INVESTIGATION

ABUSE OF TRUST

Being a person aged 18 years or over in a position of trust has sexual intercourse with a person under 18 years of age, contrary to section 3(1) and (4) of the Sexual Offences (Amendment) Act 2000.

Being a person aged 18 years or over in a position of trust engages in sexual activity other than sexual intercourse with person under 18, contrary to section 3(1) and (4), of the Sexual Offences (Amendment) Act 2000.

ASSISTING OFFENDERS

Where a person is guilty of or has committed an arrestable offence, any other person who knowing or believing him to be guilty of the offence or some other arrestable offence, does without lawful authority or reasonable excuse any act with intent to impede his apprehension or prosecution shall be guilty of an offence, contrary to section 4(1), Criminal Law Act 1967.

Arrestable offences cover the more serious offences of serious assault, the sexual offences and the theft offences. Assisting offenders requires more than simply not reporting someone's guilt or not co-operating with the investigation. It must be a deliberate act.

COMMON ASSAULT

It is an offence contrary to section 39 of the Criminal Justice Act 1988 for any person to unlawfully assault or beat any other person.

An assault is any act by which a person intentionally, or recklessly, causes another to apprehend immediate unlawful violence. Sometimes minor offences of assault occasioning actual bodily harm are reduced to 'common assault' by the Crown Prosecution Service.

ASSAULT OCCASIONING ACTUAL BODILY HARM

This is contrary to section 47, Offences Against the Person Act 1861. Actual bodily harm means any hurt or injury calculated to interfere with the health or comfort of the victim.

FALSE IMPRISONMENT

This offence is against common law. It consists of the unlawful and intentional or reckless restraint of a victim's freedom of movement from a place.

GRIEVOUS BODILY HARM AND WOUNDING

Anyone who unlawfully and maliciously wounds or inflicts grievous bodily harm upon any other person, either with or without any weapon or instrument, shall be guilty of an offence, contrary to section 20, Offences Against the Person Act 1861.

GRIEVOUS BODILY HARM AND WOUNDING WITH INTENT

Anyone who unlawfully and maliciously wounds or inflicts grievous bodily harm upon any other person with intent to cause grievous bodily harm shall be guilty of an offence, contrary to section 18, Offences Against the Person Act 1861.

ILL-TREATMENT OF PATIENTS

Ill-treatment or wilful neglect of a patient by officer on the staff or otherwise employed in, or any of the manager of a hospital or mental nursing home, contrary to section 127(1), Mental Health Act 1983.

Ill-treatment or wilful neglect of a mentally disordered patient who is for the time being subject to his/her guardianship or is otherwise in his/her custody or care (whether by virtue of any legal or moral obligation or otherwise), contrary to section 127(2), Mental Health Act 1983.

INDECENT ASSAULT ON A MAN

It is an offence for anyone to indecently assault a man, contrary to section 15 Sexual Offences Act 1956.

N.B. It is a defence to indecent assault if the person consented, but a person under the age of 16 years cannot give their consent, so even if the sexual touching occurs with their permission it is still indecent assault.

INDECENT ASSAULT ON A WOMAN

It is an offence for anyone to indecently assault a woman, contrary to section 14 (1), Sexual Offences Act 1956.

OBTAINING PROPERTY BY DECEPTION

A person commits an offence if by any deception s/he dishonestly appropriates property belonging to another, with the intention of permanently depriving the other of it, contrary to section 15, Theft Act 1968.

RAPE

A man commits rape if he has sexual intercourse with a person (whether vaginal or anal) who at the time of intercourse does not consent to it; and at the time he knows that the person does not consent to the intercourse or is reckless as to whether the person consents to it, contrary to section 1, Sexual Offences Act 1956.

Any person can commit the offence of rape if they aid, abet, counsel or procure a rape (assist or incite the other person to commit the act), this is contrary to common law and is supported in case law.

SEXUAL INTERCOURSE WITH PATIENTS

It is an offence for a man who is an officer on the staff, or is otherwise employed in, or is one of the managers of, a hospital or mental nursing home to have unlawful sexual intercourse with a woman who is for the time being receiving treatment for mental disorder in that hospital or home, or to have such intercourse on the premises of which the hospital or home forms part, with a woman who is for the time being receiving such treatment there as an outpatient, and it is an offence for a man to have unlawful sexual intercourse with a woman who is a mentally disordered patient and who is subject to his guardianship under the Mental Health Act 1983 or is otherwise in his custody or care under the Mental Health Act 1983, contrary to section 128 Mental Health Act 1959.

THEFT

A person is guilty of theft if they dishonestly appropriate property belonging to another with the intention of permanently depriving the other of it, contrary to section 1, Theft Act 1968.

UNLAWFUL SEXUAL INTERCOURSE WITH A GIRL UNDER 13 YEARS

It is an offence, punishable with a maximum prison sentence of life, if a person has sexual intercourse with a girl under 13 years, contrary to section 5, Sexual Offences Act 1956.

UNLAWFUL SEXUAL INTERCOURSE WITH A GIRL UNDER 16 YEARS

It is an offence, punishable with a maximum prison sentence of two years, if a person has sexual intercourse with a girl under 16 years, contrary to section 6, Sexual Offences Act 1956.

N.B. Prosecution for this offence is limited to 12 months after the date of the commission of the offence, but indecent assault is not. The author of this chapter had a case where he charged a man with indecent assault on a girl under 16 years of age which had occurred 20 years previously. The defence went for an abuse of process hearing stating that the police had inappropriately misused this section because the statute of limitation had run out on the more appropriate charge of unlawful sexual intercourse with a girl under 16 years. The High Court Judge held that the charge of indecent assault was appropriate and there to be used by the police. The man later pleaded guilty at his trial.

REFERENCES

Archbold (2000) *Criminal Pleading Evidence and Practice*. London: Sweet and Maxwell.

Children and Young Persons Act 1933. London: HMSO.

Criminal Procedure and Investigations Act 1976 and 1996. London: HMSO.

Crown Prosecution Service (1994) *The Code For Crown Prosecutors*. London: CPS. (The Code is available from Crown Prosecution Service, Information Branch, 50 Ludgate Hill, London, EC4M 7EX.)

Department of Health (2000) *No Secrets: Guidance on Developing and Implementing Multi-Agency Policies and Procedures to Protect Vulnerable Adults from Abuse*. London: HMSO.

Department of Health and Home Office (1992) *Memorandum of Good Practice on Video Recorded Interviews with Child Witnesses for Criminal Proceedings*. London: HMSO.

Home Office (1999) *Action for Justice*. London: HMSO.

Home Office (1998) *Speaking Up For Justice. Report of the Interdepartmental Working Group on the Treatment of Vulnerable or Intimidated Witnesses in the Criminal Justice System*. London: HMSO.

Mental Health Act 1983. London: HMSO.

National Crime Faculty (1996) *Investigative Interviewing: A Practical Guide*. Bramshill, Hants: National Crime Faculty. (This publication is not available to anyone other than police officers.)

Police and Criminal Evidence Act 1984. London: HMSO.

Police and Criminal Evidence Act 1984, Codes of Practice. London: HMSO.

Youth Justice and Criminal Evidence Act 1999. London: HMSO.

CHAPTER 4

THE ROLE OF THE GENERAL PRACTITIONER

IONA HEATH

General practitioners seeking to provide an effective and enabling response to vulnerable adults suffering abuse, work in a context that both helps and hinders them. This will be the focus of the chapter, which will also include discussion about taking action and working with primary care teams to promote good practice in working with vulnerable adults who may be victims of abuse.

HELPING FACTORS

- Almost all general practitioners aspire to offer a high standard of care to all patients whatever their health care need.

- Almost every vulnerable adult living in the community is registered with a general practice and a named general practitioner, and that general practitioner has the opportunity to establish a continuing and long-term relationship with the patient and their carers. This gives the general practitioner and the primary health care team[1] uniquely privileged access to vulnerable adults. The single largest group are older people. Patients over 65 years old consult their general practitioner on average six times a year (RCGP 1999). The minority of older people who have chronic and debilitating illnesses tend to consult much

---

1   Primary health care teams include: district nurses, health visitors, counsellors, community psychiatric nurses, occupational therapists and physiotherapists.

more often. All this means that general practitioners and other members of primary care teams have unique opportunities to identify patients who are victims of abuse and neglect.

- The general practice consultation is accessible to all and has the capacity to provide an acceptable and non-stigmatizing setting for the delivery of care in situations where people may be ashamed or embarrassed by the situation in which they find themselves.

- General practitioners increasingly regard their relationships with patients as a 'partnership of experts'. The doctor is the expert on the potential and complexity of biomedical science but the patient is the expert on the reality of their own symptoms and the context of a unique life history and a framework of values and aspirations within which those symptoms arise. This helps the doctor to value the patient's account of their own experience, and to place it within the patient's wider social and biographical setting. This should in turn make it easier for patients to tell their stories and for doctors to recognize stories of abuse.

- More and more general practitioners work within extended primary care teams and have ready access to the experience and expertise of other health care professionals. The knowledge and support of these colleagues can be invaluable in raising and sharing suspicions of abuse and in helping to unravel the complexities of potentially abusive situations.

- Primary health care teams will often have long-standing knowledge of those families and households within which there are entrenched and long-standing dysfunctional relationships, sometimes compounded by mental illness and/or excessive use of alcohol, and which are known to be at particularly high risk of abuse. Primary health care teams will also be aware of nursing and residential care homes, and even hospitals, where there are inadequate levels of staffing, with recruitment and retention difficulties and high levels of stress and staff turnover.

- The recent policy of placing social workers with responsibility for frail older people within primary care teams has the potential to provide much needed support to the gradually developing expertise of primary health care professionals.

- Professional and public recognition of the reality of adult abuse in a variety of settings is slowly but surely increasing and general practitioners and other primary health care professionals have an increasing understanding of the range of presentations of adult abuse. This gradually increasing knowledge base is supported by information provided by Action on Elder Abuse, Age Concern, UK Voice, Ann Craft Trust and other agencies.

HINDERING FORCES

- General practitioners are severely constrained by lack of time, with consultations lasting on average less than ten minutes. In addition, they have 24-hour responsibility for the care of their patients, with fixed commitments to the provision of regular surgery sessions, and, in England, an average list of 1,846 registered patients (RCGP 1999). This can make it almost impossible for general practitioners to attend case conferences and similar inter-agency meetings, particularly as such meetings are often very lengthy. It is important that the constraints on general practitioners are recognized by their fellow professionals and that lack of attendance is not routinely and simplistically interpreted as lack of interest or commitment.

- Problems arising from abuse are seldom revealed directly to the doctor but are presented or hinted at indirectly. This offers the general practitioner the opportunity of colluding with the covert nature of the presentation by ignoring the hints and this is particularly likely when the doctor is more than usually pressed for time.

- General practitioners and other primary care professionals, faced with society's inadequate investment in the care of vulnerable adults, and, perhaps particularly, frail older people, often feel a sense of helplessness about being able to improve a bad situation. Too often we see patients living in circumstances that verge on the squalid and that systematically erode the dignity of the individual.

  Most developed societies do little to enhance the image of the 'senior citizen,' who is liable to be patronised, marginalised, or simply ignored and is seen as a problem for an overburdened welfare state. (Pitt 1998, pp.1452–4)

- One sign of the inadequacy of society's commitment to the care of vulnerable adults has been the devaluing of intimate physical care, and this is why the Government's recent response to the recommendations of the Royal Commission on Long Term Care is so intensely disappointing. The Commission argued that the common diseases of frail older people, which include strokes, heart failure, arthritis and dementia, are difficult to treat but inexorably undermine the sufferer's ability to care for his or her own body. This predicament erodes dignity, and dignity is part of health. The provision of intimate personal care with skill and sensitivity can restore dignity and independence; it is the most important dimension of health care for those rendered frail and debilitated by chronic illness. Yet this type of care has been devalued, taken away from nurses, and redefined as social care which can be delivered by those who are poorly trained and even more poorly paid. Crucially, it is during the delivery of intimate personal care that signs of abuse are likely to be revealed – bruises hidden under clothing, signs of sexual trauma, unexpected tearfulness or distress.

- Through these processes older people and other vulnerable adults are systematically distanced not only from skilled care but also from expertise that could and should provide both early diagnosis and prevention of abuse. Most 'social' care is provided by carers[2] who are poorly paid and have had little access to training and it is a testament to their dedication that so much of the care they provide is of high standard. There is an urgent need for these carers to be integrated into district nursing teams so that the skills and expertise of trained nurses, and indeed those of the wider primary health care team, can support the work of carers.

- Many general practitioners have a very understandable fear of revealing a problem that will be difficult and time-consuming to resolve. This often compounds the

---

2   Carer being defined as anyone who provides a substantial amount of care and support on a regular basis to someone with significant illness or disability.

sense of helplessness in the face of society's apathy and is combined with a fear of somehow making things worse.

- The general practitioner will often have a long-standing relationship with the extended family of a vulnerable adult and the carer(s) may well themselves be patients of the same general practitioner. The effectiveness of general practice depends on the ability of the general practitioner to understand and empathize with the patient's symptoms and experience. Empathy is built on deliberate positive regard for each individual patient and this can make it very difficult for the general practitioner to see a patient as capable of abuse. It is inevitable that in such situations the general practitioner will experience difficult and painful conflicts of loyalty and it may prove impossible to sustain an effective relationship with all the parties to an abusive situation.

- General practitioners, alongside all other professionals, face huge difficulties in raising the possibility of abuse and in asking appropriate and timely questions. This situation is compounded where there is a barrier of communication between patient and doctor through learning difficulty, severe physical disability, mental illness, dementia, confusion or the lack of a shared language. In such circumstances it can be very difficult to gain a clear understanding of what has occurred.

- It is very difficult to reflect the entire content of a consultation in the medical record, but if important components are omitted the retrospective pattern of incident that becomes increasingly suggestive of abuse may be absent and diagnosis unnecessarily delayed.

- Once the possibility or probability of abuse is raised the general practitioner can be further hindered by a lack of availability of crucial information at the moment of the consultation and by the limited availability of services able to offer urgent and appropriate intervention.

AUTONOMY, NEGLECT AND PROTECTION

Whereas the responsibilities of the general practitioner in relation to both child abuse and domestic violence are relatively clearly defined, the correct response to the abuse of vulnerable adults remains elusive. In child abuse, the practitioner must prioritize the interests and protection of the child; in domestic violence, the prime responsibility is to respect and promote the autonomy of the abused woman and support her in making her own decisions. In the abuse of vulnerable adults, a delicate balance must be struck depending on the mental competence of the abused person. When the person is fully competent, no matter how physically frail or impaired, the appropriate response parallels that for domestic violence. Indeed, some abuse of vulnerable older people represents the progression of long-standing domestic violence over time so that both the perpetrator and the abused person have become old. In such cases, the abused older person's wishes must be elicited and respected, although much can be achieved by offering extra help within the home, so that stresses of daily living are minimized and the transactions of care more closely supervised. In situations where the vulnerable adult is rendered incompetent through learning difficulty, mental illness, confusion or dementia, the priority shifts towards the protection of the abused person from both abuse and neglect. However, all these situations can be complicated by relationships in which each party is both a victim and a perpetrator of abuse.

The close relationship between a vulnerable adult and their carer may easily compromise the vulnerable adult's rights to confidentiality and health care professionals will need to pay very explicit attention to these rights. When the vulnerable adult has severe learning difficulties, significant mental illness or is suffering from confusion or dementia, the situation becomes even more complicated as the imperative to protect begins to override the duty of confidentiality.

McCreadie (1996) has usefully tabulated the overlaps and differences in understanding between domestic violence and elder abuse, which can be extended to help our understanding of the abuse of all vulnerable adults:

Domestic violence	Elder abuse
Physical and sexual violence, emotional abuse	Also includes financial abuse and neglect
Violence as *criminal* behaviour	Emphasis on protection
Violence by men towards women	Violence by men and women towards men and women
Violence by partners and ex-partners	Violence by adult children, partners, siblings, friends, neighbours
Clear victim; clear perpetrator	Ambiguities over victim

(McCreadie 1996, p.18)

Olive Stevenson has emphasized the enormous variety of emotional and physical interdependence that can arise in situations involving vulnerable adults.

> One can envisage situations in which a mentally ill son is living with his elderly mother when both would much rather he had a home of his own. Such a situation might give rise to explosive abuse. Equally, it would be extremely naïve to assume that there is no emotional entanglement which prevents them from separating. (Stevenson 1996, p.21)

EFFECTIVE AND ENABLING CARE

The different categories of adult abuse (DOH 2000):

- physical abuse
- emotional or psychological abuse
- neglect
- sexual abuse
- financial abuse
- discriminatory abuse

present different challenges and simple physical abuse is probably the most straightforward and accessible for general practitioners. At the other extreme financial abuse may be very difficult indeed for a health professional to identify.

Emotional abuse is a broad and imprecise concept which has been consistently difficult to define and to identify with an acceptable degree of certainty. It is also likely that cultural context may be more influential and relevant than it is with physical abuse.

Sexual abuse raises very particular moral difficulties in relation to consent. Sexual activity between consenting adults is not illegal and societal attitudes to the sexuality of older people and disabled and otherwise vulnerable adults are undoubtedly ambivalent. This situation is fraught with conflicting dangers ranging from a view that all sexual activity involving vulnerable adults is in some way abusive, to the strong likelihood that the possibility of abuse will be ignored or minimized, as has undoubtedly happened in relation to people with learning difficulties.

CONSIDER THE POSSIBILITY

In common with all other diagnostic situations, the most powerful aid to the identification of adult abuse is an open mind that considers the possibility. Doctors can only confirm possibilities that occur to them, and so they need to foster a high index of suspicion in every situation where a vulnerable adult is dependent on the care of others. It is better to consider the possibility and explicitly discount it than to remain blind to the possibility. Suspicion should perhaps be particularly high in the situations described above where there are dysfunctional relationships, sometimes compounded by excessive use of alcohol, within families and households or where there are inadequate levels of staffing, with recruitment and retention difficulties and high levels of stress and staff turnover, in hospitals and nursing and residential care homes. However, there are dangers of developing a stereotyped view of a potentially abusive situation as this can inappropriately lower the index of suspicion in situations where some or all of these risk factors do not apply but where abuse nonetheless remains a possibility.

ASK THE QUESTION

Here again, there is both similarity with, and important difference from, the management of domestic violence. In situations of domestic violence, asking the patient whether she is being abused is crucial to all subsequent intervention and there is useful evidence to show that women who are not being abused do not mind being asked, while abused women want to be asked and to be given the opportunity to describe their situation and to seek help in changing it. Again the question of mental competence and consequent autonomy is crucial. Where vulnerable adults are fully competent, they should be asked directly, in a setting of complete confidentiality, whether or not they are being abused. Where doctor and patient do not share a common language, a professional and fully confidential interpreting service should be provided. Situations where the patient is mentally competent but so physically disabled that they are unable to speak are perhaps the most difficult. The temptation to rely on the carers to interpret the patient's wishes is enormous but it is essential to try to seek some means of communicating confidentially by accessing those with special skills in the care of the extremely physically/mentally disabled.

Practitioners often find it helpful to identify a form of words with which they feel comfortable in raising the possibility of abuse. Suggestions might include:

> 'Many patients with bruises like these have been hurt by someone close to them. Could this be happening to you?'

> 'Sometimes people who look after others want to have too much control over them. Could this be happening to you?'

> 'We know that carers can sometimes be irritable and perhaps even rough. Could this be happening to you?'

> 'Have you ever felt frightened of anyone close to you or who cares for you?'

However, in the frequent situations where the patient is not competent because of severe learning difficulty, mental illness, confusion or dementia, it is often more difficult to ask the patient a direct question and there is always the danger of leading him/her. In such situations, it is unwise to direct questions to the carers as this may serve to exacerbate an already abusive situation and further distance the vulnerable adult from effective intervention and help. It is usually more appropriate to seek advice from the local social services department before proceeding further.

RECORD THE EVIDENCE

Whether or not the possibility has been raised directly, the evidence suggesting the possibility of abuse should be carefully recorded. Physical injuries should be described in detail, alongside any discrepancy with the proffered explanation for the injuries. Any signs of neglect should also be recorded and practitioners should pay careful attention to the mood and affect of the patient as this may offer the only clue to the possibility of emotional abuse. Unusual symptoms and signs may indicate the possibility of the patient being either over- or under-medicated by their carer.

REFER APPROPRIATELY

The individual general practitioner is almost never in a position to resolve a situation in which a vulnerable adult is being subjected to abuse. Effective care is almost always entirely dependent on the appropriate involvement of other agencies. Where the patient is mentally competent, referral must be made with the patient's consent. If the patient is not competent, referral may be made in the patient's best interest.

Where the possibility of abuse remains at the level of vague suspicion it may well be helpful to involve other members of the primary health care team. A referral to a district nurse may allow the nurse to spend more time in the patient's home, carefully assessing both the physical and psychological condition of the patient and the relationships between the patient and the carer(s). This assessment can help to confirm or refute suspicions. Other professionals including physiotherapists, occupational therapists, community psychiatric nurses and, of course, social workers, can make similar assessments.

In most situations, once abuse is thought probable, the most appropriate referral will be to someone from the local social services department who has responsibility for the protection of vulnerable adults. All general practitioners should make themselves aware of this named individual and their contact details. However, when a general practitioner or another member of the primary care team discovers a vulnerable adult with severe injuries, the most appropriate course of action may be to secure the patient's immediate safety by emergency hospital admission.

General practitioners will need to be prepared to provide a full report of their findings and the basis of their suspicion of abuse, but when it is possible for further investigation to be led and co-ordinated by social services, it may make it easier for the general practitioner to remain in constructive contact with all members of the affected household. This may be particularly important when dealing with relationships in which each party is both a victim and a perpetrator of abuse. In all situations there is an ongoing need for support, particularly for the victim, but also for everyone else involved.

The availability and accessibility of general practitioners gives them unique opportunities to contribute to the provision of this ongoing support.

REFERENCES

Department of Health (2000) *No Secrets: Guidance on Developing and Implementing Multi-Agency Policies and Procedures to Protect Vulnerable Adults from Abuse.* London: HMSO.

McCreadie, C. (1996) *Elder Abuse: Update on Research.* London: Age Concern Institute of Gerontology, Kings College, London.

Pitt, B. (1998) 'Loss in Late Life.' *British Medical Journal 316,* 1452–1454.

RCGP (August 1999) *General Practitioner Workload.* Information Sheet Number 3.

Stevenson, O. (1996) *Elder Protection in the Community: What can we Learn from Child Protection?* London: Age Concern Institute of Gerontology, Kings College, London.

CHAPTER 5

THE ROLE OF
THE MEDICAL PRACTITIONER

A VIEW FROM AUSTRALIA

SUSAN KURRLE

INTRODUCTION

In 1988 Rosalie Wolf wrote in the *Journal of the American Geriatrics Society* that 'physicians can make a major contribution to the advancement of knowledge, practice and policy, with regards to elder abuse and neglect' (Wolf 1988). Unfortunately the medical profession has not, to any great degree, taken up the challenge to be involved in this problematic issue. This is disappointing when you consider the significant contribution made in the arena of child abuse where physicians have been in the forefront of research and practice. In 1995 Lachs and Pillemer made a direct appeal to the medical profession in the *New England Journal of Medicine* (Lachs and Pillemer 1995), and in 1998 McCreadie, Bennett and Tinker noted the lack of awareness of elder abuse, and the need for education and training of general practitioners surveyed in London (McCreadie *et al.* 1998).

In Australia, elder abuse was a hidden problem until the late 1980s, and there is still considerable professional and public lack of awareness of the problem. However, since those early days, research throughout Australia has confirmed the significance of abuse as a social, medical and legal problem in the Australian community (Kurrle, Sadler and Cameron 1992). Action has occurred at both Australian Commonwealth and State government levels, with development of specific policies on elder abuse and education and training programmes. Most agencies dealing with older people now have protocols in place for management of elder abuse. There is no specific legislation relating to elder abuse and there is no mandatory reporting of abuse, or provision of adult protective services. However, there is guardianship legislation in most Australian States which allows for the appointment of a substitute decision-maker for those older people who are no longer able to make decisions for themselves because of mental or physical disability. Currently the majority of cases of elder abuse are assessed and managed by geriatric health services and in particular Aged Care Assessment Teams[1] (which usually work as part of a hospital and community-based geriatric health service). General practitioners (GPs) in particular and the medical profession in general are less commonly involved.

There are a number of reasons why medical practitioners have not been involved in the past and these persist into the present:

- There is still a lack of awareness of elder abuse which is now being addressed with education and training at both the undergraduate and postgraduate levels. However, a lack of understanding of the definition has meant that elder abuse may not be recognized as such. McCreadie *et al.* (1998) noted in the London GP survey that where the abuse situation was not seen as severe, or there was no intent on the part of the abuser to cause harm, then elder abuse was not considered by some GPs to have occurred.

- Ageism remains a concern in the practice of geriatric medicine, particularly at the clinical level. Signs and symptoms of abuse may be ascribed to the ageing process or ignored; reports from older patients of abuse may be dismissed as due to dementia or psychotic illness.

- There is a lack of scientific knowledge in the area of elder abuse where other areas of medicine are increasingly relying on evidence-based guidelines and treatment. Diagnosis may be difficult, risk factors may be unclear, and there are no

1   Aged Care Assessment Teams (ACATs) are Commonwealth-funded community multidisciplinary teams usually based within a hospital geriatric health service. The team consists of a geriatrician, registered nurses, social workers, occupational therapists and clerical staff. Physiotherapists, speech pathologists and psychologists may also be part of the ACAT. ACATs assess the needs of older people with a view to provision of community services, or for entry into residential aged care facilities.

randomized trials on useful or effective interventions. For a condition with a significant rate of occurrence there are remarkably few published papers in the medical literature.

- Many doctors feel discomfort when dealing with abuse, particularly in a family situation. There is a lack of training in this area for physicians, and there is the concern that where both victim and abuser are patients, the important doctor–patient relationship will be lost.

- Therapeutic nihilism exists in the area of elder abuse, with the perception of powerlessness – nothing can be done to help or change the situation so why do anything at all?

- The structure of medical practice and time constraints on appointments mean that there is rarely time for a full exploration of problems. This is so particularly in general practice and the hospital emergency department where pressure of patient numbers means only a short amount of time is available for assessment of the acute problem.

- Fear of legal action may prevent involvement in abuse situations. Being called to testify in court is a stressful and time-consuming activity, and general practitioners, geriatricians and psychiatrists may be reluctant even to write reports for an application for guardianship.

- Some medical practitioners see elder abuse as a social problem to be dealt with by social workers or other allied health professionals and not as a medical problem. There is also a lack of orientation and skills to tackle psychosocial issues amongst some members of the medical profession.

THE ROLE OF THE MEDICAL PRACTITIONER

It is essential that the medical profession become involved in identification, assessment and management of elder abuse for a number of reasons. Older people are the greatest users of health services, and in Australia over 90 per cent of older people see their general practitioner (GP) at least once a year (McCallum *et al.* 1994). GPs are ideally placed to identify potential and actual cases of abuse and with their often long-standing knowledge of, and relationship with, the older person and their family they can have an important role in assessment and management.

It is not only general practitioners who have an important role. Impairment and disability play a significant part in the occurrence of elder abuse and there is much that can be done to improve an older person's physical and mental health and general function. Geriatricians, psychiatrists and rehabilitation physicians can make an important contribution in the areas of identification of abuse, assessment of function, treatment of illness and improvement in disability. Emergency department physicians may also see abuse presenting as trauma in their departments, and they need to be aware of referral mechanisms for these patients.

DEFINITION OF ELDER ABUSE

It is impossible to recognize a problem if we have not adequately defined it. Because ignorance or lack of understanding of the definition of elder abuse has, in the past, led to under-reporting and poor recognition, it is important to have a simple widely accepted working definition of elder abuse. The following definition has been in use amongst the medical and allied health professions in Australia for some time:

> Elder abuse is any pattern of behaviour which causes physical, psychological, financial or social harm to an older person. The abuse occurs in the context of a relationship between victim and abuser. (Kurrle 1995, p.2)

Elder abuse may be divided into the following categories:

- physical
- sexual
- psychological
- financial
- neglect.

ASSESSMENT OF RISK

Screening is becoming an important and accepted part of medical management and is now commonplace for diseases such as diabetes, hypertension and hyperlipidaemia. Any treatable disease that causes considerable morbidity or mortality should be looked for, and with community prevalence studies indicating that between 3 and 5 per cent of people over the age of 65 are victims of elder abuse (Pillemer and Finkelhor 1988), it is important that the medical profession considers asking about abuse in the patients they are seeing, and also looks for risk factors for elder abuse.

Research and clinical experience show very clearly that there are a number of factors contributing to the occurrence of abuse and a combination of these are usually involved in abusive situations. Those risk factors that are often more easy to identify in the primary care situation include:

1. *Increased dependency of the older person.* Older people are more vulnerable to abuse when they are helpless or dependent on others for assistance. This dependency may be due to physical impairments such as Parkinson's disease or stroke, or cognitive impairments such as dementia.

2. *Abuser psychopathology.* The personality characteristics of the abuser are a major factor in the occurrence of abuse. Alcoholism, drug abuse, psychiatric illness and cognitive impairment in the abuser are highly significant as contributory factors in cases of abuse. In many cases of physical and psychological abuse, abuser psychopathology is implicated as the major contributory factor. In cases of carer abuse where carers are abused by the people for whom they are caring, dementia or psychiatric illness is frequently present in the abuser. A large number of carers of people with dementia experience aggression from the person for whom they are caring at some stage in the illness.

3. *Family dynamics.* In some families violence is considered the normal reaction to stress, and it may continue from generation to generation. In some cases, the abuser was abused as a child by the person they are now abusing. Marital conflict resulting in spouse abuse can continue into old age, and in many cases of elder abuse there has been a long past history of domestic violence. When two or more generations live together, inter-generational conflict can occur due to different values and expectations.

4. *Carer stress.* The responsibility for providing physical, emotional and financial support to a dependent older family member can generate great stress. Illness in the carer, financial difficulties, inadequate support and lack of recognition for the caring role, and personal stress, can all

contribute to this stress. In many cases, other contributory factors are already present and this additional stress on the carer appears to be the factor that triggers the abuse.

5.   *Older population*. It is very important that these contributory factors are looked at in the context of a population where an increasing proportion are older people and there is an increasing prevalence of age-related diseases such as dementia. Government policies are advocating community care, and in light of the limited resources available, are possibly placing extra strain on family carers.

IDENTIFICATION OF ABUSE

One of the major problems in dealing with abuse is the difficulty we may have in recognizing it. It is necessary to be on the alert and have a high index of suspicion, because symptoms and signs of abuse are often subtle, and are attributed to the ageing process because the person is old and frail. The following symptoms and signs are suggestive of abuse. However, it is also important to remember that the presence of one or more of the signs listed below does not necessarily establish that abuse is occurring, as many of these are seen in frail older people with chronic disease. Ageing skin may bruise more readily, bones may fracture more easily due to osteoporosis, and falls may occur more often due to degenerative changes or disease in the central nervous system. The physical examination is most appropriately done by a medical practitioner, who should have the clinical experience to differentiate between those symptoms and signs due to pathological changes and those due to abuse.

Physical and sexual abuse

This type of abuse includes punching, kicking, beating, biting, burning, pushing, dragging, scratching, shaking, arm twisting, sexual assault and any other physical harm to an older person. It includes physical restraint such as being tied to a bed or chair, or being locked in a room.

Good Practice Tips: Indicators

- Look for a history of unexplained accidents or injuries. Has the older person been to several different doctors or hospitals? It is important to check on conflicting stories from the older person and caregiver, and on discrepancies between the injury and the history. There may have been a long delay between the injury occurring, and reporting for treatment.

- Any story of an older person being accident-prone should be viewed with suspicion, as should multiple injuries, especially at different stages of healing, and untreated old injuries.

- On the head, look for bald patches, and signs of bruising on the scalp. This may be indicative of hair pulling.

- Watch for black eyes and bleeding in the white part of the eye. Look at the nose and lips for swelling, bruising, lacerations and missing teeth. Fractures of the skull, nose and facial bones should always alert one to the possibility of abuse.

- On the arms look for bruising, especially bruises of an unusual shape. Consider belt buckles, walking sticks, hair brushes or ropes as instruments of injury. Look for pinch marks and grip marks on the upper arms. Victims of abuse are sometimes shaken. Look for bite marks or scratches.

- Look for burns from cigarettes, or chemical burns from caustic substances. Glove or stocking distribution of burns suggest immersion in hot or boiling water.

- Look for rope or chain burns, or other signs of physical restraint, especially on the wrists or around the waist. Older people may be tied to a bed, to a chair, even to a toilet.

- On the trunk look for bruises, abrasions, cigarette burns. Ribs may be fractured if the victim is pushed or shoved against an object or piece of furniture.

- Examine the genital area for bruising, bleeding, and painful areas. Check for torn, stained or blood-stained underwear. Look for evidence of sexually transmitted disease. Watch for difficulty with walking or sitting. Any of these signs may be indicative of sexual abuse.

- On the lower limbs look for bruising, rope burns, abrasions, lacerations, or evidence of past or present fractures.

Psychological abuse

This is said to have occurred when an older person suffers mental anguish as a result of being shouted/sworn at, threatened, humiliated, intimidated, bullied, emotionally isolated by withdrawal of affection, or emotionally blackmailed.

Psychological abuse is usually characterized by a pattern of behaviour repeated over time and intended to maintain a hold of fear over the older person.

Good Practice Tips: Indicators

- The older person may be huddled when sitting, and nervous with the family member or caregiver nearby.

- Insomnia, sleep deprivation and loss of interest in self or environment may occur.

- Fearfulness, helplessness, hopelessness, passivity, apathy, resignation, withdrawal may be evident. Look for paranoid behaviour or confusion. Look for anger, agitation, or anxiety. Many of these signs may be attributed to psychiatric disorders or delirium.

- Watch how the older person behaves when the caregiver enters or leaves the room. There may be ambivalence towards a family member or caregiver. Often there is reluctance to talk openly, and the older person avoids facial or eye contact with both medical practitioner and caregiver.

Financial abuse

This is the improper use of an older person's money, property, or assets, by someone else and may be more easily detected when older people are visited in their own homes. This may be difficult for a medical practitioner to ascertain, and may require advice from the older person's solicitor or accountant. Referral to a social worker within an aged care service may also be appropriate.

Good Practice Tips: Indicators

- There may be loss of money ranging from removal of cash from a wallet to the cashing of cheques for large amounts of money.

- Sudden or unexplained withdrawal of money from a bank account may occur.

- There may be a sudden inability to pay bills or buy food.

- Bank books, credit cards and cheque books may be 'lost'.

- There may be a loss of jewellery, silverware, paintings, even furniture.

- An unprecedented transfer of money or property to another person may have occurred.

- A new will may have been made in favour of a new friend or another family member. Power of attorney may be obtained improperly from an older person who is not mentally competent.

Neglect

This occurs where an older person is deprived by the caregiver of the necessities of life. Neglect may include the withholding of adequate food, shelter, clothing, medical care or dental care and may be intentional or unintentional. Neglect may also involve the refusal to permit others to provide appropriate care.

Good Practice Tips: Indicators

- If food or drink are being withheld there is malnourishment, weight loss, wasting and dehydration, all without an illness-related cause. The older person may have constipation or faecal impaction.

- There may be evidence of inadequate or inappropriate use of medication, for instance, the older person may be over-sedated in the middle of the day.

- There may be evidence of unmet physical needs such as decaying teeth or overgrown nails.

- The older person may be lacking necessary aids such as spectacles, dentures, hearing aids or walking frame.

- There may be poor hygiene or inadequate skin care. The older person may be very dirty or smell strongly of urine or be infested with lice. There may be a urine rash with excoriation and chafing.

- Clothing may be dirty and in poor repair; it may be inappropriate for the weather or for the person's gender.

- In some cases where the older person is immobile, they may develop pressure areas over the sacrum, hips, heels or elbows. Sometimes medical care and attention are withheld until the older person is almost moribund.

THE ASSESSMENT PROCESS

General principles for assessment

It is necessary to gain the consent of the patient for any assessment and whilst the patient may be happy to be interviewed and examined, there are often situations where the victim of abuse does not wish any further action to be taken. Older people may be reluctant to report abuse by a family member or caregiver on whom they rely for their basic needs. There may be shame where a close family member is the abuser, or there may be fear of retaliation or fear of institutionalization. If the person does not give consent to further action and is competent to make that decision, then that decision must be respected. One important issue for general practitioners is the well-founded concern that if they confront the abusive situation openly or take action in contravention to the wishes of the patient or perhaps the family, the patient will simply move to another GP.

It is important to take a non-judgemental approach to cases of abuse, and often it is most appropriate to look at the situation as one in which there are two victims, rather than a victim and an abuser. Attention must be paid to resolving the unmet needs of both victim and abuser rather than simply identifying abuse and punishing the guilty party. In many cases where the GP is involved, the GP has a good knowledge of both victim and abuser and in fact may be in a doctor–patient relationship with both parties. However, this may create problems in management preventing further action on the part of the GP, and necessitating referral to another service.

There are a number of ethical principles to be observed. Beneficence is the principle of doing good and ensuring that the best interests of the patient are promoted. Harming or destroying a fragile family relationship that is important to the older person in the process of dealing with an abusive situation is not observing this principle. This may be averted by taking the non-judgemental approach described above. Autonomy is the principle of freedom of choice, the right of an individual to make decisions for themselves that are independent and made without coercion or undue influence. There are often major dilemmas involving our duty of care, associated with the principle of beneficence and the victim's freedom of choice, when we have a victim in a situation of abuse and clearly at risk who wishes to stay in that situation. If that person is competent to make that decision then that is their right.

Confidentiality refers to the obligation of non-disclosure by medical professionals of personal information unless they have the consent of the patient. Whilst this is a basic tenet of medical practice, there are times when practitioners have to disclose information and so the principle of confidentiality is overridden. This occurs where there is a subpoena, or where the medical practitioner believes that a crime has been committed, or where it is in the individual's interest, for example if the individual is suicidal. Here the principle of beneficence might take precedence over confidentiality.

The assessment
It is important to know the past medical and psychiatric history of the patient, their present medical problems and their current medication. This should be readily available to the GP, and should be obtained from the GP if the patient has been referred to a geriatric health service. It is important to look for the geriatric syndromes that may be underlying the presentation. Cognitive decline is often not recognized, and reversible problems such as depression or chronic urinary tract infection need to be identified and treated. Delirium needs to be identified and the underlying cause treated. Disorders such as Parkinson's disease may present with the 'negative' symptoms of slowness in walking and inability to perform self-care tasks such as doing up buttons or cleaning teeth, symptoms often attributed to the ageing process. However

Parkinson's disease responds very well to medication and referral for rehabilitation. Progressive disability due to a previous stroke may also benefit from a further period of targeted rehabilitation.

Where there is any suspicion or suggestion of elder abuse, the possible victim should be asked as sensitively and tactfully as possible about the situation. Where there has been a long-standing relationship of trust between patient and doctor this may be somewhat easier than where a relative stranger is asking questions. Indirect questions are less confronting and may elicit more information than asking directly about abuse. Sometimes it may take several consultations and many assurances of confidentiality before the situation is clear.

A full physical examination may reveal untreated medical problems such as hypertension, mild heart failure, diabetes, urinary tract infection, or constipation, which may all be impacting on the patient's function, dependency levels or mental state. The examination may reveal some of the signs of abuse described above. The patient's level of speech and need for assistive devices such as hearing aids or spectacles should be noted.

As part of the examination it is important to check the patient's cognitive state and the Mini Mental Status Examination (Folstein, Folstein and McHugh 1975) is a very useful screening test. Dementia is a condition of high prevalence but is not always diagnosed early in the disease process. It is highly significant as a risk factor for abuse, as the person with dementia may be a victim of abuse (particularly financial abuse), but may also become physically or verbally abusive towards their caregiver.

It is absolutely imperative to know whether a person has mental capacity, that is, s/he is competent to make decisions. This is relevant from the taking of a history through to arranging appropriate interventions. If a person is incapable of giving an accurate history due to dementia or psychiatric illness then involvement of others (family members, friends, service providers) is essential. If there is no enduring guardian or power of attorney in place, a substitute decision-maker may need to be appointed to assist where decisions have to be made about future management. It is important to remember that capacity is task-specific, and a person with dementia may be quite able to make reasonable decisions about what they wish to wear, or eat for dinner, but may not be able to consent to a major surgical procedure or make financial decisions. Whilst it is ultimately a legal decision as to whether a person is competent or not, the opinion of the attending medical practitioner is very important.

Depression is another quite common condition in older people that can contribute to or be caused by abuse. The use of a screening tool such as the Geriatric Depression Scale (Yesavage *et al.* 1983) can reveal underlying depressive illness which may respond well to medication or psychotherapy. Chronic eating disorders have been identified in some older women who are victims of abuse, and this type of anorexia needs to be recognized and addressed (Pritchard 2000).

A functional assessment should be performed. Is the patient independent in self-care and activities of daily living or do they need assistance in some areas? This dependence on others for assistance is a risk factor for abuse and in some cases this dependence can be improved by rehabilitation or provision of aids.

Gathering background information is another very important part of the assessment process. Interviews with the caregiver, family members and friends can provide a lot of useful and corroborative information.

The role of the general practitioner

In Australia, the vast majority of older people visit their GP at least once a year, and the GP often has a long-standing relationship with their patient and the patient's family, and knows their background. As well, the GP should have detailed medical records for the patient and be well aware of both present and past medical problems, current medication and the patient's social situation. They are therefore ideally placed to identify elder abuse. In November 1999, a new health-screening and assessment item for the over-75s was introduced into the Australian Medical Benefits Schedule. This item reimburses GPs for performing screening and assessment on an annual basis for their older patients. It includes functional, psychological and cognitive assessments, enabling the GP to have a better understanding of their patients' needs. The screening for, and identification of, elder abuse will hopefully become part of this process.

The role of the GP in managing the abusive situation is a little less clear. Whilst management of the medical problems is clearly within the capabilities of the GP, areas such as counselling, arranging community services, applying for guardianship or organizing alternative accommodation may be more appropriately dealt with by the multidisciplinary staff within a geriatric health service. This also allows the GP to maintain a relationship with both parties in the abusive situation, and to remain in the role of a trusted counsellor and perhaps friend.

The GP also has an important role in preventing abusive situations from occurring. Where carer stress is evident, the GP can help the family recognize that this is an at-risk situation, that stress levels need to be monitored. The carer is often an older person who may have a medical condition or functional impairment, and they need to be cared for and treated as a patient as well.

The role of the geriatrician

Most geriatricians work within a geriatric health service, and cover both hospital in-patients and community patients. They have training in internal medicine and experience in assessment of cognitive and functional impairment, and can access other disciplines such as social work, and specialties such as psychiatry where necessary. They are used to assessing patients with non-specific, unusual or deceptive presentations and to working with families and other service providers. They are therefore well qualified to assist in the assessment and management of elder abuse.

Since the report on elder abuse from the British Geriatrics Society in 1989 (Tomlin 1989), geriatricians have been alerted to the problem of elder abuse. In Australia, the Australian Society for Geriatric Medicine made elder abuse the subject of its first position paper in an attempt to improve the assessment and management of elder abuse (Kurrle 1995). As opposed to the ongoing role of the GP, a geriatrician is more likely to be involved on a one-off or episodic basis, in providing advice about medical management, in the provision of rehabilitation or assistive devices to address functional impairment, and in the assessment of mental capacity.

The role of the Aged Care Psychiatry Service

As patients with psychological or physical abuse may present with symptoms of depression, anxiety or psychosis, it is important that staff of the Aged Care Psychiatry Service are aware of the possiblity of abuse occurring in patients they see. Psychopathology in the abuser is a significant risk factor in the occurrence of abuse, with some sufferers of psychiatric illness having very poor self-control and judgement. The involvement of aged care psychiatrists and nurses is essential in assessment and management of these patients. Neuropsychology input may be necessary where assessment of mental capacity is required, and specific areas of competence need to be tested.

The role of the Emergency Department physician

A patient presenting to the busy Emergency Department of a hospital will have the obvious injury treated but often lack of time and pressure of other medical emergencies will prevent a detailed history being taken, or further questions being asked. There is rarely any background history available and unless the referral has been made by the patient's GP with a diagnosis of elder abuse or at least the suggestion of the possibility of abuse, the diagnosis of abuse is rarely entertained. Whilst there is legislation relating to child abuse in Australia, and therefore reasonable knowledge and training in this area, there is neither legislation nor training in elder abuse. It is very important that emergency medicine physicians and nursing staff are aware of the occurrence of abuse and are able to alert the hospital's geriatric medical services to follow the patient and where necessary inform the GP.

MANAGEMENT OF ABUSE

The management of elder abuse is dealt with in detail elsewhere in this book, and this section simply touches on some of the interventions that a medical practitioner may use to address an abusive situation. Ideally interventions seek to achieve freedom, safety, the minimum disruption of lifestyle, and the least restrictive care alternatives.

Addressing underlying medical problems in both victim and abuser is essential. Two of the major risk factors for abuse are the dependency of the older person due to physical or cognitive impairment and psychopathology in the abuser. Reducing symptoms of disease, improving physical function and treating psychiatric illness or substance abuse are clearly important ways to improve a potential or actual abusive situation.

In cases of severe physical abuse, the victim often needs to be immediately separated from the abuser and this may require admission to an acute hospital bed. The GP may be involved in making this referral, and then the geriatrician, hospital social worker and other members of the geriatric health service can assist in providing assessment and advice on future management. Counselling is an important means of intervention and may involve individual counselling or family therapy. The aim is to help the victim cope with their situation, and assist them to find a way to be safe from their abuser. It is also important that the victim be given assistance to recover from the impact of the abuse. In some cases the GP may wish to undertake some of this counselling, but more often this would be done by a social worker. In cases where domestic violence is the main cause of abuse, a referral may need to be made to the appropriate services for victims of domestic violence. These services include counselling, dedicated police officers with specific training in domestic violence, and access to refuges. Unfortunately most domestic violence services in Australia are orientated towards the younger women, and many are unsuitable for a frail or disabled older person.

It is very important to acknowledge the treatment needs of the abuser. In cases where abuser psychopathology is a major causative factor, admission to hospital may be necessary to address the psychiatric illness or drug or alcohol problems. Psychological counselling which allows the abuser to talk openly about their behaviour may be beneficial.

The other interventions including provision of community support services or respite care, arrangement of alternative accommodation, and legal interventions are often arranged by social workers or other team members. However, close liaison with the medical practitioner is important.

CASE EXAMPLES

When things are not quite what they seem

CASE STUDY 1

Mrs White is a 73-year-old woman with an early dementia who was referred to the geriatric health service as a case of physical abuse at the hands of her daughter who had moved in with her some months earlier. Mrs White had quite severe bruising on one side of her face and on her arms and lower legs. Neighbours had also reported hearing loud voices frequently. It appeared to be a definite case of abuse, although both Mrs White and her daughter denied it vehemently. Mrs White was admitted to hospital because she was considered to be at risk. Blood tests showed that she had a blood-clotting disorder resulting in spontaneous bruising and the presence of obvious bruising on exposed areas. She was also noted to be quite deaf without her hearing aid and needed to be spoken to in a loud voice. Once her blood disease was treated and a functioning hearing aid was purchased, there were no further 'signs' of abuse.

CASE STUDY 2

Mr Gray is a man in his late 70s who was admitted to hospital with a several-day history of vomiting blood. He had arthritis and occasionally took anti-inflammatory drugs which are known to cause stomach ulceration. Investigations showed him to have a gastric ulcer, and he was started on treatment for this and discharged. He was readmitted a month later after a massive bowel haemorrhage from which he almost died. On admission he was noted to have very high levels of the anti-coagulant drug warfarin in his urine. His GP confirmed that he was not being prescribed this for any medical reason. As he was recovering, the patient made an off-hand comment about how his son would be glad to see the last of him. The hospital social worker investigated further and discovered that the patient's son was in fact a bankrupt solicitor who had major financial problems. He also held a power of attorney for his father. It transpired that he had mortgaged his father's home and spent most of his liquid assets, all without his father's knowledge or consent. The daughter-in-law was a nurse who in her job had easy access to the drug warfarin. It would appear that this man was being poisoned.

Dementia, financial abuse and neglect

CASE STUDY 3

Mrs Brown was an 84-year-old widow with moderate Alzheimer's disease who lived alone. She had been managing quite well with assistance from community services, and her GP visited regularly. Recently her daughter moved in with her, ostensibly to care for her. Her daughter cancelled all services and suggested to the GP that his regular visits were unnecessary. Three months later one of Mrs Brown's neighbours contacted her GP. He was concerned that Mrs Brown appeared to have lost a lot of weight and was often seen in her backyard crying. The GP visited and was reluctantly admitted to the house by Mrs Brown's daughter. The GP noted that Mrs Brown had indeed lost weight, and she appeared unkempt and had facial bruising. She was unable to use her right arm and her mental state had markedly deteriorated.

Arrangements were made for Mrs Brown to be admitted to hospital, where she was found to be malnourished, to have an untreated wrist fracture and to have bruising over her trunk and face. As she recovered, unsuccessful attempts were made to involve her daughter in discussions about future care. As it was understood that previously Mrs Brown had been a woman of considerable means, an application was made to the Guardianship Tribunal for Financial Management, and also for Guardianship. It transpired that Mrs Brown's daughter had organized a power of attorney for her mother and had moved a large amount of money into other accounts for her own use. With the making of Guardianship and Financial Management orders, much of the money was retrieved, and Mrs Brown was able to return home and could afford to pay for a live-in carer.

Carer abuse

CASE STUDY 4

Mr and Mrs Jones had been married for 45 years when Mr Jones developed Parkinson's disease and dementia. Despite Mrs Jones' general poor health and increasing frailty, she continued to provide all the care for her husband. He refused to allow the Home Nursing Service to assist in showering him until his wife fell in the shower and broke her wrist. When the visiting nurse attempted to shower him, he grabbed at her breasts and made suggestive comments. A male nurse took over care and no similar behaviour occurred.

Once his wife's wrist fracture was healed, Mr Jones insisted that his wife shower him. The male nurse continued to visit to supervise medication and noted that Mrs Jones often had bruising on her face. She explained that she had hit her head on the door during the night, or had fallen against a piece of furniture. Eventually she admitted that her husband had got angry with her and occasionally hit her. She felt that it was her fault as she must have provoked him.

The nurse spoke with the Jones' general practitioner who visited and examined Mrs Jones. He noted bruising of different ages on her face, trunk and arms.

A referral was made to the Aged Care Assessment Team who arranged regular in-home respite for Mrs Jones, as well as assistance with showering for Mr Jones. Mrs Jones underwent considerable counselling to help her to deal with the culmination of many years of low grade domestic violence. Eventually Mr Jones required nursing home placement. Mrs Jones' health improved markedly and she became very involved in a local handcraft group.

CONCLUSION

As the numbers of dependent older people in the community increase, we can expect to see more cases of abuse. As noted at the beginning of this chapter there has been a general reluctance amongst the medical profession to become involved with elder abuse to the same degree as with child abuse. This is a great pity for older people because there is so much that the medical profession can offer in the identification, assessment and management of elder abuse. As Dr Mark Lachs says:

... the proper management of elder abuse can produce improvement in quality of life that rivals or exceeds the gains made when doctors aggressively diagnose and treat heart disease, pneumonia, diabetes, and other organic illnesses. (Lachs 1995)

REFERENCES

Folstein, M., Folstein, S. and McHugh, P. (1975) 'Mini-mental state: A practical method for grading the cognitive state of patients for the clinician.' *Journal of Psychiatric Research 12*, 189–198.

Kurrle, S., Sadler, P. and Cameron, I. (1992) 'Patterns of elder abuse.' *Medical Journal of Australia 157*, 10, 673–676.

Kurrle, S. (1995) *Position Statement on Elder Abuse.* Sydney: Australian Society for Geriatric Medicine.

Lachs, M. (1995) 'Preaching to the Unconverted: Educating Physicians About Elder Abuse.' *Journal of Elder Abuse and Neglect 7*, 4, 1–12.

Lachs, M. and Pillemer, K. (1995) 'Abuse and neglect of elderly persons.' *New England Journal of Medicine 332*, 7, 437–443.

McCallum, J., Simons, L., Simons, J. and Wilson, J. (1994) *Hospital and Home: A Longitudinal Study of Hospital, Residential and Community Services Use by Older People Living in Dubbo NSW.* Social Policy Directorate Best Practice Paper 6. Sydney: Office on Ageing, 1994.

McCreadie, C., Bennett, G. and Tinker, A. (1998) 'Investigating british general practitioners' knowledge and experience of elder abuse: Report of a research study in an Inner London borough.' *Journal of Elder Abuse and Neglect 9*, 3, 23–29.

Pillemer, K. and Finkelhor, D. (1988) 'The prevalence of elder abuse: A random sample survey.' *Gerontologist 28*, 51–57.

Pritchard, J. (2000) *The Needs of Older Women: Services for Victims of Elder Abuse and Other Abuse.* Bristol: Policy Press.

Tomlin, S. (1989) *Abuse of Elderly People: An Unnecessary and Preventable Problem.* London. British Geriatrics Society.

Wolf, R. (1988) 'Elder Abuse: Ten years later.' *Journal of the American Geriatrics Society 36*, 758–762.

Yesavage, J.A., Brink, T.L., Lum, O., Huang, V., Adey, M. and Leirer, V.O. (1983) 'Development and validation of a geriatric depression screening scale: a preliminary report.' *Journal of Psychiatric Research 17*, 37–49.

CHAPTER 6

THE ROLE OF THE REGISTRATION AND INSPECTION OFFICER

ADRIAN HUGHES

INTRODUCTION

In this chapter I shall consider the two main ways in which the registration and inspection officer (RIO) has a direct role in the prevention and identification of abuse within residential care settings. In broad terms RIOs are involved with residential services both before registration is granted and post-registration, and have a specific role at each point.

In summary the pre-registration involvement provides the RIO with an opportunity to offer guidance that seeks to prevent abuse. Following registration the RIO has a statutory duty to visit and inspect services, which will include monitoring how the registered person ensures the safety and well-being of those living in the home.

Before looking at the present role of registration and inspection in preventing, identifying and investigating incidents of the abuse of vulnerable adults it is important to emphasize that legislative changes are on the horizon. This is part of the government's modernizing agenda, and will alter the structure, location and management of registration and inspection officers, and one hopes deal with some of the weaknesses in the present arrangements.

The Care Standards Act 2000 received Royal Assent on 17 July 2000 and it is proposed that the new Act will be implemented in full on 1 April 2002. The Care Standards Act 2000 will repeal the present legislation in full, however in the meantime the Registered Homes Act 1984, associated regulations and other guidance with various amendments and their inherent faults continue to provide the legal framework.

The Registered Homes Act 1984 is the primary legislation regulating residential homes, homes for children with disabilities, nursing homes, private hospitals and clinics. Currently the responsibility for the registration and inspection of residential care homes rests with social services departments, who were required in 1990 Department of Health LAC (90) 13 to establish inspection units. Health authorities provide for the regulation of nursing homes and private hospitals and clinics but are not required to maintain inspection units in the same way. The Department of Health requires social services registration and inspection units to be managed at 'arms length' from the operational functions of social services departments. This is to deal with the tension where social services are purchasers, providers and regulators of care, thereby being in conflict with the private and voluntary providers of residential homes. Registration and inspection units located in social services departments have a statutory duty to register and inspect residential care homes, small residential care homes (homes for fewer than four clients) and many now undertake the voluntary accreditation and inspection of domiciliary care agencies.

Residential care homes provide accommodation, board, and personal care to adults who need personal care by reason of disability, age, infirmity, or drug or alcohol dependency.

Health authorities register and inspect nursing homes, private hospitals, and clinics for adults in need of nursing or medical intervention. It is a general rule of thumb that residential care homes provide the type of care that a competent caring relative would provide and nursing homes provide care that would be delivered by a skilled registered nurse.

Under the present arrangements the legislation allows for each social services department and each health authority to have its own registration and inspection unit. Each unit will have its own policies and standards based on the legislation. This results in a large number of individual units and sometimes in a variation in standards although perhaps not as diverse as some would have us believe. There are a few joint units, which carry out the functions for both health and social services.

It should be recognized that a large number of vulnerable adults live in care situations in which there is no external regulation, relying at best solely on the internal auditing and monitoring processes and at worst on the endeavours of individual staff. Such settings include sheltered housing schemes, warden-controlled housing complexes, supported lodgings and hostels. Recent findings by Action on Elder Abuse (Jenkins, Asif and Bennett 2000) indicated that reports of abuse in sheltered housing complexes accounted for 4.2 per cent of all calls to their helpline. Clearly in the absence of external scrutiny vulnerable adults in these settings are subject to or perceive themselves to be the victims of abuse.

In order to understand the specific role and level of involvement of a local inspection unit the practitioner should aim to find out where the unit is located, its address and ideally make contact, seeking information regarding policies and procedures. Most units provide leaflets detailing key functions, which will often include a complaints procedure, and the unit's role in adult protection procedures (see Appendix 1 for example).

Good Practice Tip

Get to know about your local registration and inspection unit before you need support with abuse situations – find out the address, telephone number and the remit of the unit. Most provide information leaflets.

THE REGISTERED HOMES ACT 1984

There are differing views as to the primary purpose of the Registered Homes Act 1984. It can be seen from a purely legal standpoint as a licensing process with the protection of users being a secondary function. Alternatively the legalization can be seen as requiring those registered under the Act to work to a set of regulations which seek to protect users by placing legally enforceable duties on the registered person. As it stands the Act is recognised in many instances to fall short of protecting vulnerable adults to a level which society and the government would view as acceptable. However, until the new legislation is enacted the Registered Homes Act 1984 can and should be used to enhance protection of individuals in residential care.

In the broadest sense the Act offers protection to vulnerable adults by seeking to ensure the 'fitness' of those operating care homes, the premises, and the policies and procedures which shape the way in which the home is run. 'Fitness' can be assessed in two ways: pre-registration and post-registration.

Pre-registration

Before anyone provides a residential care home or nursing home they must be registered with the local social services department or health authority – or both if they intend to run a dual registered (residential and nursing) home. It is an offence to run a home for which the provider is not registered and the person can be prosecuted. The registration process is designed to ensure that only those who are considered 'fit' to operate a home are allowed to do so. A number of checks are undertaken, including police checks and references, and a consideration of policies to protect clients from abuse. It should be recognized that abuse is possible in any home, and acceptance of this is no reflection on the home itself, but is a responsible and necessary approach to the care of vulnerable people. If there is a denial or a lack of understanding of what constitutes abuse it is more likely that abuse or abusive practice will develop undetected.

When the registration and inspection unit as the registering authority is satisfied of the fitness of the applicant, the premises and the manner in which the home will operate, a certificate of registration is issued. The certificate of registration must be displayed in a prominent place within the home, with the exception of small homes. The certificate will permit a named person, persons or company to carry on a residential or nursing home in a named establishment.

There are conditions attached to the certificate of registration, which regulate the number, age, sex and category of residents to be accommodated. These conditions should not be seen as a bureaucratic burden but more of a regulatory necessity and are designed to ensure the welfare of people living at the home, for example by avoiding overcrowding that can lead to environmental abuse. Specifying categories ensures that staff understand the particular needs of those for whom they will care, and that they have suitable training and skills to minimize the likelihood of abusive care practice. In seeking to create a safe environment for residents the conditions make some provision to ensure compatibility of need. Where the needs of residents are incompatible this can result in an abuse of residents by another resident. One example could be where the behaviour of a resident who has disturbed sleep patterns may result in sleep deprivation of others living in the home. Alternatively older people who require support due to physical frailty may be put in situations of heightened risk of abuse if a younger resident with an acute mental health need were to be admitted to the home. Thus the starting principle of not mixing care needs may prevent some institutional abuse that would otherwise occur. There is always the scope to vary conditions in respect of individual residents, providing the evidence is available to demonstrate that the proposed placement would be in the client's best interest and does not compromise the needs of those already living in the home.

Good Practice Tip

When considering the placement of a services user with whom you are working, consider the conditions attached to the registration. Do these indicate that the staff will be able to meet the particular needs of the service user? Is the permitted client mix suitable, complementary to the needs of the service user you are supporting? Abusive practice can be the result of 'right service user – wrong placement' simply because the home is not equipped to meet the needs of the service user.

If the officers (usually head of registration and inspection) of the registering authority are not satisfied that the applicant, the premises or the manner in which the home will operate are 'fit', the authority can propose that the registration be refused. The present legislation places the onus on the registering authority to prove unfitness rather than the applicant to prove that s/he is fit. A proposal to refuse registration is heard in private by a panel of members of the registering authority. The panel can uphold or dismiss the recommendation of the officer and, in the case of the latter, registration would proceed and a certificate of registration would be issued. As a general principle it would not be known to third parties that a proposal to refuse was considered.

If the panel upholds the recommendation and refuses registration the applicant has the right of appeal against the decision to the Registered Homes Act Tribunal Secretariat. A tribunal is ordinarily open to the public and allows both the applicant and the registering authority to present their respective cases, calling witnesses and evidence as necessary. The tribunal can accept the decision of the registering authority and dismiss the appeal or can overturn the decision and allow registration to proceed. The applicant can only appeal against a decision by the tribunal on points of law. Tribunal decisions are published in full. The Department of Health maintains a list of cancelled or refused registrations, and this is checked when an application for registration is received.

Good Practice Tip

Find out from the Registered Homes Act Tribunal Secretariat the dates of forthcoming tribunals in your area or obtain copies of tribunal decisions. This will help to increase your understanding of what is seen as acceptable in providing services.

Post-registration

When a certificate is issued the person registered is permitted to accept residents into the home and has a legal duty to operate the home in accordance with the legislation and local standards or guidelines. The requirements of the Residential Care Homes Regulations (RCHR)(Statutory Instrument No 1345) and the Nursing Home and Mental Nursing Home Regulations (NH&MNHR) (Statutory Instrument No 1578) together with the standards of the authority seek to offer protection to all residents. Duties are placed on those who run a home to operate in a way that seeks to eliminate abuse and harm to residents. For example the registered person is required to maintain individual case records including care plans which are recognized as one way to respond to situations where abuse is more likely to occur, e.g. challenging behaviour, residents refusing or reluctant to accept help/support in personal care/ hygiene/health. If staff are supporting a resident who refuses pre-scribed medication, or one who presents in an aggressive manner it is likely that without explicit written guidance staff may respond in wholly inappropriate ways which could be psychologically or physi-cally abusive.

Regulation 9 of the Residential Care Homes Regulations 1984, which applies to residential care homes but not nursing homes, requires those registered to ensure that the conduct of the home and decisions regarding the clients are always in the client's best interest. Regulation 10 (RCHR) and Regulation 12 (NH&MNHR) require the registered person to employ suitably qualified and competent staff in numbers which are adequate for the welfare of residents. It has been highlighted in a number of inquiries and reports – Longcare Inquiry (Bergner 1998); Beech House Inquiry (Camden and Islington Community Health Services NHS Trust 1999; Sheffield Adult Protection Committee (2000) – that the quality, training and skills of the staff together with the quality of the environment can be significant factors in abusive practice and regimes within homes. If for example the right type of equipment is not available or staff do not know how to respond to a specific care need the likelihood of increased risk and therefore harm to residents is present. If staff injure a resident when they have to physically move her when in reality she needs a hoist to be transferred, is this an accident or abuse?

The statutory duty of the registering authority is to visit and inspect a home at least twice in a 12-month period. If these two visits together amount to one and a half days, this equates to an inspector being in the home for approximately 0.4 per cent of the home's functioning in one year. The regulations therefore provide for some external scrutiny of the way in which homes operate between inspection visits. Regulation 14 (RCHR) sets out a requirement for specific events and incidents occurring within care homes to be reported to the registering authority within 24 hours. This would include examples such as the death of a resident under the age of 70 years, outbreak of infectious disease, theft, burglary, fire or accident in the home, and any event in the home that affects the well-being of any resident. The reporting of these incidents provides an opportunity for the registration unit to assess the level of response by the home to certain types of events and to determine if this is acceptable. If a number of similar incidents were reported or the way in which a particular incident was handled was of concern these would be prompts for a visit to be made in addition to the statutory inspections.

CASE STUDY I

Restawhile House reports to the registration and inspection unit an incident involving Graham, a young man with a learning disability who, following an allegation of inappropriate sexual conduct, was given a caution by the police. The report indicates that the matter was neither admitted nor proven. However, as Graham had been warned by staff in the past for similar behaviours it was considered as 'firing a warning shot across his bows'.

What are the issues? Does the incident raise any abuse issues?

In looking into the matter the registration and inspection unit discovered that this involved an alleged incident during a bus journey with Graham's previous long-term partner, Susan. There had been no witnesses and the woman involved had raised the matter with her carer later in the day. She had alleged that Graham had attempted to put his hand up her skirt, she had resisted and also asked him to stop. Graham denied this saying that he was no longer interested in his ex-partner. There had been incidents in the past following which staff had addressed with him some issues regarding inappropriate sexual conduct and the general view was that Susan would have no motive to fabricate the story.

In considering the issues it is important to ensure that the rights of Susan are protected but a starting point must be to consider whether this situation would have been handled the same way if Graham did not have a learning disability. A caution by the police even in the presence of an appropriate adult still amounts to admitting guilt. However, Graham denied this. The central feature in this matter was the opportunity to 'fire the warning shot', which was more to make staff feel comfortable rather than to deal with the issue.

Was it abusive?

The first response is usually 'staff were acting in everyone's best interest' although in considering abuse the most important matter is to consider outcome. If you are thumped, the physical pain is no less because it was not intentional. This incident was abusive as it denied Graham the most basic right of being listened to and heard; his guilt was assumed because of past behaviours. The actions of the staff were less to do with the protection of Graham but more to demonstrate that they were doing something about the concerns they have about a resident in their care.

Learning point

Vulnerable residents must be offered the same protection in law as every other citizen, and corners should not be cut simply because the person is not sufficiently 'street-wise' to understand that their rights are being compromised. Abuse is about outcome not intention.

These regulations together with the visits by the registration and inspection unit provide for some level of external monitoring of the home. In addition of course there are visits by family and friends, other professionals and the clients themselves, who will be the ears and eyes, providing ongoing and regular monitoring. However, in situations in which abuse occurs it is usually behind closed doors when visitors and others have left.

INSPECTION

Under present legislation one statutory inspection is announced and another unannounced. There is a need for units to schedule all inspections to assist with their own workload planning and to ensure compliance in meeting the statutory targets. The plan is for this information to be available only within the registration and inspection unit but it should be noted that there are incidents when this information has inadvertently been made known. The ways in which dates of proposed unannounced inspections are made known vary from chance comments, individual staff sharing information with colleagues outside the unit or with friends who may be involved in the provision of care. Whilst this leaking of information is not endemic it must be recognized that in the best systems there are some flaws. In situations in which information is released, managers of units deal with it by changing inspection dates and schedules. The sole purpose for raising this here is to acknowledge that the determined abuser or abusive environments can remain well-hidden and serve as a reminder that the integrity of the unannounced inspection must be protected.

Each registration and inspection unit will have a policy regarding the inspection visits including notice period of the announced inspection. This can vary from three weeks to a couple of months but the average tends to be about four weeks. The announced visit is perhaps the best opportunity for those living in homes and those supporting them to have direct and planned access to the RIO. Again each authority will have its own policy about engaging users and others in the inspection process, which usually, but not always, relies on the registered person 'advertising' a forthcoming inspection.

Good Practice Tip

Find out from your local registration and inspection unit the policy for notifying homes and others of the forthcoming announced inspection. This is an opportunity for practitioners to support service users to give their view about the service provided.

The statutory inspection of homes focuses on three main aspects reflecting the registration process: the fitness of the premises; the fitness of staff; and the manner in which the home operates. Again the emphasis of the process is to consider the outcome for users and to ensure that the safety and well-being of residents is protected and safeguarded. During both the announced and unannounced inspection visits the RIO will create opportunities for discussion with residents to hear firsthand of their experience. In situations in which this opportunity is limited the officer will employ a range of other skills and techniques to learn of the outcome for residents. Discussion with staff is important as it gives an insight into the values of the home and what is seen as acceptable in terms of practice. Often abusive practice is not directly observed but is identified from an account relayed by a staff member. This gives the RIO the opportunity to explore these matters further by talking with other staff, inspecting records and directly observing practice.

It is not possible in this chapter to set out the whole process of inspection, as it will vary between authorities. However, suffice to say that each inspection regardless of individual style or approach will be a process which seeks to measure whether the service being inspected meets the minimum requirements of the legislation and the standards of the authority and protects those who use the service. Registration and inspection units will give cognizance to the learning from enquiries and will have modified their practice accordingly. For example, inquiry reports into settings such as Longcare (Bergner 1998), and UKCC (1994) have raised important practice issues, which will guide inspectors. The following checklist is not an 'abusive practice checklist' which when ticked will evidence that abuse is taking place but rather should trigger inspection staff and others to consider if abusive practice could develop.

Good Practice Tips: Checklist

Cause for Concern

Staffing: inadequate recruitment/selection practice; inadequate or no induction; inadequate practice guidance and standards; poor or no support, supervision, appraisal or development; poor or no training; poor pay and conditions; undervaluing of staff; staff working alone or on a one-to-one basis; working under pressure; authoritarian or laissez-faire regime; high level of sickness; high level of turnover; inappropriate alcohol consumption by staff.

Practice: failure to develop clear philosophy/purpose/aim; senior staff being in post a long time thus having a high level of authority and perhaps entrenched views; under resourcing – staff, equipment, provisions; dull or depressing lifestyle for users; poor medical/nursing/personal care; few outside contacts; no advocacy scheme or complaints procedures; poor recording; poor administration; no internal audit/evaluation; a lack of openness about practice or procedure – an air of secrecy; fixed times of rising and going to bed; bathing and toilet routines not geared to the individual.

Environment: poor physical conditions; overcrowding; lack of equipment or damaged equipment; neglected furniture and fittings; overly clean; inadequately clean.

Individual staff: lack of interest and commitment; lack of knowledge, understanding or concern for the residents; personal problems including health problems; inability to relate to a particular resident.

External contact: pattern of incidents of concern; high level of complaints but none proven; difficulties or delays in access to people and premises; over-controlling regime; strict visiting times.

It is important to stress that if these features are present it does not automatically follow that abuse is taking place but such an environment may be the right 'breeding ground' for abusive practice to develop.

During an inspection the RIO will wish to be satisfied that the registered person is complying with the regulations and the conditions of registration as specified on the certificate of registration. There may be situations in which the registered person has admitted a resident outside the current conditions. The harsh reality is that a breach of the regulations has occurred and the RIO has to determine with his or her manager whether legal action should be pursued as described in the conclusion to this chapter. However, regardless of any enforcement action some decisions have to be made in respect of the specific breach.

The most likely breach is one in which a resident with care and support needs not covered by the certificate of registration is admitted to the home. In this situation the RIO does not want to give the message that disregard of the condition will result in simply allowing the resident to stay in the home. The RIO has to be satisfied that the home can respond to specific care needs and that others living in the home are not at any increased risk, which would include diminution of their support. Sometimes the high support needs of the incoming resident is at such a level that without increase of staff there are insufficient staff to provide a satisfactory service. It would never be the intention of the RIO to displace a resident who has been placed inappropriately but in some situations might have to ask the registered person to make alternative arrangements.

In 1994 the Department of Health issued guidance under section 7 of the Local Government Service Act 1970 (LAC (94)16) to require registration and inspection units to include lay assessors as part of the formal inspection process. The guiding principle is that the lay assessor could bring a fresh, non-professional perspective to the process, making it easier and more accessible for users, their carers and supporters to gain a lay view of the quality of homes. Following the inspection the lay assessor makes their views of the home known and this can be part of the overall inspection report or a stand-alone report.

A number of units seek to include residents in the lay assessor scheme providing support, transport, induction and some administrative support to facilitate their valuable contribution. The involvement of residents obviously changes the focus and provides a number of valuable opportunities for the residents of the particular service to share firsthand their experience of the home in which they live and of any concerns regarding practice. In working with residents as lay assessors some of the myths about expectations, gratitude and power relationships can be challenged.

INSPECTION REPORTS

Following an inspection visit a report will be prepared and eventually published following agreement with the registered person as to its accuracy. The reports are public documents and in accordance with guidance registration and inspection units are required to make them available (DOH 1994). Inspection reports should provide details of the service's response to abuse and indicate whether policies are in place to prevent abuse and to respond to abuse if it is identified.

Good Practice Tip

Find out from the registration and inspection unit how you can gain access to reports. When practitioners are working with service users who are considering a placement the inspection report can give an indicator as to how well the home meets the needs of current users and complies with the requirements of the registering authority.

COMPLAINTS

Registration and inspection units investigate complaints about services which they register. It is often through the process of investigating a complaint that abusive practice is identified. The investigation will be to consider if the complaint is founded and whether the registered person is in breach of any legislation, regulation or local standard. There is often a reluctance to complain about a service whilst the resident is still living in the home for fear of comeback. However, any detriment to the residents would be abusive in itself and would not be acceptable to the registering authority. Complaints do provide an opportunity for external monitoring of unsatisfactory situations and enable the regulator to determine if the practice or conduct of the home is in the broadest terms abusive. Clearly the term 'abusive' is emotive and rejected by home-owners, who prefer the terms 'poor' or 'bad practice'. However, examples such as poor quality food, poor quality of environment, lack of essential equipment, misappropriation of finances, punitive regimes, inadequate support from staff, care from someone not trained to provide quality care may fall under the general heading of 'poor practice' but to the client the outcome is abusive.

Where a complaint is founded or raises specific areas of concern the RIO in investigating complaints is in a position to request that the registered person takes action. This can be in the form of a recommendation or a requirement. The latter is set out against the regulations and is legally enforceable.

THE ROLE OF THE REGISTRATION AND INSPECTION UNIT IN THE INVESTIGATION OF SPECIFIC ALLEGATIONS OF ABUSE

Many authorities have developed inter-agency working arrangements and with the publication of *No Secrets* (DOH 2000) these arrangements should be further developed. Where an allegation of abuse is received in respect of a residential or nursing setting the inspection and registration unit will ordinarily be involved. It is likely that within such settings it will only be the registration and inspection unit that will have ongoing involvement following the investigation stage unless criminal charges are brought.

The following case study seeks to bring out the role of the registration and inspection unit in dealing with an incident of abusive practice. Here the 'whistleblower' does not use the term 'abuse' but wants to know if it is acceptable practice or if the registration and inspection unit allows it. This terminology is crucial in understanding that even now workers are not always sure as to what constitutes abuse and whether such unacceptable practice is permitted if sanctioned by an outside body.

CASE STUDY 2

A care assistant from Dunroaming Nursing Home contacted the registration and inspection unit to ask if an incident, which she has witnessed, is allowed by the unit. A qualified nurse who has recently joined the staff team was responsible for helping Mrs Baxter, who is totally blind, to have a bath. A note in Mrs Baxter's records stated that she can become agitated when having a bath and in the past she has scratched staff. The nurse decided that in order to protect staff she will make temporary mittens by bandaging Mrs Baxter's hands, thus removing any danger to staff. The care assistant reports that Mrs Baxter was even more agitated on this occasion requiring additional staff to manage the situation. The care assistant was concerned as the incident had been distressing to Mrs Baxter but the qualified nurse was of the view that the first duty was to ensure safety of staff.

Following receipt of this information a meeting of professionals was held where it was decided that the police did not have a remit to act. It was determined that a joint care manager/registration and inspection unit investigation would be the best way forward.

The qualified nurse admitted the incident and explained that her actions were primarily to protect Mrs Baxter. If she hurt staff then it may damage the relationship and this may impact on Mrs Baxter; the rationale being that to avoid any possibility of harm to either party was ultimately in the resident's best interest. The nurse confirmed that she had used this approach in other settings and it had never been questioned before. The care assistant, who had a positive relationship with Mrs Baxter, knew that she only became agitated in the bath because she disliked being naked and exposed to others. The care assistant's practice had in the past been to cover Mrs Baxter's breasts with a warm flannel and this had avoided any lashing out or behaviour which was difficult to manage. She was unqualified and although she wasn't happy with the action of the nurse she did not like to question her decisions, as she was a professional.

In investigating the abuse it was decided that the son of Mrs Baxter should be notified that an incident was being investigated. He was of the view that his mother could be difficult and actions of the staff to manage her were acceptable to him, providing she was not physically harmed.

The manager of the home agreed that the behaviour of the nurse was unacceptable but considered that her actions 'were for the best reasons'.

Mrs Baxter herself was interviewed but due to her deteriorating mental health and memory recall she was unable to give a verbal view as to how she felt. However, the accounts of the two staff involved in the situation in addition to the qualified nurse indicated that Mrs Baxter's non-verbal communication was that she did not like having her hands bandaged as this increased her sense of insecurity associated with her sight impairment.

Was this abusive?

The general view was that the incident was abusive and the outcome for Mrs Baxter was certainly abusive. The intention of the nurse was not to harm or distress Mrs Baxter but she failed to consider all known facts and approaches before dealing with the situation. It is accepted that abusive practice is more likely to occur when staff are unsure or uncertain as to how to deal with challenging behaviour. If they are not given guidance it is likely as in this case that the response will be inappropriate and to the detriment of the resident – abuse is about outcome not intention.

Outcome

The registration and inspection unit was able to work with the home, setting out the action they should take to ensure the likelihood of a recurrence of the incident was eliminated. This included staff training and induction, revision of policies and procedures and most importantly for staff at all levels to learn that reporting incidents to the manager about which they were unsure was an expectation of them as workers.

Learning points

Abuse is not always clearly articulated as abuse but often reported in the guise of poor practice. Managers of homes must set out as part of the care plan how they expect staff to deal with and respond to any challenging behaviour. If staff are uncertain there is an increased risk that their intervention will not be thought out. Unqualified staff will sometimes acquiesce to the practice of qualified staff, considering that it is not their place to raise issues. All staff must know that even professionals abuse and if there is an incident about which you feel unsure or uncomfortable you must report it to your manager. Abusive regimes may grow from incidents of abusive practice.

The RIO have within their remit a range of interventions in dealing with abuse in regulated services, and the Registered Homes Act also gives an inspector the right to enter and inspect at all times premises used or believed to be used as a residential care home. The Registered Homes Act 1984 sections 17 and 35 make it an offence to obstruct an inspector, not only to bar entry but also to prevent them from doing their job. Section 35 in respect of nursing homes goes further, making it an offence for anyone to refuse to withdraw when requested so that a service user can be interviewed by an RIO in private. The offender is liable to prosecution that on conviction could lead to imprisonment for up to three months or to a fine.

In addition to the partnership working with other agencies there is scope to work with homes and offer advice and guidance to the registered person to assist them to change practice. Often the discussion and heightened awareness of abusive practice is sufficient to persuade the registered person committed to providing a quality service to change practice. In other situations in which the registered person is perhaps not so receptive the scope to use the legislation to enforce specific action may be necessary. This can include remedial action such as serving an improvement or enforcement notice, or a proposal to cancel registration, and always ongoing close monitoring.

CASE STUDY 3

16 Carter Street is a registered care home accommodating 10 young adults with learning disabilities. There have been concerns about the regime in the home based primarily on the owner's and the staff team's ability and willingness to accept and support the residents' rights to independence. This has manifested itself on occasions when staff have misinterpreted challenging behaviours as 'naughtiness' and have responded in that vein.

During inspection visits this has been discussed with the owner and a requirement made for him to secure staff training and development opportunities for staff. It was recommended that the core element of the training should be about values and how to respond to challenging behaviour in age-appropriate and productive ways.

Despite discussions with the owner and some evidence of attempts to secure training the situation is drifting. Following an investigation into a complaint made by the carer of one of the residents in which it was proven that he was denied attending a social event at the day centre because of an outburst in the home. The owner was of the view that it was the fault of the staff because he had told them not to respond in this way. The staff felt they had always responded in that manner and until they were told to do otherwise they could not be expected to change.

In discussion with the registration and inspection unit manager it was decided that a notice should be served. This is a legal document and failure to comply with the notice in the timescale given is an offence against the regulations and the registering authority can initiate a prosecution in the magistrates' court. The prescribed period cannot exceed three months.

In this example the notice was served relating solely to Regulation 10 (RCHR) which is concerned with the provision of competent staff, and described the outcome to be achieved. This was to secure training for staff to ensure they understand the theory of good practice in providing services for people with learning disabilities. This had to be achieved in two months.

In order for the matter not to drift it was agreed that the inspector would closely monitor the situation so the owner could provide evidence that the training had been undertaken.

Without the input from the registration and inspection unit and the judicious use of the legislation it is possible that an abusive regime would have continued. Staff may have continued to use inappropriate power to control the residents' behaviour, and sanctions would perhaps have had to increase to maintain the control.

Learning points

It is likely that the situation would have continued to drift as the regime was useful for the owner and his staff. The full weight of the legislation could have been considered, resulting in the home closing, but, in doing so, along with the poor elements of the service many positive elements would have also been lost.

In dealing with the situation in this way the primary objective of protecting users from abuse is achieved. If the owner maintains compliance the notice becomes less important over subsequent years. Best practice would suggest that the home continues to be monitored to ensure the training and emerging new practice become the established pattern and regime. If not the registration and inspection unit may have to consider further action.

SUPPORTING LEGISLATION

All practitioners should be aware of two important statutes, which should guide and influence their practice: the Crime and Disorder Act 1998 and Public Interest Disclosure Act 1998. These two pieces of legislation not only offer protection to the practitioner in the event of reporting abuse but also complement other legislation such as the Registered Homes Act 1984 in dealing with and responding to abuse of vulnerable adults.

Section 115 of the Crime and Disorder Act 1998 provides for anyone to pass on information where they consider it necessary to aid or assist any provisions of the Act. One provision of the Act places a duty on local authorities to do all they can when discharging existing functions to prevent crime and disorder. In addition local authorities, the police and probation are required to develop and implement a strategy for reducing crime in their area. As set out in the chapter on *No Secrets* it is accepted that all forms of abuse can be a criminal act and therefore any disclosure about abuse or suspected abuse would provide for the legitimate passing-on of information under the provisions of section 115 of the Act. Information, which is considered to be important to prevent or reduce crime, can be disclosed to any of the police, the probation service, and a local authority or health authority. Practitioners should consider the following factors such as:

- What is the evidence? What is the source? How strong is the evidence?
- Is the potential victim a vulnerable adult and does the person have a 'right' to be protected?
- Who are the potential victims? Where do they live, in which authority area?

The practitioner may decide before full disclosure to liaise with local authorities and the police, presenting the scenario without disclosing identifying details. However, before doing so the practitioner should if possible discuss the information with their employing organization.

Good Practice Tip

Find out from your local registration and inspection unit or from the co-ordinator for the protection of vulnerable adults the policy or protocol for disclosure of information under section 115 of the Crime And Disorder Act 1998. In addition find out the agreed inter-agency protocol for reducing crime in the area. If the prevention of abuse is not on the agenda, ask why?

The Public Interest Disclosure Act 1998, which was enacted in July 1999, has been referred to disparagingly as a 'whistleblower's charter'. This is regrettable because in reality good employers do establish internal reporting systems, which staff can use and have confidence in, thereby removing or minimizing the need for staff to disclose to a third party. The Act establishes a framework for staff to raise serious concerns without the fear of victimization or recrimination.

The Act is only intended to be used for disclosing serious and genuine concerns and does not offer protection to those who seek to misuse it by making malicious allegations or disclosures for financial gain. Under the Act an employee is protected if they reasonably believe there is evidence of one of the following:

- a criminal offence – past, present or potential
- failure to meet a legal obligation
- a miscarriage of justice
- health and safety being compromised
- risk of environmental damage

or

- intentional concealment of any of the above.

In response to this Act a number of employers have established procedures for staff to report concerns. In some settings, policies carrying titles such as 'Speak out' encourage every employee to adopt a corporate responsibility to report poor or bad practice.

The Act encourages internal mechanisms for reporting incidents of concern to senior staff within the employing organization. However, it is also recognized that for a variety of reasons this may not be possible. The Public Interest Disclosure Act 1998 offers protection if the disclosure is to a third party. The general rules of thumb would be that they reasonably believe that:

- she/he will suffer some detriment for disclosing to their employer
- the employer will destroy, contaminate or lose evidence if they are 'warned' of the concern
- the employer is aware of the failure but has not taken action.

In disclosing to a third party it is expected that the employee will act reasonably and this would include considerations such as:

- to whom the disclosure is made – a report to the registration and inspection unit in respect of a care or nursing home would be seen as reasonable but a disclosure to the local press or television station would not
- the seriousness of the concern, whether it was a one-off or an ongoing activity – if it was the first occasion that health and safety was compromised and the employer did not know about it, it may be that the first approach would have been to use the in-house procedure where it exists
- the existence of an in-house disclosure policy and whether the employee had attempted to use it
- the seriousness of the activity, action or omission. If it is exceptionally serious and a considered disclosure is made directly to a third party, the employee would be protected.

The Public Interest Disclosure Act 1998 therefore provides a framework for staff to report acts of omission and commission, which result in abuse of vulnerable adults. These would include criminal activities including financial, physical or sexual abuse, any failure to comply with regulatory requirements such as duties under the Registered Homes Act, and any abusive practice, including neglect, which compromises the health, safety or well-being of clients.

All practitioners should make themselves familiar with the Crime and Disorder Act 1998 and Public Interest Disclosure Act 1998 and find out how these have been incorporated into local practice.

LIMITATIONS

There are limitations within the role of the registration and inspection officer, which must be considered. However, this should not be a deterrent to the proper investigation of concerns about practice within a home. Under present legislation RIOs do not have a statutory right to interview staff if the registered person states that they do not want the staff interviewed. It is therefore important that all staff are aware that they have a right to approach their local registration and inspection unit.

As set out in Case Study 2, staff sometimes do not know what constitutes abuse and there remains secret practice within the home. The nurse in the case study alleged that she had used this practice in a number of settings and it was not commented upon and therefore by default was seen as acceptable. While she may not have seen her practice as unacceptable, other staff obviously had concerns.

There are three 'evils' that exist in many settings and institutional settings in particular – *fear*, *power* and *loyalty*, and these will often work against abuse being reported. Staff and particularly managers are powerful – they create the jobs, pay the salary, offer the extra hours, allow time off at short notice – and some staff will be reluctant to challenge them. Managers and owners who wish to perpetuate poor practice will abuse this power, rendering staff unwilling to report incidents.

The working relationships and patterns of staff in care settings are such that managers in particular get to know staff very well. In situations where abuse is reported there is sometimes an inability to reconcile abusive behaviour with the staff they have recruited, inducted, supervised and supported, often through personal as well as employment matters, and loyalty to staff sometimes overrides independent or critical analysis of concerns.

Within care settings the feelings of fear at all levels cannot be underestimated. Staff and residents may be fearful of reprisal or of the unknown, and such fear inhibits people from speaking out, allowing abusive regimes and practice to continue.

These three 'evils' will prevent registration and inspection units from hearing about and therefore investigating complaints, often because of the power of the regulatory role. Abuse is generally seen as a social issue rather than what most often it is, a criminal act, and it is the fear of the registration and inspection unit closing the home that is seen as the worst that can happen. In this context the continued abusive practice is seen as preferable to reporting the matter, action being taken and the risk of the home being closed.

Staff in homes are often concerned about reporting abuse and staff are sometimes asked to sign confidentiality clauses. The importance of confidentiality cannot be underestimated in care settings. Staff often have access to detailed, personal and intimate knowledge of residents and it is therefore important that this is treated with respect and sensitivity. In most homes the reason for such a clause is self-evident, allowing the employer to take action if there is a breach of confidentiality. However, this can deter some staff from reporting concerns, believing that to discuss matters outside the home may result in a charge of breach of contract.

The reporting of suspected or actual abuse in care settings does not have to be kept secret, in a climate of fear and retribution, but can now be reported in such a way that the vulnerable adult and the 'whistleblower' can be protected.

CONCLUSION

It is accepted generally that registration and inspection units are only one agency involved in preventing, identifying and dealing with abuse in residential and nursing home environments, where abuse is often denied and overlooked. The work of inspection units through the registration process seeks to establish safeguards to minimize the likelihood of abuse occurring. However, it is accepted that in personal services the possibility of abuse is always present. The general understanding of abuse is such that it is often described in ways which avoid using the term, thereby making it difficult for external agencies to fully grasp what goes on behind closed doors. Those who live in care homes, the staff who work there and friends, family and practitioners who visit must be ever vigilant and check out any incidents which cause them concern or about which they are uncomfortable. The role of registration and inspection officers extends beyond regulation and closure of a home. Inspectors can provide guidance and support to ensure that abusive practice or regimes are investigated and where necessary action is taken. It is accepted that in extreme cases this may lead to the closure of a home but in most cases homes will be supported to establish systems to ensure that abusive practice is challenged and dealt with. In considering whether or not abuse has occurred practitioners must always remember that it is the consequence of the practice which is the determining factor, not the intention (or ignorance) of the perpetrator.

Appendix 1

The Joint Registration and Inspection Unit

What is it

The Joint Registration and Inspection Unit (JRIU) was set up as a requirement of the National Health Service and Community Care Act 1990. Its main responsibility is to carry out the statutory registration and inspection of private, voluntary and local authority residential care homes, nursing homes and dual registered homes. Created as a joint Unit, it operates independently of both the Health Authority and the Social Services Department.

The Unit was formally established in January 1991, under the management of Mrs Dawn Cousins, Head of Service, Registration, Inspection and Complaints.

The Unit also has responsibility for the Guardian ad Litem and Reporting Officers' function and for the Departmental Complaints procedure for the Social Services Department.

Where is it

St Thomas Chambers
147 High Street
Newport
Isle of Wight
PO30 1TY
Tel: (01983) 822185 Fax: (01983) 822186
Opening Hours:
Mon – Thurs 8.30 a.m. – 5.00 p.m.
Fri – 8.30 a.m. – 4.30 p.m.

What it does

The main task of the JRIU is to regulate the service provided in Residential Care, Small Care and Nursing Homes, and to ensure all statutory requirements are met under the Registered Homes Act 1984 and the NHS and Community Care Act 1990.

In October 1991 the Children Act 1989 placed further duties on the JRIU: the inspection of community children's homes; the registration and inspection of private children's homes; and the inspection of independent boarding schools.

What all this means is that the JRIU is responsible for ensuring a high quality of service is provided to those people living in residential care and nursing homes, small group homes, boarding schools and children's homes with fewer than 4 residents previously exempted from the requirements of the Registered Homes Act. We are also responsible for ensuring that residents' needs are met and their rights are protected. To that end we promote and help to develop good practice in all residential establishments in partnership with the home owners/managers and we operate a complaints procedure for residents and their advocates.

The registration and inspection of homes and the investigation of complaints requires a wide range of skills and a broad knowledge base on the part of the inspection staff employed at the unit. In addition there is a need for expert advice in various areas and we maintain close liaison with health authority services, Environmental Health and Building Control Services, Planning Unit, Fire Service, Dept. of Social Security, Police etc.

All of the work undertaken by the JRIU has a financial cost. Originally the government's intention was that inspection units should be self-financing, through monies provided by registered homes from statutory fees levied for registration and on an annual basis. It has been shown that such fees are insufficient to cover the costs of inspection units, and the shortfall is made up from Social Services and Health Authority budgets. The JRIU is exploring income generation possibilities.

In conclusion, the registration and inspection unit is a statutory body with a wide range of responsibilities towards people living in residential settings. The world of inspection units is a fast-changing one, and the profile of the JRIU is sure to increase in the years to come. People living in residential care are entitled to the highest quality of service and the JRIU exists to help ensure that this is achieved on the Isle of Wight.

Complaints

There are more that 2,000 people living in Residential and Nursing Homes on the Island. To help ensure that the rights of these residents are maintained, the JRIU operates a complaints procedure. If you, whether as a resident, an advocate, or other interested party are unhappy with any aspect of the service in a Home, you should raise your concern first with the Home.

If this approach does not produce the result that you desire, you may contact the JRIU directly. (There is a leaflet specifically about the complaints procedure available in all Homes, or at Social Services' offices and in libraries). The JRIU will do its utmost to resolve your concern

REFERENCES

Bergner, T. (1998) *Independent Longcare Inquiry*. London: HMSO.

Camden and Islington Community Health Services NHS Trust (1999) *Beech House Inquiry; Report of the Internal Inquiry Relating to the Mistreatment of Patients Residing at Beech House, St Pancras Hospital During the Period March 1993 to April 1996*. London: Camden and Islington Community Health Services NHS Trust.

Care Standards Act 2000. London: HMSO.

Crime and Disorder Act 1998. London: HMSO.

Department of Health (1990) *Community Care Implementation: Inspection Units* LAC (90) 13. London: HMSO.

Department of Health (1994) *Inspecting Social Services* LAC (94) 16. London: HMSO.

Department of Health (2000) *No Secrets: Guidance on Developing and Implementing Multi-Agency Policies and Procedures to Protect Vulnerable Adults from Abuse*. London: HMSO.

Jenkins, G., Asif., Z. and Bennett, G. (2000) *Listening is Not Enough*. London: Action on Elder Abuse.

Local Government Services Act 1970. London: HMSO.

Nursing Home and Mental Nursing Home Regulations 1984 – Statutory Instrument No 1578. London: HMSO.

Public Interest Disclosure Act 1998. London: HMSO.

Registered Homes Act 1984. London: HMSO.

Residential Care Homes Regulations 1984 – Statutory Instrument No 1345. London: HMSO.

Sheffield Adult Protection Committee (2000) *Annual Report 1999/2000*. Sheffield: Sheffield Adult Protection Office.

UKCC (1994) *Professional Conduct: Occasional Report on Standards of Nursing Home Care*. London: UKCC.

CHAPTER 7

'WISH WE WEREN'T HERE'

A CONVERSATION BETWEEN
A REGISTRATION AND INSPECTION OFFICER AND A SOCIAL
WORKER ABOUT ABUSE IN RESIDENTIAL SETTINGS

PURPOSE OF THE CHAPTER

This chapter is presented as a dialogue between **Janice Griffin,** an experienced registration and inspection officer (RIO) and **Jacki Pritchard,** a qualified social worker who now trains and researches within residential settings where vulnerable adults live. What follows is a presentation of a live discussion that took place about the current problems in addressing abuse within residential settings. This format has been used previously in training sessions and at conferences; we feel it is a very powerful medium by which to make people aware of current dilemmas surrounding practice issues.

THE DISCUSSION

Jacki: We are here today to talk about abuse in residential homes. We have both been involved in dealing with abusive situations, but before we start it may be helpful for the audience to understand our backgrounds. I worked as a social worker for 13 years, during which time I dealt with both child and adult abuse cases. I now divide my time between training people on abuse issues and working with victims of adult abuse. I spend many hours of my working life either in residential settings or training care staff.

Janice: I have been a registration and inspection officer (RIO) in a large city for the past nine years. I have a responsibility for the registration and inspection of residential services within the local authority, the private and voluntary sectors. The client groups I cover are: children, young physically disabled, older people, people with special needs (e.g. dementia, learning disabilities, mental health problems). I

140

also have an individual responsibility to register and inspect dual registered homes, that is, care homes that provide both nursing and residential care.

Jacki: A fundamental question to begin with – what does abuse mean to you?

Janice: Any event or activity which could affect the health, safety and well-being of individual people.

Jacki: Would you like to talk about the types of abuse you see most often in your day-to-day working life?

Janice: There is obviously institutional abuse. Some typical examples are:

- Locking the doors (internal and external) to restrict movement around the building.
- Use of equipment to restrict movement – cot sides, straps on wheelchairs, geriatric chairs.
- Restricting residents access to their property, money and valuables or forcing them to hand them over. For example, one home encouraged residents on admission to care to bring in with them things of value (ornaments, jewellery). Following admission they were made to hand over the possessions to managerial staff, the reason being to keep them in a secure place. However, they became a little nest egg and it was alleged that the managers sold these things without the knowledge of the residents.
- Not allowing residents food and drink. One example of emotional abuse was when a care assistant put a male resident on a diet. She deliberately used to walk by the man, wave cream buns in front of his face, and say 'You can't have this.'
- Rigid meal times and drink times. Staff not asking people if they have milk and sugar.
- Heating is often controlled centrally, that is, temperatures are dictated by the system. Sometimes it is extremely cold in rooms and the temperature cannot be altered. Another thing which concerns me is in winter when I am driving round the city I see residential homes where nearly every window is open in the building. This is done to get rid of the smells. What always strikes me – I look at the other houses on the road and none of their windows are open.

- Regimes – strict times for toiletting, rising and bed times.
- Restricting access to general practitioners (GP), opticians, dentists, chiropodists – for general health care. On the other side of that is not giving people choice. For example GPs coming and giving flu jabs to all residents whether they want it or not. I have seen residents lined up outside the doctor's room.
- Not reassessing for nursing care when a resident's health deteriorates. The priority seems to be about keeping bums in beds; they are scared of losing income.
- Medication – residents are told 'You will have medication when we say.' Night sedation is often given at 8.00 p.m. because afternoon staff are finishing their shift.

Jacki: People think we have moved on and the things you have mentioned do not happen any more. What is frightening is that staff sometimes do not realize that what they are doing is abusive. I was recently shown round a home which I was told was 'the pride of the authority'. Staff knew I was being shown around. When I walked into the main lounge and looked to the top of the room where toilets were located, I saw women sitting in the toilet cubicles, the doors had been left open. This should never happen. Staff often disclose to me on training courses. They talk about 'rules' or 'systems'. Very often they have known that 'it is not right' to do something but have been frightened to speak up. One common practice I still hear about frequently is the padlocking of fridges and freezers so that residents and staff cannot access food. These locks are removed when an inspection is due.

Janice: I often think about whether institutional abuse has become more widespread or is it just that we are more aware of it now. We used to think of institutional abuse happening in mental hospitals, but this form of abuse occurs in many other settings. I can sometimes understand why staff abuse – one of the reasons can be the stress of the job. Residential care homes often operate below the minimum staff levels; for example the staffing ratio could be two care assistants to care for as many as 25 residents. Often the residents are very frail, confused and ill. In a lot of cases some homes employ very young staff who have little experience, and training may not be provided either before they commence duties or whilst they are employed at the home.

I can think of a recent case where in a unit there was an adult with learning disabilities. He had severe behaviour problems – he constantly was shouting, screaming, scratching, thumping. One staff member was working with him on a one-to-one basis all day long. Sometimes, the staff member locked the door and he was allowed to wander around the building. When I came out of that unit I said to my colleague 'I know it is a dreadful thing to say, but I can understand how a staff member might abuse him.'

Jacki: When we talk about abuse everyone thinks of *physical* and believe it is easy to identify. What do you see most often?

Janice: I see a hell of a lot of older people with bruises. I saw one the other night. When I establish why – it is often not that someone is hitting them but because there are not enough staff on to supervise residents. They are being left unattended trying to get in and out of chairs and end up falling, or it can be that staff have no idea how to care for frail, sick or confused residents.

Jacki: Another problem is that people may not have proper training on how to lift and handle. Even though this is a legal requirement, I know of young people employed to do night shifts and 'fill in as required' but they are never given any formal training.

Janice: Those staff who are not trained are so frightened of dropping residents that they grab far too hard in order not to drop them. They actually bruise them. It is not intentional. Another thing which is a growing problem is the number of young staff wearing big fashion jewellery which causes residents to get tears in their skin. There are rarely policies about staff wearing jewellery – there is one for cooks but not care staff. Another thing I am coming across a lot is resident abusing resident. Some residents maybe with dementia or a mental health problem become aggressive and attack other residents. Although residents with dementia should be in specialist homes, they are often cared for in mainstream residential care homes. As previously mentioned, staff are often not trained to deal with residents with difficult behaviour. I have also experienced residents sexually abusing each other. This again can be due to dementia; often the resident can forget who their wife or husband is but they don't always forget the desire for sex. Consequently, they may sexually abuse another resident to overcome their sexual frustration.

Jacki: Similar situations can arise where adults with learning disabilities are living together and maybe one of them has sexualized behaviour and work on sexual/sexuality issues has not been undertaken.

Janice: Managers rarely request a reassessment and move them. Again it can be about keeping bums in beds.

Jacki: It is unfair to the resident and other residents, but staff should not have to put up with being abused either. I know a group of staff who kept asking their manager to get the social worker to reassess an adult with learning disabilities who was becoming increasingly violent. They were told: 'Don't complain. If you don't like the job get out.' Action was only taken when the resident stabbed one of the staff with a bread knife.

Janice: Medication abuse also comes under physical abuse. The experience I have is of older people being on medication to control difficult behaviour. I have found situations where GPs have prescribed large doses of medication to control aggression. The medication is not always reviewed and it can be increased subject to the resident having an aggressive outburst. Finally the residents can become like zombies.

Jacki: I worry about collusion. Managers being overly friendly with the GP who is the doctor for all the residents. There should be choice about GPs for the residents. Because of this cosy relationship, the manager may ask for medication and it is prescribed without the resident being seen by the doctor. I visited one home where 83 residents out of 90 were on Melleril.

Janice: Melleril is a medication often used to control difficult behaviour with old people.

Jacki: Years ago *sexual abuse* used to be included within the category of physical abuse but now it is recognized as a category on its own – rightly so. It worries me that sexual abuse in relation to vulnerable adults is still very much a taboo subject. It is understandable that people do not want to think about it, but it will remain hidden if people do not acknowledge how prevalent it is. Also, so many stereotypical pictures are presented. People do not want to

think about men as victims of sexual abuse and women as
perpetrators. Also I do not think enough thought is given to
how abusers groom their adult victims; it is very similar to
the way paedophiles groom children.

Janice: The general public just do not relate sexual abuse to older
people. There has been so much coverage in the media
about child sexual abuse, they do not think about older
people, adults with learning disabilities, adults with mental
health problems. I believe it is quite common to discover
staff abusing resident, but it is probably more resident
abusing resident.

Jacki: In these cases have the police been brought in early?

Janice: Not always. Some just do not get reported. There is the
attitude of 'He's just a dirty old man. He has always been
like that – touches people up.' In other cases, staff do not
realize how they are contributing to the abuse. As in the
case of Sally, a 30-year-old adult with learning disabilities,
who had been in care for many years. I have known Sally
for 15 years. There had always been problems regarding
fulfilling her sexual needs. Even to the point of using
certain instruments (coathangers, brushes) to satisfy
herself, which caused internal damage. In the past, staff
took her to the doctor for treatment; she was told how dirty
she was and to stop it. During the past two years she has
been in a new unit where staff quite rightly had positively
tried to manage her sexual needs. They encouraged sexual
activity; they got her a vibrator. To help her to try to
understand about sexuality they bought her pornographic
magazines and videos. You can understand why they did it;
but this made her worse. She started learning things she
never knew and started practising on other residents. She
thought what she was doing was acceptable. After she had
watched a video she said to me 'Doesn't it make you want
to shag people?'; from reading magazines she learnt 'If I
want to go with a woman I can use a vibrator.' We then
moved onto a hygiene problem – she didn't wash the
vibrator. She was then anally raped by a male member of
staff who had seen all the pornographic material in her
bedroom. This man had left the job but came back to take
Sally out to the pub. Sally did not understand about anal
sex and said she would not have consented if she had
known what he was going to do to her. She said to me 'He
put it up my arse. I wouldn't have minded if he had done it

the proper way.' The male worker told the police that: 'She was begging for it.' Sally got into the situation because of her misunderstanding of sex. After this staff called her a nymphomaniac. They didn't realize how they had contributed to the situation. This is back to lack of training again.

Jacki: I do have concerns about the quality of care given in residential settings and I think this goes back to the type of person being employed. Some (not all) care staff just see it as a job; they are not actually committed to working with people they care about. This is hardly surprising when the level of pay is so low. The other concern is offenders who deliberately get jobs in residential settings because they know this gives them access to vulnerable people, who may not have the ability to disclose or are unlikely to be believed.

Janice: Certain people know it is easy to get a job in residential care. Sometimes there are no checks at all made prior to starting work at the home – they have an interview and then told to start tomorrow. We have got some individuals who want to abuse older people – like paedophiles they get themselves into positions where they can do that. Quite often when I talk to managers/owners about this they say 'Never – I don't believe that.' There is general widespread ignorance.

Jacki: This is also true for adults with learning disabilities. I identified a paedophile on a training course who was then working in supported accommodation. When the agency undertook a formal investigation staff disclosed that there had been concerns from his first shift when he brought in a pornographic video for the young men to watch. Staff had never voiced their concerns to management. No police checks had been done.

Janice: It is often very hard to prove sexual abuse because we cannot get the evidence needed. There was a situation where there was an allegation that a 40-year-old male care assistant had either raped or indecently assaulted 26 older females in a nursing home. There were so many indicators – report book entries that residents were displaying a general fear of men; residents with blood and discharge in their knickers; bruising round the groin area; some residents becoming withdrawn. All the alleged victims were confused. It came to light when the manager phoned me one day – her exact words were 'There is something fishy here. Nearly all the staff are noticing lots of changes in the females...quite a lot of them have bruising round the vagina and bleeding.'

I visited the home with another RIO; on our way there we talked about sexual abuse and the need to cross-reference. We thought about the things we needed to find out – if there was a new carer; what time of day the bruising/bleeding was discovered – for example when getting up. It was established that a male worker had been there just eight weeks. When I was given his name I remembered he had been dismissed from another job. Letters had been sent out to all units in the area about two years previously saying to contact the registration and inspection unit if he applied for a job. The manager in this home had filed the letter. An emergency strategy meeting was convened. In the end no evidence could be brought forward because the older women refused to be examined by the male police surgeon. Also, some had been showered and bathed. The alleged perpetrator was a Schedule 1 Offender. The manager had not asked for references nor had she checked her file with letters from the registration and inspection unit. She had asked him to sign the Rehabilitation of Offenders Declaration but he stated that he had no convictions. He had also changed his name, but no checks had been asked for re-identification.

Jacki: So we are back again to the need for training and checking. People changing their names is not uncommon. It was purely a coincidence that a secretary in a hospital social work department recognized a woman who was visiting older people on the wards to talk about the new residential home she was opening up in the area. The secretary knew that this woman and her husband had previously owned two homes in another city. Both homes had been closed down because of abuse. This woman had changed her name by deed poll. How can we prevent this practice?

Janice: Owners and managers have to improve the recruitment process, ensure that prospective staff provide a birth certificate and proof of identity. We have had problems with some people from other cultures who do not have birth certificates. In cases where people with British nationality apply we ask to see their nationality papers. We also look at marriage certificates, decree nisis. We check documentation with a photograph – for example a passport. We also ask questions about previous names/marriages, check the curriculum vitae and we request proof of qualifications.

Jacki: Residents can also be put at risk when a known sex offender is placed in a residential setting as a resident. Management and staff face all sorts of dilemmas when they are torn between the rights of the offender and the rights of the other residents. I have seen this in units both for young and older adults who are vulnerable.

Janice: It was recently brought to my attention that a known sex offender had been admitted into a residential care home. The younger staff had become concerned when he was asking them to touch his penis. He had also been observed asking visitors' children into his bedroom, enticing them in by offering them sweets. At the time of his admission his past was not brought to the attention of the staff. It was only after a case conference that a police check was done and it was found that he was a convicted sex offender. The home did produce a protection plan to supervise him on a one-to-one basis. However, this did not work out due to staff shortages and lack of understanding of the individual care needs; the man was moved to a specialist unit after eight weeks.

Jacki: For as long as I have been working in the field, I have always believed that *financial abuse* is probably the most common form of adult abuse. This was borne out in a recent research project too (Pritchard 2000). Do you think it is as common in residential settings?

Janice: Yes, financial abuse is very common. The things I have come across recently are:

- Abuse of residents' personal allowance, monies, assets.
- Charging residents for goods (for example 35p for one cigarette; taking a group of residents out in a minibus and charging each resident 30p per mile for the round trip). An owner was putting a £1 mark-up on the cost of a shampoo and set.
- Charging for services which should be part of contract – £5 to push residents in a wheelchair round the block; £2 for a bath; 50p for a cup of tea; paying for bottles of milk. Charging for gas and electricity – having meters in residents' bedrooms.
- Family taking all personal allowance, bank books etc.

- A manager purchasing new clothes for herself, which were paid for by the residents and her giving the residents her old ones.

Jacki: How can we prevent this happening?

Janice: Part of our standards is that advocates are to be used. There are private companies which charge a small amount per year (*c.* £100) and in return they manage residents' finances. It is a requirement of our standards that residents' accounts are audited by an outside auditor. It is also a requirement that staff and managers are not made appointees. We require that all financial transactions made on behalf of residents are witnessed by two staff.

Jacki: When staff are asked to witness transactions I am concerned that many of them do not know what they are witnessing. I know of many care staff who have sat in whilst a solicitor has brought legal documents – perhaps to do with Court of Protection – but they have no idea what their role is in this. Few of them would question a professional person, who they consider to be of higher status. In a recent case, a man signed over his house to a neighbour; he had no idea what he was doing. Care staff sat in and never questioned what was going on, even though they knew this man had previously been abused by the same neighbour. Again, questioning identity is important. The solicitor who came to the home with the papers in this case turned out to be the neighbour's daughter.

Janice: Residents often don't understand what they are signing – because of difficulties with language, age, confusion, infirmity etc. Some nursing and residential care homes are limited companies and therefore have company bank accounts. I have come across some occasions recently when it has come to my attention that residents' savings have been banked in the company's account. In the event of the company going bankrupt, then the residents' savings could be swallowed up by the receivers.

Jacki: I have always been worried about the more subtle forms of abuse which occur within residential settings. Time and time again managers or staff will say to me 'Jacki that is only a bit of bad practice, it's not abuse.' This begs the question, when does bad practice cross that fine line and become abuse? I am currently very interested in considering working with *neglect*. Neglect can be physical or *emotional,* but it is incredibly difficult to identify or prove. So many times, no one will be present when the emotional abuse occurs. The subtle forms of abuse can be in the form of name calling, over-familiarity, infantilization, regularly ignoring someone so in fact they become very isolated. Also I do not think enough attention is given to the concept of bullying – especially emotional bullying.

Janice: I have heard residents say:

- 'It pays to know your place in here.'
- 'If the staff get to know you have told inspectors about bad practice then you get no food or food you don't like. They won't let you go on the next trip out.'
- 'Staff ignore you when you ask for assistance to the toilet.'

A new one for me in relation to emotional abuse and neglect is where more people are being placed in residential care when they should have been placed in a nursing home. The reason for this being it is a cheaper option. Policies within local authorities and health authorities have contributed to this. There has been a big increase in complaints from relatives, for example in cases where residential staff did not get doctors in time. They did not see the changes in the resident's health soon enough. In one case a resident who was diabetic started vomiting, which would affect the diabetes. The staff did not realize that the resident could dehydrate more quickly and a doctor was not asked to visit for over a week. The resident became weaker and consequently died. The case went to the Coroner's Court. Her GP gave evidence and stated that the woman had a heart condition and this led to her death. No mention was made that she died in discomfort and pain that could have been avoided had a doctor been called sooner. The police were asked to investigate but they could not find any legislation that would be relevant to the case. The registration and inspection unit could have investigated and prosecuted under the Registered Homes Act but it would have been costly and difficult to prove. We did however de-register the manager for being unfit in this case.

In other cases staff have not realized that a resident has not been taking food and consequently urgent medical attention has been needed when s/he has ended up in a coma. Other examples of neglect we have repeatedly identified are:

- Not recognizing signs and symptoms, e.g. effects of certain medical conditions; side-effects of tablets.
- Not caring for skin, e.g. not using creams, turning people regularly. I seem to be seeing an increasing number of bed sores.
- Related to food. Cheap food being bought and no attention being given to nutritional value. Residents needing to be fed but staff don't have time to feed them. So food is left, given to them cold or thrown away. Liquidizing food en masse, not liquidizing it individually. In some cases it has been identified through risk assessment that a resident needs a soft diet (maybe because of difficulty swallowing after a stroke) but s/he is still being given solid food.

It is my view that more attention needs to be paid with regard to poor nutrition and older people. I have observed cheap brands of food being given to residents. Small portions of food. Some food left on the table for residents who are too frail to feed themselves; staff on duty did not attempt to feed them. The food was removed later by other staff who assumed the residents did not want the food.

I have noted residents losing weight after admission to care. Our standards do not require that the older people are weighed on a regular basis. The reason for this is we don't want residential care homes to become too medically orientated. However, weight checks might act as an indicator that residents are not getting enough food.

Jacki: I totally agree. I worry that we do not monitor vulnerable adults' health properly. An annual check is not enough. How do we monitor if someone (either young or old) is failing to thrive? The answer is we don't. I hate the term 'frail, elderly'; it is always said as though it is normal for an older person to be thin and frail. I remember a GP who identified classic physical neglect in a nursing home. He had gone in to see a patient who had recently gone into this home. He was astonished at how the other residents looked. He reported this to the local registration and inspection unit. It came to light that the residents were not being fed properly. They had the same menu everyday – for breakfast they had half a slice of toast; lunch was one slice of cold meat, peas and a potato; for tea – half a sandwich.

That home was owned by a consultant and the manager was his wife.

Janice: It is not just about training staff but about resources. More staff are needed to supervise residents. I have already mentioned about residents falling. In the event of an older person fracturing their femur, then the obvious physical sign would be the shortening of the leg. Care assistants don't know this and a fractured femur can be overlooked by staff. I have seen staff try to make a resident walk with a fractured femur. This is agonizing pain.

Some health authorities would argue that district nurses can provide a network of health care support to residential care homes. I am sure the district nurses would love to do this but there are not enough resources to allow this. A trend up and down the country is that more dependent people are going into residential care with greater needs. Typical examples: with the closure of large mental health hospitals, many patients are placed in mainstream residential care homes because there is nowhere else to put them. They are not getting the specialist mental health care support they need. An adult with Down's Syndrome may have been cared for by mum and dad for years, but then s/he develops special health care needs. The current training offered to staff to equip them to deal with these needs is not adequate.

There is also emotional abuse from other residents towards adults from ethnic groups. A black worker was telling me the other day about when black elders are admitted to residential care, diets/religious needs are not met. Recently, I went into a room of a Polish person, who cannot speak English, and found a bottle of bleach on the windowsill – which should not be there. The staff on duty when questioned stated that they genuinely believed that Polish people clean their teeth with bleach. This reminded me of when I was a young naïve nurse, my mother had told me that when Jewish people die they had to be stood up and buried in the standing position. One night a Jewish person died and I said to another first-year nurse what my mother had told me. After the doctor had certified the person dead, I struggled with my colleague to get the body to stand up against the wall. I feel a real idiot when I think of it now. I trusted my mother – she seemed to be knowledgeable. Thank God the ward sister came along and stopped me doing this.

This incident makes me think about how young staff may abuse or develop practices which are abusive because they have been told to do something in a certain way. They do this in order to be kind but in fact they are being cruel. I think it is the more experienced care staff telling new or inexperienced staff 'This is the way we do this round here.' Power and control can be a root cause of abuse. Some people go through life being so insecure – in order to make them feel good they need to have or be seen to have power over other people. The victims are so weak they would never ever challenge that person. In order to fulfil themselves they have to pick on weaker people. Nearly everyone in residential care is vulnerable. The subtle stuff gives staff the control rather than shouting and bawling, for example locking the front door; refusing to take residents to the toilet; controlling their portions of food; forgetting to offer them a cup of tea from the drinks trolley; putting sugar and milk in the tea/coffee when the staff member knows full well that the resident does not take sugar. Knowledge is power. Confidence is confused with power. Young staff will often do what they are told by someone who is seen to be in a position of power.

Jacki: Another side of this is when a manager bullies staff either emotionally or physically; s/he exercises power and control over certain individuals or the whole staff group. A manager often knows that certain staff need the job and will put up with anything rather than leave. Again, if the manager has run the unit for a long time and staff have never known anything different, then often they think what they are doing is right. I am often asked to undertake team-building after an abusive manager has left; it can be soul-destroying to see how traumatized some of the staff have become. It takes a long time to work with them and build their self-esteem.

Janice: I took over a badly managed residential care home in the 1980s. I could not believe how some staff treated the residents. When questioned about their behaviour some staff would say 'Well they're only old people, why don't they go to live with their own relatives?' I have heard white staff say 'Why should black people expect to be cared for by white staff? Why don't they go back to where they came from?' Often the culture of a home is that it is run for the staff not the residents. For example, residents are got up, put to bed, given meals etc. to fit in with the staff's hours of duty.

Jacki: I frequently think about how adults with mental health problems do not get a high profile in the adult abuse literature. When we mention institutional abuse in regard to adults people used to think mainly in terms of older people; nowadays more recognition is being given to the fact that adults with learning disabilities are a high-risk group. It strikes me that very rarely do people consider adults with mental health problems who may be living in institutions. It is an area of work which is not given much attention.

Janice: When I think of adults with mental health problems I think of medication abuse. One of the things I particularly do with mental health units is always to check what medication the residents were on when admitted. I then cross-reference it with what they are on now. In my role as inspector I am looking for indicators of medication abuse. The reason I do it is that I am very aware that people with mental health problems can be managed by medication. One case I can recall involved three residents whose medications had increased tremendously after their admissions to care. I contacted the community psychiatric nurse (CPN) and asked if the medication was an acceptable level; the answer was 'No, it's far too much.' I had to establish *why* they had ended up on these levels. The medication had been prescribed to be given 'when required'. Care assistants had phoned the GP on several occasions to say the residents' behaviour was unmanageable. The records stated that the GP over the phone on each occasion had instructed them to increase the medication but he never kept a record himself of the telephone conversations or the amounts the three residents were taking. I checked for formal medication reviews but there were none. I went to see the GP myself and asked if he was aware of the amounts of medication the residents were now on; he had no idea. His response was that the staff cannot cope with the residents' behaviours. He was dismissive so I had to urge him strongly to immediately review all patients in the home. If he hadn't have done that I would have taken it further by taking the evidence and voicing my concerns to the police. The outcome was that the home-owners decided to voluntarily close after three months.

Jacki:	How do you break the chain or cycle of abuse?
Janice:	From the view of the RIO I read care plans, report books and get staff to tell me how they are meeting needs. I talk to residents, staff and managers about this. I observe. I talk to old and new staff – individually and collectively. I always try to spend some time with staff in the staff room; I try to keep it relaxed so that they will open up. I get a lot of disclosures at that time: 'Don't tell them I have told you but...' Staff know me, they trust me – it works for me.
Jacki:	But couldn't the other side of it be that if an RIO becomes too familiar with staff, there could be collusion? I believe that it would be better if an RIO had never worked for the local authority or health authority in the area they are inspecting. They need to be neutral; not inspecting former colleagues or current friends otherwise there can be cover-ups. Because I work in different parts of the country I see that the length of inspections differs tremendously – anything from half a day to three days per inspection.
Janice:	I spend a minimum of a day and sometimes a half-day on inspection follow-up. I still don't think that is enough. We used to spend two days but found we did not have the staffing resources to continue. Furthermore, there were so many other demands on our time, for example, investigating complaints.
Jacki:	How can you make staff feel safe to whistleblow? What should be in place?
Janice:	There needs to be a proper complaints procedure in place and staff must be aware of this. Staff should have access to RIOs; they need to know they can come to us or ring up. It is also crucial that staff read the inspection report; it must be accessible to them. There should be a formal whistleblowing policy. Supervision is important. There should be forums where an individual can talk about issues of concern to them. Then we are back to training again – staff need to attend courses to raise awareness about abuse; they need to have an understanding about what they are doing and how they may be abusing residents.
Jacki:	The Public Interest Disclosure Act, which was introduced in 1999, may help to support whistleblowers in the future. It is expected that employers should establish procedures so that staff can voice concerns to nominated people, not

necessarily within the organization. The Act covers disclosures about criminal offences, any breach of regulatory duty, any abuse or neglect which endangers an individual's health or safety. As well as thinking about their own practices, staff need to understand why abuse may happen. It is a very complex issue and they need to learn that there can be various causal factors contributing to the abusive situation. Training courses need to allocate time to considering the issues around power and control.

Janice: It is not just care staff who need to understand the effects of power and control – it is anyone who may agree to care or protection plans. An example which springs to mind from a recent investigation involved Jo, an adult with learning disabilities who is 40 years old and has lived in a dual-registered care home for about 2 years. She has no verbal communication. She can write and she can sign. The home had an individual restraint policy for Jo, which supposedly had been produced by a number of different professionals (social worker, police, residential workers). The policy stated that in the event of her aggressive behaviour there were to be five staff (in practice it was always males) to get together and form a ring round Jo. Two to three staff were to hold her down whilst another member went to get a quilt, which was to be laid on the floor; Jo was then rolled in it. Once she was tightly rolled in it she became quiet – usually this took five to ten minutes – before the staff took the quilt off her.

When I looked at Jo's case notes the one thing that immediately stuck out was the fact that this aggressive behaviour had only really occurred during the last eight months. When I cross-referenced the incidents with the staff rota, it was clear that it always happened when the same two female staff were on duty. If the manager had done the same exercise he would probably have picked that up. Rather than do that he went straight into managing the behaviour rather than looking for the causes. The other side of this dangerous practice was that none of the staff had had training in First Aid. Therefore they could not recognize when things start to go wrong, which we have mentioned already.

Jacki: Surely First Aid training is a legal requirement?

Janice: Yes it is. The 1984 Residential Care Homes Regulation 10 (1) (j) states that the registered owners must take adequate precautions against the risk of accidents including the training of staff in First Aid. The five staff who were on duty in actual fact weren't the abusers. Their task was to manage the challenging behaviour of the resident.

Jacki: Who were then?

Janice: Two women who were suspended never actually took part in that restraint procedure. When Jo was being restrained, they stood and laughed. They would wind her up – other staff said this. This made her worse. On most report entries the first words were: 'Jo was KICKING OFF again.' Most reports said 'Had to restrain her using the quilt method.' Therefore it was clearly recorded.

Jacki: So what about the future, Janice. Is it going to get better?

Janice: There are going to be a lot of changes in the regulatory systems brought about by Care Standards Act 2000.

Jacki: So what will this mean for you in your role as RIO?

Janice: Care Commissions will be set up. We will no longer work within the local authority system. RIOs will be regionally based with new management structures. The main changes under the Commission will be:

- national standards
- care homes (not residential or nursing homes)
- better regulations
- local authority provision for the first time will need to be registered and inspected
- domiciliary services (home care) – local authority and private providers must be registered and inspected
- better regulation of children's homes
- regulation and inspection of adoption and fostering agencies
- a register of those deemed unfit to care for vulnerable adults
- abolition of nursing agencies.

For me it will mean working to national standards and inspecting a wider range of care services.

Jacki: Will you have to have special training for this?

Janice: Yes. Currently each RIO will have come from different backgrounds, therefore will have different training needs.

Jacki: What are your hopes and fears?

Janice: It is fair to say I currently work for a head of registration and inspection unit who has developed me and insisted that I check things thoroughly. She has always been very keen that we listen and develop ways of inspecting that covers as much as we can. She is not frightened when challenged by powerful people. When the service providers have threatened legal action, this has never put her off. Each local authority is expected to develop its own standards – we were keen to develop the best. New standards are coming in – the first draft I have seen is not as detailed as the standards that we use now. It is early days and there may be room for local flexibility. However, the new standards are more specific – about certain aspects of the building, e.g. room sizes, equipment, fixtures and fittings. The draft standards I have seen are more specific on staffing levels required and the training that staff must have. These are major improvements to what we have had nationally. My worry is that after consultation with owners, managers, other professionals, that the standards do not become diluted. Some RIOs may not want their workloads increased and this may affect the consultation process.

Jacki: So you are saying that the standards should help to improve things, but what still worries you?

Janice: Recruitment. We need to ensure that we get the right people for the job – that to me is RIOs who are keen and have the skills and experience to do the job.

Jacki: What do you think is needed?

Janice: Experience in the caring professions – the need to understand what constitutes good care. Other things would be:

- good observational skills
- good analytical skills
- organizational skills – being methodical
- ability to see the situation for what it is rather than what it should be

- ability to communicate with people at all levels (staff in coffee room and owners) – to see that everybody makes a contribution is important
- ability to be assertive and resilient.

Jacki: What about being creative – flexible in approach?

Janice: It is about being committed to the job – no good doing the job if you don't care.

Jacki: Time and time again I see people being put in jobs because there is nowhere else for them to go.

Janice: The other thing we need – wouldn't it be wonderful if all service providers' main objectives were to provide good quality services rather than big fat bank accounts or meeting budget targets? We need service managers who have the experience and knowledge; they have responsibility for developing policies and procedures. A good manager will be looking at new policies and systems to prevent institutional abuse. We need managers who are committed to recruiting the right staff. The recruitment process needs to include all the things we discussed earlier, for example checking police records and identity, qualifications and medical fitness.

Jacki: How do we get rid of staff who are not good enough?

Janice: The reason they do not get rid of staff is they are frightened of employment legislation. Scared of being sued. Often managers have not done what they should have done, that is offered training, supervision, development etc. There is also a national shortage of staff – so we have the attitude of 'better the devil you know'. Better to have six bad staff, than only four OK staff. We are back to the argument for training owners/managers on staff development. They need to be made aware of what is expected of them. Owners have to invest in the staff. In general there is a low expectation by managers; low wages so what quality of staff can you expect? They are not valued financially. Seen as not professional. Within local authority, managers are frightened – too much trouble to go through the process. It is not just sacking today – there is the whole legal baggage. Some cannot be bothered. Others have had a bad experience where things have not been followed through. So they say 'What's the point?' Good support is very necessary.

Jacki: In the private sector where do they get support from?

Janice: They should get support via the adult abuse procedures and the RIO. Also other professionals need to support; by this I mean social workers, district nurses, GPs, primary health care teams. All agencies must see it as their duty to ensure good quality care is offered to frail or vulnerable people. Some organizations provide advice for a fee on legal aspects of employment. Our unit has set up a Managers Advisory Group – a forum where the managers from all the sectors meet with us. They get information about the future but also it is a sort of support group. We meet every three months. This has been very positive and used to promote good care standards.

Jacki: It is not enough to just develop the adult abuse policy and have the bit of paper, it has to be implemented properly – ongoing training, monitoring, and evaluating are needed. Managers need to use supervision sessions and staff meetings to ensure that staff are aware of the policy and HOW to implement it. I believe we need to improve the training about abuse. Basic awareness training needs to cover what abuse is and how to recognize it. I feel very strongly that there needs to be a commitment to ongoing training programmes – not just for managers and staff within the units but for RIOs too. The odd day's training here and there is not enough; there needs to be a thorough rolling programme.

Janice: I agree. There needs to be training for staff on all aspects of care:

- health and safety
- safe lifting practices
- understanding and dealing with difficult behaviour
- what constitutes good basic physical care
- recognizing and dealing with abuse
- understanding special health care needs (conditions – people who have arthritis) – sexuality
- what medication is given for and the side effects
- rights of individual – Human Rights Act 1998
- nutrition
- emotional needs – religion/cultural needs
- staff understanding sanctions

- training on restraint – what is legal
- how to complain
- law – understanding people's rights
- why residents need a care plan
- why residents need to be reviewed.

Jacki: Do you need more powers?

Janice: I am not convinced we need more powers – it is back to workloads. I think the legislation is there. Individuals have got to put it to the test. It takes a lot of time and costs a lot of money. We need support from the local authority and good advice from its solicitor. Some individuals are powerless to fight the systems. A local authority solicitor gives advice but he or she cannot tell me what to do. There are always risks involved. I think the risk of costing a lot of money and losing the case is one of the greatest. The risk of exposing the situation that residents had been left in a home that the local authority has a contract with would make them look bad. In one particular case where a home was providing poor care, a group of politicians asked 'Where are we going to put 39 residents with mental health problems on a Friday afternoon if we use emergency closure procedures?' The outcome was that pressure was put on after discussion with the home-owners. They decided on voluntarily closure; it was easier for them. It resolved the situation but it did not address their unfitness. They were not exposed and could carry on with their other homes. Although I did visit the other homes which were for older people, the service they were providing was good. They had gone into a different field (adults with learning disabilities) and were out of their depth. This qualifies what was said earlier, that is the importance of recruitment, training etc.

What I worry about personally is proving all of it. The systems are there but it is bigger than me. As an RIO I am prepared to work day and night to stop abuse and take whatever action I have to to stop the abusers – but I cannot do it on my own. I need all the support networks – police, social workers, community psychiatric nurses, GPs, managerial support, and legal support. Sometimes I do not get support from relatives. Some would rather their relative would be in an abusive situation than be back living with them. They think 'What they are getting is better than what I can offer them.' Or sometimes there is denial from relatives: 'This is a wonderful home.' I also need support from residents. I have heard residents say: 'This isn't right – this is our home. You have no right to interfere.' Often residents are frightened of the repercussions. To get the evidence, quick responses from *everybody* are necessary. To take action against unfit owners and staff it is necessary to obtain evidence for prosecution. It is no good trying to collect evidence after several days; the evidence could have been destroyed.

Jacki: So, Janice, we have both seen a lot of abuse over the years. What do you think the future holds for working with abuse which is occurring in residential settings?

Janice: I have worked in the caring profession for over 30 years. In my view abuse today is possibly worse than when I started my career. Well I intend to carry on trying to stop the abuse. I now think of the days when I will be retired and old, perhaps in a care home. Maybe when a resident I will become a victim. What I dearly hope is that I will be a strong victim; one who will whistleblow, keep a record, of the abusive practice, maybe I will secure a solicitor to take legal action against the abusers. Whatever, I will continue my work to stop this bad practice and maybe I will be successful in securing the attention of those in positions that can help stop abuse.

Jacki: I totally endorse what you say and I certainly won't give up trying to stop abuse either, but you and I know that we are both very mouthy and strong people, who fight systems. I worry about the vulnerable people who cannot speak up for themselves and that is why I continue to advocate that we need a statutory framework to protect vulnerable adults. Maybe as you and I get older we will become vulnerable too. So who is going to help us?

Janice: Well I hope that I will be healthy enough to help myself and *not* be in a care home. I am hoping to live in the sunshine, perhaps go to Spain and drown my sorrows with Sangria and whiskey. Seriously, I have spent a lot of vacations in Spain and I do believe the Spanish provide better care homes than we do in England. Often families still look after their older people. I am told the Spanish Government pay for their older people to spend time in Benidorm as part of their package of care. Who knows, as a European citizen maybe my care will be funded in Benidorm.

REFERENCES

Care Standards Act 2000. London: HMSO.

Human Rights Act 1998. London: HMSO.

Public Interest Disclosure Act 1998. London: HMSO.

Pritchard, J. (2000) *The Needs of Older Women: Services for Victims of Elder Abuse and Other Abuse.* Bristol: Policy Press.

Registered Homes Act 1984. London: HMSO.

Residential Care Homes Regulations (1984). London: HMSO.

CHAPTER 8

ABUSE IN EARLIER LIFE

OLDER WOMEN SPEAK OUT

JACKI PRITCHARD

INTRODUCTION

Debates about the cycle of violence have taken place for years and will continue into the future. Some researchers have focused on the transgenerational transmission of violence (House of Commons 1975) whilst others have considered the three stages of violence in the cycle – build up, explosion, and honeymoon (Walker 1977–8; 1979). In my years spent working as a social worker I met with a considerable number of older people who had experienced abuse earlier in life. Later in my career I wanted to research further into this aspect of working with abuse in order to consider whether the cycle of abuse does exist. This particular cycle would include *all* forms of abuse, not just physical violence. I wanted to explore whether people did experience abuse through different stages of their life cycle. I felt this was an important subject to research because I have always worked adopting the psychodynamic model and support the idea that older people need to resolve certain issues or come to terms with past trauma before they die (Hunt, Marshall and Rowlings 1997).

Between 1997 and 1999 I worked on a research project which considered the needs of older women who had been abused (Pritchard 2000). The purpose of this chapter is to present some of the findings from that project which were not presented in the final report, that is, regarding the abuse experienced by older women earlier in life. The findings of the project identified the need for workers across the disciplines and sectors to offer support in order for victims to come to terms with abuse they had experienced:

Human and practical resources were needed for long-term work to adequately address the emotional needs of victims. This could include social workers, care workers, nurses, counsellors within day-care, day hospitals, community centres, women's centres, trauma centres.

(Joseph Rowntree Foundation 2000, p.4)

THE PROJECT

The project *The Needs of Older Women: Services for Victims of Elder and Other Abuse* was carried out in three social services departments in the north of England:

- Churchtown
- Millfield
- Tallyborough.

The aims of the project were to:

1. identify women who were victims of elder abuse

2. carry out a small study to identify the extent to which victims of elder abuse have also experienced abuse earlier in their lives

3. identify the types of abuse experienced (in childhood and adulthood)

4. identify the needs of victims

5. consider what resources/services should be provided for victims.

In order to obtain data from victims themselves a variety of research methods were adopted, which included running focus groups for over 300 older people and in-depth unstructured interviews conducted with 27 female victims of elder abuse. This kind of interview allowed victims the opportunity to talk about their own perceptions of abuse and experiences, using their own terminology. The following broad subject areas were introduced, so that there was some consistency within and between the interviews:

- life history
- definition of abuse
- previous experience of abuse (in childhood/younger adulthood)

- experience of elder abuse
- knowledge about other victims
- what help/advice/support the woman received/needed at the time of abuse and currently
- current needs.

This chapter is concerned with the themes which emerged from the in-depth interviews relating to the victims' lives and the abuse experienced in childhood and young adulthood. In the conclusion I shall argue that it is important to deal with the long-term effects of past abusive experiences, which may have been left unresolved for many years.

THE WOMEN

The criteria for interview was that the older woman should be a victim of elder abuse and be aged 60 or over. One woman, Jessie, aged 54, was included in the project when the manager of a day centre asked me to interview her as she had recently been abused and had a very interesting history. The women were aged, therefore, between 54 and 98, the mean age being 79. The majority (75%) were aged over 75 years:

Age	Number of women
50+	1
60–64	5
65–69	-
70–74	1
75–79	5
80–84	7
85–89	2
90–94	4
95–99	2

At the time of interview, two women were in nursing homes, six in sheltered accommodation and the remainder in their own homes. The interviews, which were conducted either at home or in day-care settings, lasted between 30 minutes and 4 hours. The majority of victims were interviewed on more than one occasion. Table 8.1 presents details of the women interviewed.

TABLE 8.1 The interviewees

Victim	Age	Type of elder abuse	Abuser	Previous abuse
Agnes	78	PEF	Husband	CA/DV
Beatrice	91	F	Carer/gangs (M)	CA(M)
Bertha	91	F	Carer	?CA
Catherine	60	PEF	Son-in-law	
Daphne	79	F	Granddaughter	
Dorothy	62	PE	Grandson	
Emma	80	PEF	Husband	DV
Ethel	95	PEN(?S)	Son	
Eva	77	PEF	Husband/son (M)	DV
Florence	80	PEF	Grandson	
Georgina	85	F	Stranger	
Gertrude	92	F	Neighbour	
Gwen	98	F	Stepdaughter	CA/DV
Harriet	90	S	Neighbour	CA/?DV
Hilda	64	EF	Son	DV
Irene	84	PF	Two sons/grandson	
Isabella	76	EF	Carer/nephew (M)	DV
Jessie	54	EFS	Stranger/brother (M)	CA/DV
Joan	78	PEF	Grandson	
Lilian	73	PEF	Son	CA/DV
Margaret	81	PE	Husband	DV

Martha	81	F	Son/daughter/stranger	DV
Mary	60	PE	Husband	CA/DV
Rose	81	EF	Gangs	
Sarah	81	PEN	Sister	
Stella	89	E	Husband/family	
Vera	63	PEFNS	Husband	DV

Key: P= physical; E = emotional; F = financial; N = neglect; S = sexual;
? = suspected abuse; M = multiple victim; CA = child abuse; DV = domestic violence

EARLY LIFE

There was little migration years ago: most victims remained living in the area where they had been born. The exceptions were Vera, who had been born in the north-east and moved to Scotland after she married to live with her husband's parents, and Jessie, who had been born in the south of England, but had moved north when she ran away from her husband. Most women had been born into large families and had experienced extreme hardship, which continued into adulthood. Poverty and hardship was a constant theme through the interviews; all the women had struggled to make ends meet. Consequently, basic things like food and warmth are most important to them in later life. They had worked from an early age in order to help support the family:

> My father married again to a woman who had got two children of her own... I was a nursemaid to them. I didn't have much of a childhood because I had to go and help her clean the house before I went to school in the morning and when I came home from school in the afternoon I had to go to the school where my Dad was school caretaker. Help sweep and dust there and then go back home and look after the two kids again... When I was 14 my Dad put me into domestic service. (Agnes)

In Churchtown, children used to get up early to go pea-picking in the summer months:

> [Brother] and me slept together when we were kids in this big bed. I used to get up about 4.00 a.m. because we loved to go out 'cos there were lorries waiting to pick you up to pick peas ... I was about 12 and he was 3 years younger than me. (Martha)

The expectation that they would contribute to the family's income was a pattern that was to continue throughout their lives. Even when Martha was married and had children of her own: 'I used to give my mother half that I earned.' Some women felt responsible for their parents all through their lives: 'I had my mother while she was 93. I looked after her all my life' (Harriet). This sense of loyalty and pulling together probably stems from the fact that families did stay together, either living in the same house or living nearby. It is ironic that in spite of this closeness, the victims could not talk about the abuse or seek help from family members.

With the exception of Harriet (whose father said: 'You can stop at home and help your mother') and Eva (who went to technical college), all the women had left school to go to work and had worked through their married lives so they could provide enough food and clothing for their children: 'Money was very strained at home and we had to get out to earn as soon as possible' (Eva).

We tend to think of the 'working mother' as a wartime and post-war phenomenon, but in fact it is not. Many of the women looked after the children during the day (and some additionally undertook daytime activities that would bring in extra money, e.g. baking which could be sold) and then went to work at night: 'I have had to bake to bring mine up' (Martha); 'I worked at the theatre as an usherette. I used to go out to work every night' (Margaret).

The women worked locally. On leaving school, most either went into service or to a local industry (e.g. mills, glassworks). Once married they may have undertaken a variety of other jobs: over the years the women interviewed had been in the following employment:

- bakery
- catering

- hairdressing
- hospitals
- in service
- librarian
- mill
- nursing
- office/secretarial work
- raincoat factory
- steelworks
- theatre.

Most willingly talked about how they had met their husbands and their courtships. What was striking and also sad was that very few women married for love:

> I accepted anything more or less because I'd got nobody, you know, no sisters or brothers and I just wanted to belong to somebody. (Agnes)

> Well my brother took me to a dance at the Town Hall and he was there. That is how I met him. But he hadn't had a very happy life. He lived with his gran. He wanted to get married. I didn't have anyone so we both got married, but it hasn't been easy going. I have had a lot to put up with. He was hot tempered. (Martha)

> I think it was after my mother died and needed someone to hang onto 'cos my family, my aunts had taken my brothers away and told me because I was 19 I could get on with my life, I didn't need any help. I suffered a bit of a breakdown. I took some tablets when she died. I came back. Someone brought me round and I first met my ex-husband... He took me out and he was as nice as pie. He never had a temper or anything, but as soon as we got married within two hours he beat me up. (Jessie)

> I was 19 and felt flattered and somewhat light-headed because someone wanted to marry me. (Vera)

Most married because it was expected at a particular age (usually late teens) and remained living with their parents. Many had married for companionship rather than passion. Agnes, who became a widow in her 30s, had advertised for a husband because she was lonely:

> I used to stand at the back door watching husbands and wives going out and I think it made me more lonelier than ever... I said I don't go out to meet anybody well I'll have to advertise for one...[cousin] put an advert in the Free Press... I decided to write to this other chap with two young girls... I thought I'd belong to a family again.

It seems that they had few expectations and just got on with things as best they could. This may help to explain why many of them put up with so much violence and abuse. Religion may also have played a part in this, related to a belief that God had put you here to suffer and eventually you will go to somewhere better. Religion has been very important to many of the women and has helped them to cope with intolerable situations: '...when you have faith it helps' (Beatrice).

EARLIER ABUSE

Of the women surveyed, 14 had been abused earlier in their lives; 7 had experienced child abuse; 13 had experienced domestic violence.

Child abuse

Five of the women (Agnes, Beatrice, Harriet, Jessie and Mary) talked readily about the abuse experienced in childhood; this included physical, emotional and sexual abuse. They found it very easy to recall in detail the physical violence, possibly indicating that it was therapeutic for them to talk about it. Agnes remembered vividly the day she had been taken away from her stepmother:

> One day she was thrashing me and I was on the floor, crouched on the floor and she was hitting me and there were three garages in the yard and one of the chaps who came to fetch his car heard her through the back kitchen window, which was open. He looked through it and saw her. Well we didn't know but he went and fetched the cruelty inspector. He came, that was the first thing we knew when he knocked at the door and she opened it and I was still crying and he took me away there and then to his home.

Some also recalled the violence they had witnessed towards their mothers:

> My father was in a foul temper many times especially if he had been drinking and I have learnt to expect it from him the violence... I know I used to think he's going to hit her [mother] and if I stood in front of her he wouldn't. (Eva)

> My father did the same thing. He kicked my mum down the stairs. She finished up with six broken ribs, two black eyes and a broken arm and I ran all the way for the police...came back in the police car and they took him away. Three weeks later he was dead. Killed in a road accident and when the police came to tell me my mum was out working and I just laughed. It was a relief because he threatened to get me and everything. (Jessie)

Victims also spoke readily about emotional abuse, which they tended to refer to as 'mental abuse' or 'mental cruelty'. They seemed clear about what they meant whereas social workers are often not clear about what constitutes this type of abuse. Harriet resented the fact that her father would not let her go out to work in the mill like her sisters. She talked about being isolated and emotionally abused:

> ... I had no friends. I was always at home and I never had a good happy life. I never had no friends and I liked dancing. I never could go 'cause I never had no friends to go with.

I found during some interviews that victims suddenly had a clear insight about what had happened to them or saw things differently when they put their thoughts into words. For example, Mary suddenly realized that her mother had abused her emotionally in similar ways to her husband later on. She said she had never realized this until talking about them in relation to abuse:

> They both use emotion. My mother has always got her own way... My brother died... I was 9...she [mother] lives her life in as much as what it would have been if he was here. Everything would have been wonderful if he had lived... She said I have two children, one is dead and the other one might as well have died... He wouldn't have been a let down you see ... She doesn't like people knowing things because that's an embarrassment... She thought I would have married a nice person.

When Mary left her husband she returned to live with her mother, who now controls her in much the same way she did in earlier life. Mary felt that she has become more assertive since leaving her husband; she commented that Anne Dickson's book *A Woman In*

Your Own Right had helped her after leaving her husband but 'it is not appropriate for women living in abusive situations'. However, Mary openly admitted she could not be assertive with her mother: 'She is 80. I might end up killing her one of these days.'

It was more difficult for victims to talk about sexual abuse. I suspect that Harriet and Bertha had been sexually abused by their fathers; they hinted at this but would not be drawn into full discussion about it, whereas they talked easily about other forms of abuse. A phenomenon discussed in the research project when considering elder abuse is that of 'multiple victim' (Pritchard 2000); Beatrice was just such a victim in childhood and her teenage years. She had been physically and sexually abused by her brother from a very early age and then she was bullied at school by pupils and teachers:

> I suffered a lot with my eyes when they blinded me at school – she hit me with the duster... I was terrified. Everything I seemed to do was wrong. They attacked my legs with the cane and all that. I have been black and blue many a time.

Domestic violence

Of the 13 women who had experienced some form of domestic violence earlier in their lives, 9 had through their own choice and actions left the situation. Similar to the victims who talked about child abuse, victims of domestic violence could recall what had happened to them and gave numerous accounts of the horrendous attacks they had experienced.

A common memory was how abusers often destroyed possessions, which were important to the victim or of sentimental value: 'I also had a cuckoo clock and he pulled it off the wall and smashed it up' (Martha).

For those victims later in life it was important to be surrounded by 'nice things'. Martha, for example, took great pride in her house and asked me what I thought of it at the end of the interview. Possessions give a sense of security and sometimes it is important for the victim to leave behind certain possessions and their memories. It was important to Eva that she had new furniture in her bedroom after her husband died: 'I can't see him here at all. New bed. All the furniture has gone.'

During the interviews victims were asked to talk about what abuse meant to them. All were clear about how they defined abuse, but there were different interpretations. Eva did not think her husband had physically abused her when he hit her:

> No, it was always something minor, like a dishcloth, nothing hard or heavy but he used to pick up things and I used to feel threatened... I used to have to think what I was going to say... He used to get violent tempers and I never knew what he would do with these tempers. He would throw a chair from one side of the room to another.

Like many women, Vera thought it was her 'duty' to have sex with her husband, but later in life interpreted it as sexual abuse.

All regretted marrying: some recalled not listening to their mother's warnings:

> My mother never wanted me to marry him. She didn't like him from the beginning...but you know what you are like when you are younger you think you know everything. (Margaret)

> My mother kept saying 'Are you sure you want to go through with this?' (Vera)

Most of the physical violence started very soon after the woman had married. Just after Vera had moved to Scotland her husband said:

> 'I'll teach you to have fun' and that was when it started. I was punched in the face a few times, in the body. My mouth was all cut and my mouth was busted open. I had black eyes. My nose was bleeding at one side where he had laid the fist in...

> I think it started the week after we got married... He threw a pint of beer over me. He stubbed a cigarette out on my arm and I was really shocked and horrified. (Mary)

> It started about a fortnight after we got married...he played hell, he was really annoyed. (Emma)

For Jessie it was even sooner: 'Within two hours he beat me up.'

The frequency of abuse varied. Some were physically attacked on a daily basis:

> Every time I remarked about it, wham. It was more or less daily. Any little excuse... Him coming out with a mouth full of filth, it got to be a normal daily procedure. (Vera)

In others situations, there was a certain regularity; for example, Margaret's husband always got drunk on Friday and Saturday nights. For others like Mary, there were long gaps when the physical violence stopped but there was always the fear that something would happen, so it felt like the abuse was constant.

Some described how they knew when they were going to be attacked:

> I used to do quite a lot of knitting. He got where he couldn't do with the needles clicking. (Emma)

> I knew when he was going to turn. No matter where I was I would know... There was always the fear that you were going to be hit... If it didn't happen you were always in fear it would happen. It is the anticipation because you know what is going to happen. (Mary)

> I had to be very careful what I said and how I said it. (Agnes)

When women talked about being abused by their husbands, I asked them if husbands had also been abusive towards the children. Some had abused the children in exactly the same way, that is physically, others had abused the children emotionally:

> He used to hit [son] a lot with the belt. (Martha)

> He never used to buy anything for the boys at Christmas. This was one way he was cruel to them, but he had a way of getting to you mentally that affected you physically as well because you were afraid to do certain things in case he got the wrong idea about it... (Vera)

> He gave [son] a terrible time. I think because it was another male in the family and he got jealous and because he used to give [son] such a bad time I used to go out of the way which I know was a mistake because it used to give him leeway for more abuse but there we were. (Eva)

Some women denied that their husbands had abused the children when asked the direct question, then contradicted themselves: 'No ...he has hit Simon a couple of times. I don't mean beaten him, but Simon was scared of him and his tempers' (Mary).

Mary decided to send her son away to boarding school to protect him:

> He was all for it...that was probably the best thing that had
> ever happened to him because he shone from there on and
> they knew – there were Benedictine monks – what he had
> been through... The other two started to board when we
> lived on the mountain...

It was important to victims to try to explain why the abuse had
happened; it was as though they wanted to excuse the actions of the
abuser. Many thought the cause lay in the fact that the abuser had
himself been abused in childhood or he had witnessed violence
within the family – therefore, it was learnt behaviour. Often they
would refer back to what had happened to the abuser in his
childhood:

> He didn't like his mother...he used to see her with other men
> and his father used to drink and he used to see her in alley
> ways with men and things like that...she considered him to
> be the most evil person she had ever met. (Mary)

> He has never been wanted and I think that is one of his trou-
> bles... His father was in his 50s and his mother in her 40s and
> I think the next one to him was about 12 and they couldn't be
> bothered with him...they used to go to the pub every night
> and lock the door and he was left playing and he said one time
> he got in through the pantry window. (Emma)

Jessie and Eva who had been abused by their sons as well as their
fathers gave the same reason, that is they had seen what their fathers
had done and did the same.

All who had been abused by their husbands explained in detail
how men had controlled them over the years. In many cases this had
been achieved by not allowing the women to have social contacts:

> He didn't let me talk to anybody. I couldn't ring up anybody.
> If anybody came to the door he told me what to say and what
> not to say. (Emma)

> I felt if I spoke to a male or female he'd half kill me when I got
> home... He didn't allow me to have friends... I'd finish work
> and if he was on late shift I used to go to the bus station and sit
> on the bus until he finished. I couldn't go home. (Mary)

> He wouldn't let people in the house... I got on with every-
> body I worked with, but I daren't let it turn into a friendship

and even using the phone I would have to say to him 'Is it al-
right if I ring for a prescription?' (Vera)

In Mary's case her husband isolated her by making her go to live in a
remote part of Wales:

> The total control was unbelievable. We bought a house on
> top of the golden mountain... I didn't want to go there be-
> cause the nearest neighbour was five miles away and I didn't
> drive. I had lessons and I came out the door one day and he
> had bought me a car with bows on and everything and this
> was my gift you see. Anyway, morning of my test came and I
> said 'Come on'. It was early. He said 'You're not going.' I said
> ... 'What do you mean? Have they cancelled it?' and he said
> 'No. I have. There is no need for you to drive.' So I ended up
> stuck on top of a mountain... He'd pull the phone's wires out
> and things like that and it was really scary.

Another pattern for husbands to maintain control was to keep their
wives pregnant: 'We had [two children] and he said "Well I made
sure that you had [3rd child] because I knew you were really tied"'
(Mary).

Lilian had been in several abusive relationships and had had 17
children; Vera had had 10 pregnancies.

Many of the men expected their wives to wait on them, so they
were really treated like servants:

> But he nagged at me to do everything, expecting me to wait
> on him hand and foot and everything he wanted... I had to do
> what he said... But he always arranged everything, domestic
> arrangements and everything. If we wanted something he
> would go and buy it. I had no choice in anything... Domi-
> neering, yes, right from the beginning when I look back. I
> didn't realize it and I was a silly fool. Just a country bumpkin
> and I ought to have stood up to him before I did. He wanted
> me clean away. Jealousy really. Just like the princess in the
> tower locked away. (Emma)

> I used to bow and scrape to him. I used to do things for him
> and try to make life easier for myself. (Margaret)

When they were younger none of the victims talked to friends or
family about what was happening to them, because it was expected
that you kept your problems to yourself and accepted the situation.

They did not consider talking to an outsider: 'No because I didn't know who to talk to' (Margaret).

Eva had talked to an educational psychologist when her daughter had been referred for help and said that had helped because she was 'neutral'. Agnes had gone to a marriage guidance counsellor once but was terrified that she would be seen going in and out of the office, so never returned. Both women were middle-aged before they could take the step of admitting the abuse to an outsider.

Other reasons for not telling anyone about the abuse was the fear of not being believed; many thought they were unique – that this could not be happening to other women. Jessie had spoken to her brothers but had not been believed, so trusted few people after that. A common trait in child and adult abuse victims is 'self-blame'. In the majority of interviews, the women at some point blamed themselves for what had happened to them:

> My stepmother just didn't seem to take to me or I didn't take to her. I think it was a bit of both really. I realized she wasn't my mother and I think part of the blame should be with me I suppose. (Agnes)

> He got more and more bad tempered. He flew into vile tempers all over nothing. I didn't know what I had said or what I had done that was wrong. (Emma)

Agnes considered herself to be a very strong woman who had had to survive independently for much of her life. She felt this was the root cause of the abuse in that her husband did not like her being able to manage, he wanted to control her:

> I think that is what he disliked in me. I was if you like wearing the trousers as he put it. I said I'm not, I'm only too pleased to hand over...I've been having to do this for so many years. I said just accept me as I am... But that's how I think it started. We have never spoken of it like that. In fact it's the first time I've put it into words, but I think it might have been the start of not getting on.

Similarly, Mary blamed herself for her husband's outbursts:

> He liked a jacket and I tried it on and he said 'Yes we will have that' and I said 'No I don't feel comfortable in it. I don't want it' and he said 'Well we will take it' and I hung it back up. He threw all the shopping up the shop and was swearing and

shouting. It was awful. It was embarrassing and I blamed my-self. I thought I should have had it. What difference does it make?

All the victims who experienced abuse earlier in their lives were asked why they stayed. The main reasons were:

- nowhere to go
- no money
- need to keep the family together.

But loyalty also played an important part in the victims' lives and sometimes they put others before themselves:

> Left to myself I would probably done it years ago ... There wasn't anything because in those days if you left your hus-band you couldn't claim money from him. You were in the wrong. (Emma)

> You have a family and you don't want to split them up, so I just stuck it out... But where could I go with four children? (Margaret)

> I was brought up to believe that a wife was to be wife to her husband so I followed the trait that I was put into and was taught. No matter what you must always stay put. You don't get up and run. So I did. I suffered for it. (Vera)

Both Emma and Agnes were responsible for caring for children who had learning disabilities and said that they had stayed until they were adults for this reason:

> I have stuck with him all these years because of [stepdaugh-ter] because I have always thought a lot about her, that's his mentally handicapped daughter... I think it was my con-science that played a big part. I felt I'm running out on them and I shouldn't leave [stepdaughter]. It was [stepdaughter] and my conscience that were the main things. I felt I was do-ing such a wrong thing. (Agnes)

In later life Agnes felt physically incapable of leaving and, added to this, she felt she had grown into being dependent, that she could not live elsewhere without help:

> I had that in mind a long time back leaving him but I thought 'Where can I go? How can I look after myself?' I couldn't get out of the house without my wheelchair. I was just stuck...

Husbands often threatened their wives about what would happen if they did leave and fear kept them in the abusive situation: 'I was so scared of him because he used to say to me if you try to part I'll kill you' (Mary); 'It's one of the worst things is fear. Fear of the unknown and what you are going to see next' (Jessie).

For some there was a feeling of resignation, that is, there was no way out 'till death do us part':

> Anyway I suppose judging by a lot of marriages it wasn't too bad, but it wasn't happy really. I was full of resentment because he had no initiative only leadership and things were left to me. It was 'you have used them, you pay for them', the gas and the electricity. (Eva)

Even though some women talked about the fear, on occasions the fear had been so overridden by anger that they had retaliated with physical violence:

> I shoved an iron in his face. (Emma)

> He is quick tempered and when his temper flared I'd think to myself I'm not letting him put on me like that. I'm not going to be a doormat and then I would start and that's it you see, instead of being a little meek woman that would suit him – being someone who wouldn't answer him back. (Agnes)

> He once tried to hit me like his father in the kitchen and I just went bang and knocked him straight out and when he came round he had these horrible evil eyes like his father had. He looked at me and I said 'Don't you dare' 'cos he thought he could do the same thing as his Dad did... (Jessie)

Both Martha and Vera discovered that their husbands were having relationships with women who lived opposite them:

> I went to sleep in another bed and he came pulling my clothes off me...so I found the poker in the bedroom and he had to have his ear stitched. (Martha)

> I picked up the meat tin and hit him over the head with it. I dented it anyway... I got him onto the floor and I set about him. I was just saying I am fed up with you always knocking me about. Now see what it is like to receive it. (Vera)

IMPLICATIONS FOR CURRENT AND FUTURE WORK

The women interviewed come from a generation who were taught to keep things to themselves. If you had a problem you did not talk about it and you put up with whatever faced you: 'Our silly mothers – my mother said it to me, "You make your bed you must lay on it"' (Emma).

It may be difficult for an older woman to discuss very private matters because she is not used to doing so. She may also be reticent because of:

- the fear of not being believed
- feeling disloyal/guilty if the abuser was a family member
- feeling embarrassed/ashamed.

It is important to give the victim 'permission to speak' (Pritchard 2000). Many workers in different settings dread working with abuse and lack confidence in dealing with disclosures. Consequently, they may avoid giving a victim the opportunity to talk because they 'do not want to open a can of worms'.

All the women interviewed plus other women who participated in focus groups said that it *did* help to talk. This was one of the main current needs identified by victims themselves. The women said it was easier to talk to someone 'outside', that is, not the family or the worker(s) they saw regularly:

> I was so ashamed that it was my own family had touched me; no I couldn't talk... I couldn't discuss it. This is the first time I have discussed it from beginning to end but I am getting over it now. (Daphne)

The timing of the need to talk can vary for each individual. Some just needed to tell their story once, others needed ongoing support and counselling to come to terms with what had happened to them. Beatrice had indicated for quite some time to day care staff that something awful had happened to her, but the workers lacked confidence to pursue this. When interviewed by the researcher she disclosed about the sexual abuse she had experienced from her brother and the secret she had never told anyone:

> I had a baby when I was 16. It's true. I don't know how it happened. It lived, but there was nobody there to see it. It should have been in an incubator. It was a girl.

Beatrice had been slightly confused before this disclosure; staff had thought it was the onset of dementia. After talking about this just once, her confusion went away completely and Beatrice presented as mentally sound. She did not want to talk about it again. In contrast Vera had been a victim of domestic violence throughout her married life and had nearly died through her husband's gross physical neglect of her in later life. She needed to talk frequently about the abuse. The social worker continues to visit on a weekly basis to counsel Vera, who also attends a survivors group for older people.

In the current climate where social workers are under pressure to get through a large number of assessments, there is the danger that long-term emotional needs may not be identified as frequently as short-term practical needs. All workers need to be trained in identifying abuse and its long-term effects. Without the understanding of why abuse happens, long-term needs may not be identified. Another concern is that under vulnerable adult/adult abuse procedures, investigating officers may be focusing on the current abuse being inflicted upon an older woman and may not consider the fact that some of the indicators being presented are a result of the abuse she may have experienced earlier in life.

The research findings of this particular project clearly indicate that older women may have needs related to abuse experienced either in childhood or earlier adulthood. Workers may feel very uncomfortable in addressing these issues; if they have no experience of working with child abuse or with women living in domestic violence situations they may feel out of their depth. This has implications for training, and consideration must be given to training workers across the specialisms in order to broaden experience.

The healing process can take years not months to complete. Victims of abuse need to be able to talk to people they trust, but those people also need to be able to help them work through the healing process. If social workers are not being allowed to undertake long-term work, then support must be identified elsewhere. The assessment process must identify what the problem is and the most appropriate way of resolving it.

The final project report (Pritchard 2000) suggested that when thinking about long-term help, consideration must be given to the following factors:

- specific problem(s) to be addressed
- underpinning philosophy of helper
- experiencing and understanding of elder abuse (and other abuse, e.g. child abuse, domestic violence)
- methods to be used
- gender of helper
- age of helper
- frequency of contact
- appropriate venue for sessions (some victims may be housebound, others may still be living in abusive situations).

(Pritchard 2000, p.98)

Over half the women interviewed in this project had experienced abuse in earlier life; few of them had received support to address unresolved issues. Past abusive experiences should not be ignored. The project found that 'many services which are currently exclusively provided for younger victims could benefit older victims, but current practices do not encourage this flexibility in provision' (Pritchard 2000, p.6). The words of Agnes should encourage us to be more proactive in helping these victims:

'Why couldn't someone just ask me if I was being hurt?'

REFERENCES

Dickson, A. (1982) *A Woman In Your Own Right*. London: Quartet.

House of Commons (1975) *Report from the Select Committee on Violence in Marriage*. London: HMSO.

Hunt, L., Marshall, M. and Rowlings, C. (1997) *Past Trauma in Later Life*. London: Jessica Kingsley Publishers.

Joseph Rowntree Foundation (2000) *Findings: The Needs of Older Women: Services for Victims of Elder Abuse and Other Abuse*. York: Joseph Rowntree Foundation.

Pritchard, J. (2000) *The Needs of Older Women: Services for Victims of Elder Abuse and Other Abuse*. Bristol: Policy Press.

Walker, L. (1977–8) 'Battered women and learned helplessness.' *Victimology 2*, 3–4, 525, 534.

Walker, L. (1979) *The Battered Woman*. New York: Harper and Row.

ACKNOWLEDGEMENTS

The research project *The Needs of Older Women: Services for Victims of Elder Abuse and Other Abuse* was funded by the Joseph Rowntree Foundation.

I would also like to thank the three social services departments and the older women who participated in the project.

CHAPTER 9

DOMESTIC VIOLENCE – DOMESTIC TERRORISM[1]

MARILYN MORNINGTON

> Domestic violence can be seen as any form of physical, psychological or sexual violence that takes place within an intimate or family-type relationship.

> (Women's Aid Federation of England 1998)

The history of the world and the story of family violence are inseparable. Despite differences in language, religion and custom, women have been beaten by their male partners the world over. In most societies we know anything about, men have considered themselves superior to women. When one group considers itself superior, it presumes the right to oppress the other. Sooner or later, oppression takes the form of physical abuse. The links with child abuse, adult abuse, elder abuse and racism are obvious – they are all linked by power and control and also by the ability to escape punishment for the abuse that the perpetrator is inflicting:

> Most of us have probably been bullied by someone on occasion – at school, in the workplace. Imagine living with a bully all the time, but being too scared to leave.

> (Women's Aid Federation 2000)

Domestic violence is a scourge on our society. I shall commence by giving you just some of the horrifying facts.

---

1   Mark Wynn – US Justice Department – Adhikar International Conference 2000.

THE BACKGROUND

UNICEF

- More than 60 million females are missing from population statistics around the world – killed by their own families deliberately or by neglect because of their gender.
- Domestic violence continues to undermine the lives of one out of every two women in some nations.

> (Reported at the Adhikar International Conference 2000 by the Metropolitan Police – Race and Violent Crime Task Force, New Scotland Yard)

British Crime Survey 1999

- A woman is murdered every three days in the UK in a domestic violence setting.
- For women, risks were particularly high for those who were separated from a spouse.
- Over their lifetime, 22.7 per cent of women and 14.9 per cent of men reported being a victim of domestic assault.
- Women were significantly more severely affected than men:
  - they were twice as likely to have been injured in attacks
  - they were much more likely to have been subject to frightening threats
  - they were more likely to have suffered multiple assaults.

> (Home Office 1999a)

Criminal Statistics for England and Wales (1997)

- Forty-seven per cent of female homicide victims were killed by their partners (compared with eight per cent of men).

> (Home Office 1997)

Home Office Crime Reduction Series 2000

- The overlap between women and abuse and child and physical abuse is variously estimated at 30 and 60 per cent (Hester and Pearson 1998).
- There is also substantial overlap with child sexual abuse; nearly half the cases in one study (Abrahams 1994).

- Up to one-third of children on child protection registers live with domestic violence.

Metropolitan Police Project Adhikar

'Snapshot' of 24-hour period on 28 September 2000 – in which 39 UK police forces and RUC and many voluntary agencies took part revealed:

- Every minute in the UK police receive a call to a victim of domestic violence.
- Injuries reported included – rape, cuts, stabbing, bleeding due to being kicked in pregnancy, 'throat slashed with a razor blade', and bruising.
- UK police receive more than 1300 calls per day – more than 570,000 each year for domestic violence.
- Three per cent of all calls to police for assistance are for domestic violence. Of these:
    - Eighty-one per cent are female victims attacked by male perpetrators.
    - Eight per cent are male victims attacked by female perpetrators.
    - Four per cent are female victims attacked by female perpetrators.
    - Seven per cent are male victims attacked by male perpetrators.
- A domestic violence incident occurs in the UK every 6 to 20 seconds.
- Nearly 1 in 5 counselling sessions held by English Relate mentioned domestic violence as a feature in the marriage.

(Adhikar International Conference 2000)

Massachusetts Coalition of Battered Women Service Groups (Jane Doe Inc)

- There are nearly three times as many animal shelters in the USA as there are for battered women and their children.
- Over 3.3 million children in the USA will witness violence at home this year.

(Adhikar International Conference 2000)

Russian Presidential Commission Report

- Annually 14,000 women in Russia are killed by husbands and relatives.

(Adhikar International Conference 2000)

The cost of domestic violence is enormous in both financial and human terms. Many thousands of families are torn apart every year. As many as one in three marriages that end in divorce involves domestic violence. This has cost implications by way of rehousing; in 1993 17,000 abused families in the UK were rehoused because of domestic violence (Borkowski, Murch and Walker 1983). In 1997 refuges helped and accommodated 54,000 women and their children and assisted and advised a further 145,000 (Women's Aid Federation 1998). There are court costs and legal aid costs, and the casting of the mother and children on to State support. Four in ten homeless young women have left home because of abuse (CHAR 1992). Thirty per cent of homeless cases result from domestic violence (Stockley *et al.* 1993).

The physical injuries received by the victims amount to one-third of all female patients seen in hospital casualty wards. General practitioners' time is taken up with dealing with the physical and emotional damage caused to the victims. The severe short- and long-term emotional damage to victims and their children is only now beginning to be understood. In many cases this leads to traumatic stress syndrome or the development of depression or other mental illness which deprives the mother of her abilities to protect herself and her children and to properly parent them either emotionally or physically (Abrahams 1994). Many women turn to drink, drugs or even suicide in their despair. Sixty-four per cent of mental health cases in hospitals are women who have experienced domestic violence; most have no prior symptoms (DOH 1995).

If a woman is being abused there is a high probability that her children are also being abused. A study of hospital cases of child abuse found violence to the mother from the father in 45 per cent of the cases. A study in one London Borough found that 20 per cent of allocated cases in the social services department had domestic violence on the mother as factors (DOH 1995). Women consistently fail to disclose the abuse suffered by their children out of shame that they have been unable to protect them and that they have failed to remove them from the violent situation earlier and also out of fear (often with some foundation) that if they do disclose, their children will be taken into care.

Even if they are not physically injured themselves the children of victims suffer severe damage to their mental, emotional and educational development. In 90 per cent of incidents, the children are in the same or the next room (Hughes 1992). Some fathers insist that they watch. One in ten mothers has been sexually abused in front of her children (Abrahams 1994).

Audrey Mullender, co-editor of the first major text on the subject of children living with domestic violence, stated:

> The development of any individual young person can never be predicted, – many react against the violence that they have seen, and vow never to emulate it, whilst others are influenced by a violent society as by a violent home-life, the challenge to us is to react to children's needs now, not to second guess the future. (Mullender and Morley 1994)

Boys who grow up in a home with domestic violence are 100 times more likely to be an abuser as an adult (Widom 1989). Any police officer, probation officer, lawyer, social worker or forensic psychiatrist will be able to confirm that our prisons and regional secure and special hospitals are full of offenders who have come from a background of domestic violence which they have gone on to inflict on others at great cost to their victims and to the State that detains them. Whilst 30 per cent of imprisoned sex abusers were themselves victims of sexual abuse, 90 per cent of them were victims of severe domestic violence as children.

Up to one third of sexual assaults are committed by children under 18. Dr Eileen Vizard runs a pioneer clinic at Great Ormond Street Hospital to try to treat such offenders whose crimes often involve severe violence. The average cost of each referral is £25,000. The average age of her patients has in three years gone down from 15 to 10 years of age. Without exception these offenders have themselves been the victims of dreadful multiple, long-term abuse, usually within their families.

Research conducted by the Metropolitan Police shows that a woman endures an average of 30–35 assaults before she contacts the police, and although the reported statistics are in themselves horrifying the crime is accepted as being vastly under-reported and that only one in five assaults at the most are reported (Adhikar International Conference 2000).

On the positive side, over the last 20 years the problem has become widely acknowledged and the relevant services are developing. There are now 284 Women's Refuges annually accommodating 54,000 women and children (Women's Aid Federation 1998). Research is being carried out into the effects of domestic violence and the services required to combat them in the UK and throughout the developed world. In 2001 the Metropolitan Police Race and Violent Crime Task Force received a grant of £300,000 for the Crime Reduction Programme for a fully funded research programme to compile up-to-date independent statistics on domestic violence. The team is led and advised by Profesor Betsey Stanko. Inter-agency co-operation and training programmes are daily being developed and expanded. I am presently engaged in a joint initiative called 'Raising the Standards', to share and improve best practice between the government agencies of England, Eire, Northern Ireland, Scotland and Wales. The UK and US governments have given the issue a very high priority. The US Senate in 2000 passed a $3.3 billion program for domestic violence. Zero Tolerance campaigns, originally developed in the USA, are being planned (with local and national government financial and other support) in many cities.

In order to attack the problem from both ends offender programmes are being developed worldwide. The Merseyside programme run by the Probation Service is a Home Office Pathfinder Programme and it now deals with 70 men at any one time with a course of challenging behaviour that extends for 12 months. They have achieved excellent results and I believe it is essential to develop effective programmes that challenge abusive behaviour, with the sanctions of the courts behind them for non-compliance, to stop offenders moving on from victim to victim, and I recommend that such programmes, under constant evaluation, be expanded countrywide and be available for referral from the Civil and Family Courts. On 7 March 2001 the National Umbrella for perpetrators programmes – RESPECT – was launched in the House of Commons. It must always be remembered that perpetrators are not mentally ill, they do not need treatment or counselling (although their victims may well) but their beliefs and behaviour need to be challenged by society and its agencies: 'In order to reduce violence, the behaviour and attitudes of perpetrators must change' (Home Office 1999b).

Of course, as with many other of society's ills, there is a vast under-resourced, unmet need. Those of us who have had the privilege of being aware of the problem can only continually press for priority to be given for education and funding within the individual service provider in which we work. In Britain there are 200 times as many sanctuary places for animals as there are for women and children.

Battered women come from all walks of life. Social class, family income, level of education, occupation, ethnic and racial background make no difference. But some groups of women are more vulnerable to the abusers and have greater difficulty in leaving them or in accessing help. I now intend to concentrate on the particular difficulties faced by some of those groups.

First, perhaps the biggest vulnerable group of adults in this field is mothers.

The British Crime Survey (Home Office 1999a) suggests that children increase levels of financial and emotional stress or that women intervene on behalf of their children and are assaulted as a result. Women are also more dependent on men when their children are under five years of age. Domestic violence is all about the abuse of power and perpetrators will take advantage of dependency and vulnerability wherever they can find it. The dependence is financial and emotional and exacerbated by widely held views on family life and the power structures therein. It is less acceptable for women to leave men, whatever their behaviour, after children are born. Children may be seen as triggers to or justification for violence. In particular, pregnancy or failure to produce a son may lead to violence.

THE USE OF CHILDREN AS A TACTIC

Men often use children as a way of abusing their partner. Ways in which this is done include:

- threats to harm the children
- threats to report as an unfit mother to social services
- threats to abduct the children if she leaves
- carrying out those threats
- saying he will gain custody if she leaves
- turning the children against their mother
- being constantly critical of her abilities as a mother
- keeping the mother and her children short of money
- abusing the children physically, sexually or emotionally
- threatening and/or carrying out threats to injure family pets.

Domestic violence can affect a mother's feelings and behaviour towards her children. Women sometimes use violence themselves towards their children either to pre-empt harsher treatment from the father or because of a build-up of frustrations and distress caused by the abuse. A woman's children may be connected to the abuse she has experienced, for example:

- children may be conceived through rape
- abuse often starts during pregnancy
- children may be encouraged to or choose to side with the aggressor
- children may join in the abuse of their mother
- the woman may switch off emotionally and therefore be unavailable to her children.

The particular problems of mothers who are victims of domestic violence and their children must be addressed. Examples of this are:

- The development of a wide range of counselling and therapy suited for the needs of mothers and their children, and the advertising of services available through the appropriate avenues in order to make the services accessible to them.
- Education of the police and the legal services and in particular the judiciary, as to the particular emotional, social and economic pressures that cause mothers to stay

with and return to abusers and the impact of the violence on them and the development of appropriate responses to them to empower them to leave and to protect them thereafter.

- Support in the process of prosecution of perpetrators and the availability of giving evidence through video link etc.
- Availability of decent rehousing.
- Expansion of refuge places (currently 60 per cent of women needing those places are turned away because of lack of availability), numbers of outreach workers, self-help groups and family centres.
- Sensitivity to the dangers, physical and emotional, to victims and their children, caused by perpetrators, in the granting of residence and contact orders.

Until recently our family courts did not deal effectively with the issues involved in child contact and residence where domestic violence was raised. The problem was largely swept under the carpet and our courts failed to protect mothers and their children from ongoing abuse perpetrated through contact.

Recently reflecting on her years of experience in the Family Division, Lady Justice Hale states in *The View From Court 45*:

> Most of my time was spent in oppressing women: specifically, mothers... The most troubling aspect of my perception is that some women are being pursued and oppressed by controlling or vengeful men with the full support of the system. (Hale 1999, p.385)

A sea change began about two years ago led from decisions of the High Court and, in particular from Mr. Justice Nicholas Wall. Due to mounting disquiet the Children Act Sub-committee of the Lord Chancellor's Advisory Board on Family Law put out a consultation paper on contact between children and violent parents which resulted in a much acclaimed report with recommendations for change to the Lord Chancellor and this was accompanied by proposed guidelines on good practice (on contact and domestic violence) for the courts. These guidelines were subsequently endorsed by the Government on 6th March 2001 and one effect of the President's decision in *Re L and others* (see below) was partially to incorporate the guidelines into law.

Most recently, on 19th June 2000, the President of the Family Division Dame Elizabeth Butler-Sloss, together with Lord Justice Thorpe and Lord Justice Waller gave judgement in four such cases (Re L (contact domestic violence) [2001] 4 ALL ER 609). (See also Contact and Domestic Violence – May [2001] Family Law 355. President of the Family Division, Dame Elizabeth Butler-Sloss DBE. In this revolutionary decision the Court, for the first time ever in English law, instructed leading psychiatrists to advise them on the effects of domestic violence on children and in which circumstances contact would continue to be in the child's best interests and with what protective mechanisms in place. The masterly judgement runs to 57 pages and warrants careful reading.

- Professionally supervised and safe contact centres need to be developed countrywide to replace the present haphazard voluntary system, which cannot offer the necessary protection to victims and their children. The new Children and Family Courts Advisory Service (CAFCASS)[2] may well be ideally placed to develop such centres. (In Eire there are no contact centres or proper methods of supervising contact.)

- Priority given to, and funding of, social services and other state-funded services in the handling of domestic violence referrals.

- Sharing of information between the RSPCA who are often the first people to know of domestic violence in families due to what is happening to the animals and the other caring agencies.

- A rolling, interdepartmental public educational programme to increase awareness of the unacceptability of domestic violence and its impact and of the services available.

- Teaching packs for schools.

- Co-ordinated multidisciplinary response.

- Access and entitlement to adequate welfare benefits.

- Top up education programmes for children who have missed schooling because of domestic violence.

2   CAFCASS – from 01.04.01 the English Court Welfare, Guardians Ad Litem and Official Solicitors' Services were amalgamated.

- Access to childcare and education and retraining for mothers to make them financially independent.

WOMEN WITH PHYSICAL DISABILITY

Perpetrators, as a result of the ease with which the perpetrator can exert power over them, physically or emotionally, and their difficulties in escaping the violence, particularly target women with a physical disability. As a disabled woman may be getting higher rates of State benefit the perpetrator can fund his own lifestyle and drinking by taking those benefits from her. Many refuges are in older types of buildings and are unable to accommodate the disabled. The home may be specially adapted to meet the disabled woman's needs, making it particularly difficult for her to leave and seek rehousing. The victim may be housebound, making it more difficult if not impossible for her to obtain help. The victim may be dependent on the perpetrator to have her physical care met. The perpetrator's presence in the home may be required to assist with childcare and he may threaten that he or the authorities will remove the children if the victim seeks help. In 2001, Wirral Children and Women's Refuge will open a new purpose-built, totally ensuite refuge; with two family units specifically adapted for the disabled.

MOTHERS WITH DISABLED CHILDREN

Women who have disabled children may also find it very difficult to leave a specially adapted house and thus disrupt the child's life. The needs of the disabled should be addressed by:

- the establishment of specialist subgroups in Domestic Violence Fora
- the production of specialist information and literature
- ensuring fully accessible venues for all activities/events
- developing specific projects for groups such as the blind and the deaf
- targeting disabled groups in Zero Tolerance and other public education programmes
- bringing disabled women into the domestic violence fora
- building or adapting refuge accommodation for the disabled

- increasing awareness of health care professionals
- separate interviewing of the woman and her carer.

MENTAL DISABILITY AND ILLNESS

Women with mental disability and illness who are now largely 'cared for' in the community are vulnerable to abusers who pray on their inability to access help. They are also liable to threats by the perpetrator to remove their children in the event of separation. Their needs can be met by:

- domestic violence training as part of their education and care package
- awareness again of the health care professionals
- the factors I have raised under physical disability above.

DRUG ABUSERS

A drug abuser or addict is often dependent upon and supplied with drugs by her abuser. She is likely to be particularly lacking in self-esteem. The illegality of her habit makes it very hard for her to call upon the aid of the police, social services and legal system. She is vulnerable again to threats from the perpetrator that he will gain custody of the children or have the children taken into care. Most refuges are unable to accommodate drug abusers due to the issues of safety for other residents and their children.

The needs of this group can be perhaps addressed by:

- specific information and literature distributed and displayed at needle exchange/drug abuse services
- support for drug abuse mothers to care for their children when they leave the abuser
- the provision of refuges specifically aimed at drug abusers.

ALCOHOLICS

Many of the problems faced by drug abusers and the solutions thereto are also those of alcoholics. It should also be borne in mind that women may have become alcoholic/drug abusing or mentally ill in response to domestic violence and this should be investigated by the professionals dealing with them, particularly in regard to issues such as residence. The perpetrator, having destroyed the woman, may well come across, superficially, as the person better able to care for the children.

PROSTITUTES

This group of women face many of the problems and obstacles in the way to seeking help of the groups above. They are very unlikely to seek official help. Their partner, who may also be their pimp, is frequently an abuser. Prostitutes may also have drug abuse problems. Many are isolated from their families and may have been brought up in care so that they have little or no family support. Many have been physically and/or sexually abused as children themselves and have therefore suffered long-term damage to their self-esteem and their ability to protect themselves.

WOMEN BROUGHT UP IN CARE

These women often had damaged childhoods making them vulnerable to and dependent upon abusers. Their family and community links may be lacking, reducing the support system for them and their children. Their unhappy experiences of the authorities may make them unwilling to seek help from State agencies or able to trust that help will be available. They form a large percentage of those seeking refuge places and often require intense support in the refuge in emotional and practical terms. These women have already been let down by society and have particular call on its resources.

- We need specific awareness training for girls brought up in care of domestic violence, of power and gender issues and of the services available to victims.
- They need priority for housing, counselling and support.

OLDER WOMEN

Older women of all social classes are particularly hidebound by outmoded attitudes of women's roles in marriage and society. They may have difficulties because of lack of financial independence from the perpetrator. Their feelings of duty to stay in the marriage and to keep the family together and of shame and guilt may well prevent them from seeking help. They may have little or no knowledge of the services available to them. Older black women, in particular, often have a very negative view of social services. Many of these women have suffered abuse for decades and only feel able to leave when their children have grown and the perpetrator has through age or illness become weak and is no longer able to exert control over them.

In many cases when the partner/perpetrator is too old, too ill or dead, one or more of the sons will take over the abuse of their elderly mother due to their conditioning. She is after years of ill-treatment particularly vulnerable to this exploitation and those investigating elder abuse should extend their enquiries to a full family history of domestic violence. They require:

- specifically focused literature distributed through the media, doctors surgeries, post offices, pensioners groups, pension books etc.
- housing suitable for older people
- counsellors trained to understand their feelings of guilt and responsibility
- health care workers, police and other relevant professionals being trained to pick up abuse in this age group.

LESBIANS AND GAY MEN

There are unique problems that gay and lesbian people face that make domestic violence more difficult to address. These can all be lumped under the heading of homophobia. It is particularly difficult for gay people to seek help from the police, as many do not believe the police will be sympathetic to them. The court system did not, until the coming into force of Part IV of the Family Law Act 1996, give them adequate protection (for instance there was no power of arrest available to them). Their needs can be addressed by:

- the development of a sympathetic, understanding approach by the Legal system and police
- specialized literature and counselling services available in gay and lesbian places of recreation and generally.

WOMEN FROM STRICT RELIGIOUS GROUPS

Sadly, many religions emphasize the power of men over their wives and children rather than their responsibilities to them and the fundamental equality of human beings. It is still part of many Anglican wedding services that women promise to obey their husbands, with the imbalance in power that that creates from the outset. It is particularly hard for women from very strict religious sects, within all the major religions, to report domestic violence or to bring upon themselves and their children the 'disgrace' and possible rejection from the group that leaving their husbands will entail. Many of these groups are in denial that domestic violence applies to them. Religious officials who are called upon by victims are prone to tell the woman that she and her husband are together until death do them part and to pray for God's help. The woman may find it particularly hard to find out about her rights or the services available to her. By way of example, the members of the Exclusive Brethren, a Christian sect, are forbidden to read newspapers or listen to the radio or watch television. They avoid contact with outsiders, making it difficult for women to be aware of recent developments and awareness campaigns.

In some way the leaders of these groups must be encouraged to address the issue, but I am not presently optimistic. London has however recently seen the opening of its first specifically Jewish Refuges. In 2000, the Catholic Church in Eire published a ground-breaking report *Domestic Violence* condemning domestic violence and fully accepting its share of responsibility in failing to protect Irish victims in the past (The Irish Commission for Justice and Peace and the Pastoral Commission of the Irish Bishops 2000). Sadly, it does not seem as ready, despite ongoing pressure from governmental and voluntary organizations, to release unused land and buildings to be used for refuges and drop-in centres or to be sold to fund necessary services.

BLACK WOMEN AND IMMIGRANTS

Unfortunately, being a victim of oppression does not create an automatic sensitivity to others who are also oppressed. This has meant that black men, who are struggling themselves against racism, sometimes continue to abuse women while using racism as an excuse for their abuse behaviour. But if racism is a reasonable excuse for being violent then black women should be the most violent of all in our society (Deltufo 1995).

In Black African countries, which have so recently freed themselves from colonial oppression and the denigration of their cultures, there is a tendency for cultural traditions not to be open to review and criticism. Women are suffering from this in the form of domestic violence or female genital mutilation, which is regarded as an inviolate cultural tradition, above intervention by human rights and national legislation.

Hannana Siddiqui of Southall Black Sisters has noted that there is a myth that only Asian women have religious or cultural expectations that make it difficult for them to leave a violent situation, and she pointed out that all women have such expectations. However, Asian women tend to live in tight-knit communities, where family pressure can leave them with few options for escape. If they leave they may well be ostracized by their community. Such pressure is increasing in other communities alongside the growth of religious fundamentalism, which is based on orthodox behaviour, conservatism and patriarchy. In the Midlands, gangs of Asian men have been formed to hunt down women and their children who have left home.

The report of the UK Government working group on forced marriage, *A Choice by Right*, led by Baroness Uddin and Lord Ahmed of July 2000, addressed this growing abuse of women in our visible minority communities. The report makes it clear that this is but another form of domestic violence that has resulted in injury and indeed death to many women.

Perceived and real racism within institutions may inhibit women from seeking help, while immigration problems can mean that a woman must either stay in the relationship or leave and be deported to her country of origin where she will be destitute and ostracized. A particularly vulnerable group at the present moment are asylum seekers. As fleeing victims they may be turned away from refuges as they cannot receive housing or social security benefits.

There is still a tendency within the police and other services to see domestic violence in ethnic communities as best left to be dealt with by the community itself. The result is that women cannot get the help they need. Black women and their children who have left abusers may be further damaged or forced to return by racism and lack of cultural awareness in predominately white refuges.

Black women need:

- refuges that are specifically for their racial groups
- female-run interpreting and translation services
- agencies gaining the confidence of women from ethnic communities by communicating with women's groups as well as their leaders
- the establishment of specialist sub-groups within domestic violence fora
- the production of literature and resource material in different languages and formats
- the representation of black women on domestic violence groups
- special support groups sympathetic to cultural needs
- refuges that understand that women may not be able to leave and need support within the marriage
- support groups and counselling to address the needs of black children.

CONCLUSION

A lot to be said, a lot to be done, but progress *is* being made. The size of the problem is enormous; the cost of not facing up to that problem is even worse.

Research is being carried out into the effects of domestic violence and the services required to combat them in the UK and throughout the world. Inter-agency co-operation and training programmes are being developed and expanded daily for all relevant bodies including, judges, lawyers, the police, healthcare workers, social workers etc.

In November 1999 the UK Home Office convened a special conference on domestic violence, bringing together concerned experts from all disciplines to aid the government in planning the way forward (Home Office 1999c). The overwhelming recommendation was to set up a national task force to investigate and co-ordinate the myriad of initiatives and develop best practice and networking. Such a body would mature and unify our responses and prevent the waste of money and resources from people 'reinventing the wheel' through lack of information, helping to end short-term approaches to a long-term problem.

The Metropolitan Police Adhikar Project held a global conference in London in October 2000 with 47 expert world speakers and 500 delegates and, through 20,000 CD-ROMs sponsored by Polaroid, access to this wealth of information will spread to a worldwide audience. The conference members have petitioned for a change in UK criminal law, similar to that already in force in Cyprus (Republic of Cyprus 1994), to make domestic violence an aggravating feature in a criminal offence and to add domestic violence to the welfare checklist contained in Section 1 of the Children's Act 1989. The work of Adhikar in promoting UK and worldwide best practice continues.

> With all the best intention in the world and all the laws and resources available to governments and to businesses, we will not prevent domestic violence until all of us wants it to stop. (John Howard, Prime Minister of Australia)
>
> United we can truly say 'Enough is Enough'. (Adhikar International Conference 2000)

REFERENCES

Abrahams, C. (1994) *The Hidden Victims: Children and Domestic Violence.* London: NCH Action for Children.

Adhikar International Conference (October 2000).

Baroness Uddin and Lord Ahmed (2000) *A Choice By Right.* London: HMSO.

Borkowski, M., Murch, M. and Walker, V. (1983) *Marital Violence: The Community Response.* London: Tavistock.

Butler-Sloss, E. (2001) 'Contact and domestic violence.' *Family Law*, May, 355.

Children's Act 1989. London: HMSO.

CHAR (1992) *4 in 10.* London: CHAR.

Deltufo, A. (1995) *Domestic Violence for Beginners.* London: Writers and Readers Ltd.

Department of Health (1995) *Domestic Violence and Social Care Report.* London: HMSO.

Hale, L. J. (1999) *A View from Court 45.* CFLQ 377.

Hester, M. and Pearson, C. (1998) *From Periphery to Centre: Domestic Violence in Work with Abused Children.* Bristol: Policy Press.

Home Office (1997) *Criminal Statistics for England and Wales 1997.* London: HMSO.

Home Office (1999a) *British Crime Survey – Domestic Violence.* Research Study 191. London: Research, Development and Statistics Directorate, Home Office.

Home Office (1999b) *Living Without Fear*. London: HMSO.

Home Office (1999c) *Violence Against Women*. Criminal Justice Conference. London: Special Conferences Unit, Home Office.

Home Office (2000) *Crime Reduction Series*. London: Research, Development and Statistics Directorate, Home Office.

Hughes, H. (1992) 'Impact of spouse abuse on children of battered women.' *Violence Update*, August 1, 9–11.

Mullender, A. and Morley, R. (eds) (1994) *Children Living in Domestic Violence: Putting Men's Abuse of Women on the Child Care Agenda*. London: Whiting and Birch.

Republic of Cyprus (1994) *Violence in the Family (Prevention and Protection of Victims) Law 1994*.

Stockley *et al.* (1993) *Young People on the Move*. University of Surrey.

The Irish Commission for Justice and Peace and the Pastoral Commission of the Irish Bishops (2000) *Domestic Violence*. Report from Conference August 2000.

Widom, C. S. (1989) 'Does violence beget violence – a critical examination of the literature.' *Psychological Bulletin 106*, 1, 3–28.

Women's Aid Federation Campaign 2000.

Women's Aid Federation (1998) *Families Without Fear*. London: Harwin.

CHAPTER 10

IS IT A DOMESTIC?
OR IS IT ADULT ABUSE?

RUTH INGRAM

INTRODUCTION

Over the past 20 years or so there have been separate strands of development of work to improve all of our responses to 'adult abuse' (also known as 'abuse of vulnerable adults') and 'domestic violence'. This has led to a situation where many areas of the UK have both a 'Domestic Violence Forum' and an 'Adult Protection Committee'. Where that work has lead to policies and procedures being developed workers may find that the organization they work for has both domestic violence guidelines and an adult protection procedure.

This chapter aims to explore the questions:

- What does this mean to the practitioner?
- Do we need a different set of skills and a different knowledge base to work with people experiencing domestic violence than we do to work with those experiencing adult abuse?
- What can 'adult protection' workers learn from 'domestic violence' workers and vice-versa?

I will explore these issues through considering a fable about how a social-care worker in the fictional town of Welston might offer a service to meet the needs of Carol, a victim of abuse.

You have been asked to assess Carol's needs before she returns home from her latest stay in hospital. You have realized, from the notes you have been given that Carol may be experiencing abuse,

CAROL

Neighbours called the police to Carol's flat last week. The police called an ambulance that took Carol to the accident and emergency department of the local hospital. She had extensive bruising on her face and on the back of her hands. She had a fracture in one of the bones of her right hand. Carol stayed in hospital over night. In the morning Chris came to collect her and took her home. Two weeks later Carol was admitted to hospital again. She was dehydrated and hungry. She had a vaginal infection and there was bruising, a few days old, around her neck. She was weepy and seemed confused.

including physical violence. It also seems that her health and physical well-being has been neglected.

Before you meet her you want to check your agency's guidance on working with people experiencing abuse. On your team leader's shelves there are three files that might be relevant. You disregard the '*Multi-Agency Child Protection Procedures*' because Carol is over 18 years of age (and almost immediately put aside your passing thought 'What if she was 17 years old?') and does not have children of her own. You turn to '*Good Practice Working: Domestic Violence*' and the '*Adult Protection Procedures*'. Which one should you use? Are either of them any use? Does it matter, to you or to Carol, which one you choose?

You might reach for the one that is designed using your favourite colour or the one that looks easiest to read. If you had ten minutes to spare you might sit down with a cup of tea and consider the difference between 'domestic violence' and 'adult abuse'.

DOMESTIC VIOLENCE

'Domestic Violence' is a phrase that has been adopted for use by the women's refuge movement (e.g. CRAWC 1984). Whilst the phrase 'domestic violence' is in itself gender-neutral, the refuge movement grew out of the response of women, to women's experience of violence, from their husbands and male partners. Starting with the provision of a network of safe houses using their own homes, funding was sought that has, 30 years later, established more than 400 refuges. The words 'domestic' and 'violence' combined together help break the myth that home is always a place of safety, that husbands are protectors of their wives and children and can be assumed to be acting in the best interests of all the family. It replaced the term 'battered wives', a term which fails to give sufficient importance to the emotional and sexual abuse that women experience (Women's Aid Federation 1988).

'A domestic'

The phrase 'a domestic' arose from the experience of those women who called the police. Historically a husband had a legal right to chastise his wife, his legal property. For example, English Common Law (as proclaimed by Judge Buller in 1782) gave men the right to beat their wives with a stick, as long as the stick was no thicker than the width of the man's thumb. This precedent was upheld in England until 1891. Despite the changed legal situation and the additional levels of protection available to women following the Domestic Violence Act 1976 many women found that the police were unwilling to intervene in what were seen to be the private matters of a man as head of his household. Women calling the police, in the hope of getting support to protect themselves from violent men, reported that they were told 'Sorry, we can't help you, it's just a domestic.'

So domestic violence is violence that occurs in a domestic situation, most often the home of the person who is experiencing the abuse. The perpetrator of the violence is not named or gendered in the term 'domestic violence' or indeed, within more detailed definitions such as that quoted by the Home Office:

> Any form of physical, sexual or emotional abuse which takes place within the context of a close relationship. In most cases the relationship will be between partners (married, cohabiting or otherwise) or ex-partners. (Home Office Affairs Select Committee 1993)

Nevertheless, domestic violence is commonly assumed to be carried out by a man with whom the woman is, or was in a sexual relationship. The term covers situations where the woman freely chose the original sexual relationship or those into which she was coerced or forced. If there are children living in the home they will also be affected by the 'domestic violence'. Studies have shown that up to 98 per cent of children who live in homes where domestic violence take place are in the same or the next room when the violence occurs (Hester and Pearson 1998).

One project working to improve the response of agencies to 'domestic violence', the Leeds Inter-Agency Project (Women and Violence) (LIAP 1996), are explicit that the aim of their work is to promote good practice in relation to 'women experiencing violence from men that they know'. This definition makes it clear that the type of 'domestic violence' they are working to prevent is perpetrated by men towards women. Their definition also extends the possible relationships between the perpetrator and the woman he is abusing. These relationships include son–mother, uncle–niece, community leader–community member, psychiatrist–patient and pimp–working woman. By focusing on 'violence towards women from men that they *know*' LIAP are recognizing several other facets of 'domestic violence'. These include the interlocking of the lives of the perpetrator and the person experiencing abuse (which is often reinforced by strong social and community pressures), the dependency (emotional, social and financial) that the person being abused has on the perpetrator, the length of the relationship (giving time for abuse to build up gradually) and the fact that there has often been, or still is, a feeling of love or trust from the person being abused towards the person who is perpetrating the abuse.

Violence

Having thought about the term 'domestic' what about 'violence'? In my experience as a trainer on these issues, when most people hear the term 'violence' they interpret it as meaning acts of physical violence. They also think of one event, or one in a series of events. They picture scenes that a woman could avoid or leave or manage, except perhaps if it happens very frequently or is very severe.

The term 'abuse', however, is associated with a greater range of experiences of being violated including: rape, forced marriage and sexual abuse; grooming, psychological torture, mental and emotional abuse; exploitation, slavery, theft and financial abuse. It is also associated with something that is ongoing and long term.

Something that may have crept up on a woman through a gradual process of compromise, acquiescence and defeat of her sense of self to the ways of 'her' man.

Whilst the commonly held image of someone fleeing domestic violence may be of women arriving at a women's refuge in the crisis aftermath of 'a domestic' with a black eye, the refuges are clear that there do not have to be any physical bruises and scars. So too is the Home Office (2000 para 1.15): 'Some (forms) are non-physical such as destructive criticism, pressure tactics, breaking trust, isolation, oppressive control of finances and harassment.'

Sometimes the physical result of the violence is permanent physical impairment. However, the damage that is often the hardest to heal and takes the longest time to heal is the damage the violence and abuse does to the woman's sense of herself; to her sense of her power; to her sense of herself as a person who deserves to live happily; to her sense of her ability to act in the world and make changes to benefit herself.

Violence, within the phrase 'domestic violence' has come to mean all behaviours towards a woman which violate her. Violence is any violation of her physical body, her sexual integrity, her sense of self, her feelings, her soul, her relationships with other people, her relationship with her God, her money or her resources. As it is most commonly used, 'domestic violence' includes all violence and abuse carried out towards a woman by a man she knows.

Except, where the woman is having a sexual relationship with a woman. Following a definition of 'domestic violence' that is based in the experience of women who are seeking safety and the means to break away from an abusive relationship, the women's refuge movement also recognizes that domestic violence, in all its forms, can be perpetrated by a woman towards 'her woman'. Being recognized within the definition does not, in itself, prevent a lesbian leaving a violent female partner feeling unwelcome or experiencing homophobia in refuges dominated by heterosexual women.

So let us return to Carol:

- Is her situation 'a domestic'?
- Is it violence towards her from a man she knows or from a woman she has a sexual relationship with?
- Who is Chris?
- And what is his/her relationship to Carol?

Clearly you do not know. There are two things you do not know in order to make that decision at this stage. The first is that you do not know whether the injuries that Carol sustained (the bruises and the broken bone) or the symptoms for which she admitted to hospital on this last occasion (the vaginal infection, dehydration and confusion) were the result of violence or abuse. If they were the second thing you do not know is who is perpetrating the abuse and what their relationship is with Carol.

There is one person who you have a remit to talk to who knows the answers to these questions and that is Carol, and after all you were going to talk to her anyway to carry out the assessment of her needs when she returned home. You need to think about the following:

- Do you take the 'Domestic Violence' file or the 'Adult Protection' file with you?
- What forms do you take?
- Are the forms you have to use different if it is 'a domestic' or if it is adult protection?
- What leaflets do you take to refer her to other agencies if that is what might be appropriate?

You decide to look inside at the summaries of both sets of guidelines.

The list of contents of the *Good Practice Procedures: Domestic Violence* includes:

- the who, what, why's and how often's of domestic violence
- the impact of domestic violence on women and children
- police and legal remedies
- safety and confidentiality
- additional issues for women from black and ethnic minority communities
- safe housing
- money

- recovery
- useful phone numbers.

As you are flicking through the guidelines the page referring to cultural needs and language barriers catches your attention. You double check the notes about Carol. There is nothing to suggest that she does not use spoken English as her method of communication; her religion is listed as 'none'.

You glance down the list of 'useful phone numbers'. It seems very comprehensive, including organizations providing safe housing and others providing ongoing support to women who choose to continue living with a violent partner. It is written in a way that you could show to Carol and work through the possible options together. You put it in your bag.

You pick up the *'Adult Protection Procedures'* with the intention of giving them a quick glance:

> The adult protection procedures are to be implemented in the protection of all vulnerable adults. This includes people with physical and sensory impairments, learning disabilities, mental health problems and older people. It is also recognised that carers of vulnerable people can experience abuse and this is included in these procedures… These procedures represent this agency's commitment to protect vulnerable adults in accordance with the guidance produced by the Government. *No Secrets* (DOH 2000).

The procedures themselves seem quite dense, but there are flow-charts and there is a clear statement that all staff have a duty to report any suspicions of abuse of a vulnerable adult to their line manager.

So is Carol a vulnerable adult? You go back to the notes and discover that Carol is 60 years of age. There is also a note of a report from an occupational therapist's assessment, six years ago, recommending that a level access shower is installed in Carol's flat. It seems likely that she is a 'vulnerable adult', according to the policy. You wonder briefly to yourself whether Carol thinks of herself as a vulnerable adult and if she does not, whether that makes any difference to whether or not you use the adult protection procedures.

You are about to start reading the policy in more detail when the hospital ward rings. They want to know when you are going to assess

Carol. They think she is getting depressed being in hospital and they need to know how many beds they will have over the weekend. You arrange to go to meet Carol in one hour. You ask the ward if you can talk to Carol in a private room and they agree to put a notice on the staff break room saying it's booked for that time.

CAROL'S THOUGHTS

It was quite an effort wheeling myself up the ward. I'd told Chris to get them to bring my powered wheelchair from home, but it never happened. Still I expect the exercise will do me good.

She seemed OK, the social worker. She wasn't like the last one I saw. I hadn't dared tell her anything. She didn't seem up to dealing with this mess. Anyhow, I promised myself that I had to put a stop to this. I can't take any more. Things have just gone from bad to worse since I had the flu last winter. It's like the flu made the M.S. worse. Now, on a bad day, I can't lift the smallest thing.

She introduced herself and we went into the nurses' tea room. That was nice of them. She wasn't 'funny' about me being in a wheelchair either, some of them are. They try not to show it, but you can feel their embarrassment. She explained she'd come to see if I needed any support to go back home. She said the doctor had been worried because I'd been dehydrated. She said that I could tell her anything that would help her understand my situation and that it would stay confidential unless I gave her permission to tell someone else like the district nurse team. She said the only time she'd tell someone something without my permission was if she thought I or someone else was in serious danger. Well I am, if I go back.

So I asked her what she'd do if I told her someone was hurting a friend of mine. She said she'd try to help by giving me information about who might be able to help, like the police. She said they've got a lot better at taking action when there's violence like domestic violence and harassment. She also said there were safe places to go like women's refuges and that the housing could offer you a new tenancy.

I hadn't thought about that. I knew the women's refuge. It was a big old building with lots of steps. I could get round the ground floor but that was it. But getting a new flat with the council or a housing association, that could really help. Not only would I get away and be safer but I'd get away from the memories too.

I must have looked pleased or something, I don't know how she guessed, but she just asked straight out 'Is that what you'd like?' and I burst into tears. Then I told her. It all came out in a big rush, all higgledy-piggledy, but she understood.

Whether Carol's situation is 'adult protection' or 'domestic violence', you have done well. Some of the good practice guidelines you have followed include:

- Interviewing the person before doing anything else.
- Interviewing them in a safe, confidential, sound proof place.
- Winning the person's confidence in your abilities and 'safety'.
- Being clear about why you are there.
- Being clear about your confidentiality boundaries.
- Letting them know you know some useful information about dealing with violence and abuse.
- Not being scared to hear what the person is experiencing.

But what do you need to do now? You've now got the basic information for your assessment of Carol's needs on leaving hospital.

In amongst her story of violence and abuse she told you about her day-to-day needs assistance with health care and daily activities. Part of the abuse has been that she has been deliberately humiliated by being left dirty and helpless to do anything about it. She has been blamed for her dependency, for being a nuisance, for being useless. She thought she had become weaker than she really is because she has not been able to eat or drink properly. Although drinks have been put by her bed she has not been able to reach them. She knows the pain of the pressure sore she developed from not being able to move herself has been clouding her ability to think.

Carol seems very mentally alert now. She is scared of having to go back 'home' and get into the same state again. She needs support to work out where she is going to live safely and then you can get going arranging a care package.

You make a mental note to talk to the ward sister before you leave about keeping Carol in hospital as a place of safety until a safe housing option can be found. If that is not possible or if it is going to take too long you might have to get a respite placement in a nursing home.

So what are the options open to Carol? And does it make any difference if it is a 'domestic' or if it is adult abuse? The answer at this point is 'yes'! But the answer has nothing to do with the label given to the violence or with who the perpetrator is.

There is a difference because the options open to Carol at this point are influenced by her physical impairment and by the duty of the health and social services to assess her needs and to provide services under the NHS and Community Care Act 1990. In some ways Carol's options are limited by the lack of access to some services that would meet the needs of a woman without mobility impairments, e.g. Carol's knowledge of the lack of access for her at the women's refuge. In other ways her options are more varied in that she does have the possibility of a temporary placement in a residential home or a respite facility that offers the level of physical care she needs.

The options that are open to Carol should include the following:

OPTION 1

Carol could stay in her current home, receive appropriate assistance with daily living and protection from the person who is abusing her.

Protection

Protection can include physical measures (e.g. new locks and video surveillance) and legal remedies (e.g. the prosecution of the perpetrator and the serving of a non-molestation order under the Family Law Act Part IV 1996). It may also include a plan for summoning help, e.g. access to a telephone and a one-touch dial number to an agreed source of emergency help. Another option used within the West Yorkshire police force's repeat victimization programme includes neighbours being made aware of the situation and agreeing to telephone the police if there is any sign of trouble.

Where the perpetrator of 'adult abuse' is a paid member of staff or a volunteer, they can be prevented from meeting Carol through their employment if they are dismissed or moved to other work. If they choose to persist in attempting to contact Carol in a personal capacity then legal remedies can be sought, for example under the Protection from Harassment Act 1997.

Violence and harassment are crimes. The police have a duty to pursue court action against those they consider to have committed a crime. In Carol's case the crimes include rape (Sexual Offences Act 1956) and grievous bodily harm (Offences Against the Person Act 1861). If the perpetrator received a custodial sentence Carol would be protected from direct attack on a temporary basis. If there is no forensic evidence and there are no other witnesses a police case against the perpetrator will rely strongly on Carol's statements and testimony in court. The Youth Crime and Criminal Evidence Act 1999 introduced new measures to protect witnesses who are victims of domestic violence and sexual assault. The aim is to enable the victims to give evidence to the best of their abilities without opening them to intimidation from the alleged perpetrator.

Carol could also choose to take civil action against a perpetrator. This would take the form of suing the perpetrator for damages done to her person. She may also be eligible for compensation from the Criminal Compensation Injuries Board.

The ultimate protection is for the person who is being violent and abusive to Carol to choose to stop behaving in that way. In an increasing number of areas of the country there are programmes for men who want to stop behaving abusively to their female partners (Dobash et al. 1996; Burton, Reagan and Kelly 1998). Perpetrator programmes have not, however, been developed to change the behaviour of other perpetrators of 'adult abuse' or 'domestic violence', e.g. domestic violence within same sex relationships or 'adult abuse' by a relative or neighbour.

OPTION 2

Carol could move to a place of safety on a temporary basis and then return to her current home.

A place of safety

A place of safety can include a women's refuge that is accessible to Carol and which will allow personal assistants to visit to provide care. (In the case where a personal assistant is needed through the night there needs to be somewhere for them to stay too.) It can also include respite care with a 'family placement' or a residential home.

If either of the last options are chosen it is crucial that those providing the placement are aware of Carol's need for protection. Standard procedures should include:

- Not telling anyone where Carol is.
- Not having her place of safety address written down anywhere that can be easily seen.
- Not telling anyone on the phone that Carol is in unless their identity has been checked (e.g. by calling them back through a switchboard).
- Always checking who is at the door.
- Not allowing anyone in that Carol does not want to have access to her.

OPTION 3

Alternatively, Carol could move to a new place to live, either from a place of safety or directly from her old home. Options for Carol might include a tenancy of an accessible flat with the local authority or a housing association, warden-assisted 'sheltered' housing, living with a relative or friend, or in a residential home.

A new home

Local authorities have a duty to provide temporary accommodation whilst they are carrying out an assessment of anyone who may be statutorily homeless and in priority need.

Section 177(1) and 178 of the 1996 Housing Act makes it clear that domestic violence 'means violence from a person with whom he or she is associated'. This would include anyone living in the same household as Carol, a partner or ex-partner and relatives, including extended family. The experience of domestic violence is now accepted as a reason why it is not reasonable for a person to continue to occupy their previous home. Carol would therefore be defined as homeless.

If someone is homeless and has priority need the Local Authority has a duty to provide accommodation for up to two years. Section 189 gives Carol priority for housing because she would be defined as 'vulnerable as a result of physical disability'. Carol therefore has an option open to her that might not be open to an able-bodied single woman. However, local authorities vary in the resources that they use to fulfil the requirements of the Act and in some areas all women fleeing domestic violence are given housing priority.

Wherever Carol chooses to live, measures for her ongoing protection from abuse should be an integral part of the plan. Her choice may depend on how confident she feels about being protected in each option. Carol may also need short- to medium-term advice, support and advocacy to rebuild the basic fabric of life: housing, money, employment, leisure, relationships and friendship networks.

Advice

Before she decides whether or not to return home Carol may need legal advice about her rights to occupy the property and the potential for obtaining an occupation order requiring the offender to leave (Family Law Act Part IV 1996).

She should also seek advice about her financial affairs. If she has been in receipt of benefits she should pass information about her change of address to the Benefits Agency as soon as possible. If there has been any misuse of (theft of) her benefits by someone else she may want to take action through the Benefits Agency. If there has been the loss of other monies or property she could take action by reporting these thefts to the police.

Advocacy support

A person who has been abused may have been made to feel that they have no skills and no power to control their own life. This lack of confidence can be a big impairment to managing all the practical changes that need to take place when someone chooses to end a violent or abusive relationship. In addition, dealing with violence and abuse on an ongoing basis leaves the person emotionally and physically exhausted.

Advocacy is an important service that gives a person information about the options open to them and enables a person to define which services they want. Advocates can then support the person to get the service they need to get back in control of their life. This often involves negotiation with complex bureaucracies and with people who do not understand the nature or impact of violence and abuse. A good advocate will support the person to regain their confidence through enabling the person to speak for him/herself, but who will also take some of the weight by carrying out tasks on their behalf.

Emotional support

Emotional support is another vital aspect of the process of escaping from an abusive or violent relationship. Sometimes a person will choose to return to a violent or abusive relationship because they feel lonely and as if there is no one on their side. Emotional support can enable someone to put the impact of the abuse behind them and move on with their life.

Carol may want to meet other women who have had similar experiences. She may also consider whether to spend some time having counselling about her experiences. For Carol it could be important that any counsellor has a good understanding of disabled people's issues. This should include an understanding of how abuse targeted at weaknesses brought about through physical impairment can reach and undermine a disabled person's identity and self-esteem.

Support groups

A major, almost universal, impact of the experience of violence and abuse is an enduring sense of shame and responsibility for the violence. 'It was my fault', 'I don't deserve any better'. Some of these beliefs can arise from the struggle of the person who is experiencing abuse, who has lost control of key aspects of their lives, to hang on to some sense of having control over the situation. More straightforwardly there can be a direct internalization of a key perpetrator's message. Many perpetrators overtly tell those they are abusing that they are behaving that way because of something about the 'victim'. 'You provoked me', 'You know I don't like it when you don't do as I say', 'You're clumsy and stupid', 'You should be able to wait to go to the toilet'.

For people who feel too ashamed to speak to 'normal people' about what they feel they 'allowed to happen', meeting other people who have also experienced violence and abuse can enable them to really talk about what happened with less fear of judgement. Where there is the opportunity for several people to meet together, the realization can dawn that perpetrators of abuse use (consciously or unconsciously) tactics that blame the victim rather than take responsibility for their own actions. However it happens, the realization that what happened was the responsibility of the perpetrator and that it 'wasn't my fault' is a key moment for the victim in gaining freedom from the abuse they have experienced.

But first things first. You suggest to Carol that you go and get you both a cup of tea and then discuss where she wants to be living this time next year and where she wants to go when she leaves hospital. She agrees.

DOMESTIC VS. ADULT ABUSE

Does it matter whether it's a domestic or adult abuse for Carol or for the worker? The short answer is no! Good Practice guidelines for working with adults with community care needs ('vulnerable' adults) are the same as those that have been developed through work with women experiencing domestic violence.

Table 10.1 Label given to abuse according to type of relationship

Chris's relationship with Carol	Label given to the abuse
Husband, boyfriend, ex- boyfriend	Domestic violence /woman experiencing violence from a known man
Lesbian partner	Domestic violence
Grandfather, father, uncle, brother, son, nephew	Domestic violence /woman experiencing violence from a known man/adult abuse
Grandmother, mother, aunt, sister, daughter, niece	Domestic violence/adult abuse
Male nurse, home care worker, social worker, doctor or other service provider	Adult abuse/woman experiencing violence from a known man
Female nurse, home care worker, personal assistant, social worker, doctor or other service provider	Adult abuse

Table 10.1 lists some of Chris's possible relationships with Carol and how this might change the label that the abuse she has experienced is given.

The differences emerge in three areas:

1. *The use of the law and professional de/registration to protect a person from a paid service provider who is perpetrating violence or abuse.* Whilst they are not comprehensive and are currently under review, there are specific offences and professional codes relating to the conduct of staff providing care to people with community care needs that should be used to help prevent the perpetrators access to people to abuse. These include the Registered Homes Act 1984, specific parts of the Mental Health Act 1983 and the Sexual Offences Act 1956 as well as *Caring for Young People and the Vulnerable* (Home Office *et al.* 2000).

2. *The use of community care service as part of the protection package to a person with community care needs who has experienced violence or abuse.* Where an adult with community care needs is experiencing domestic violence, community care services can be used as part of a protection plan. A residential home where the staff have been briefed can be used as a place of safety, a day centre can be used as the venue for confidential advice, counselling, self-defence training or support groups and an appropriately trained personal assistant can act as a body guard.

3. *The impact of the person's impairments on their ability to take action to protect themselves from violence and abuse.* All people should be enabled to take part as fully as possible in decisions about their safety and the degree of risk they want to take in their life. Where someone is unable to do this there is an increasing duty on agencies to take action on behalf of the person to protect them from violence and abuse (DOH 2000) and in some situations the Mental Health Act can apply and be used as part of a protection plan, e.g. use of guardianship to state where a person should live.

My conclusion is that it should make very little difference to Carol or to the practitioner whether the social worker used the domestic violence good practice guidelines or the adult protection procedures with them. Both should have lead to a similar outcome.

In the case I have in mind as I have been writing this (where Chris was Carol's husband), Carol moved from hospital to a residential home where she took three weeks to gather information and advice. She then took legal action under the Family Law Act Part IV 1996 that resulted in her gaining sole occupancy of the marital home and there being a restraining order on Chris's contact with her. She quickly regained control of her financial situation and used the direct payments scheme to employ personal assistants of her choosing. She is able to get out and about and visit friends (who Chris had prevented her from seeing) and her co-ordination improved to the level that she was able to take up her hobby of pottery again.

One implication of there being so few differences between the two areas of work is that there needs to be close co-operation between those working on the development of adult protection work and those who have developed good practice in working with women experiencing violence from men that they know (domestic violence). Whatever the label (if there has to be one) given to Carol or to the abuse she has experienced, the support and services that she receives to protect herself from future violence and abuse and to recover from her previous experiences should be the same.

For the practitioner and policy maker there remains one further question. What if Carol was Carl?

There is much less information about the incidence and impact of domestic violence experienced by able-bodied and disabled men. The law relating to domestic violence, harassment and the provision of housing would be the same for Carl and Carol. However, there are far fewer dedicated resources to address the support needs of men who experience abuse. Carl would have far fewer options for refuge, advice and counselling. It is possible that your agency's 'domestic violence guidelines' do not apply to men. One area in which there has been some development of resources has been for gay men experiencing domestic violence from a same sex partner (Kibblewhite 1999).

We do know that the incidence of abuse of disabled men and in particular of learning disabled men is high (MENCAP 1999; Brown and Craft 1989). If Carl is disabled then the adult protection policy will be applicable and, as with Carol, it will be possible to use community care services as part of a protection package.

Will Carl's need for support be the same as Carol's? Are men affected by violence and abuse in the same way as women? Evidence about men's reaction to other abusive traumas such as being taken hostage indicate that they are (Herman 1992). It is also possible to theorize that disabled men who are abused experience the abuse as part of the consequence of their disability and therefore as a consequence of their identity in an able-bodied dominated society. If this is correct Carl is likely to internalize the message that the abuse is his fault.

One way to think about this issue is to check the following good practice tips. They apply to Carol whether she is able-bodied or disabled. Are all the points equally applicable to Carl?

GOOD PRACTICE SUMMARY

For the policy maker:

1. Ensure that your adult protection procedures and your good practice guidelines for domestic violence are consistent.

2. Ensure that a woman who is also a 'vulnerable adult' receives the same service if either set of guidelines are followed.

3. Ensure that the definition of violence and abuse used in each document is consistent.

For the practitioner:

1. Have a working knowledge of your agency's good practice procedures for 'domestic violence' and 'adult protection procedures'.

2. Interview any woman who may be experiencing violence or abuse in a setting where it is safe for her to disclose experiences of violence and abuse if she chooses to.

   Safety includes physical safety and confidentiality. Research shows that violence increases, and becomes more dangerous, if the perpetrator suspects that the person they are controlling is trying to leave. She will be worried about whether he could find out she is talking to you about what he does.

Safety also includes emotional safety. Safety from judgement, safety from discrimination, safety from being patronized.

It is better to take time to find a way of meeting the woman in a safe space than to compromise safety. Be creative!

3. Be clear about your agency's confidentiality and information-sharing policies. Ensure that the woman understands your duty to disclose information if she indicates that other people are at risk or that an agency has a duty to stop the abuse or if you consider her to be at serious risk.

4. Safety includes your safety. Assume that this is a potentially dangerous situation. Follow your agency's procedures. Make sure your manager knows about the work you are doing and you log your whereabouts. Do not carry out home visits on your own.

    The dynamics of a violent relationship can mean that the woman may be or can feel forced to tell the perpetrator that you are helping her. Do not give her information that will allow her to pass on knowledge of where you live or other details, e.g. home phone number.

5. Provide whatever is necessary to enable you to communicate with her effectively, e.g. a venue that is accessible to her where she is safe, a trained professional interpreter, a key worker that understands her communication, a signboard, or a laptop computer.

6. Develop the skills and experience that enable you to ask about, respond to and explore her experiences of violence and abuse to the level that is needed to fulfil your role.

7. Develop your knowledge of services in your own and other agencies that may be able to provide support to people experiencing violence and abuse.

STATUTES

Domestic Violence Act 1976. London: HMSO

Family Law Act Part IV 1996. London: HMSO

Housing Act 1996. London: HMSO.

Mental Health Act 1983. London: HMSO.

NHS and Community Care Act 1990. London: HMSO.

Offences Against the Person Act 1861. London: HMSO

Protection from Harassment Act 1997. London: HMSO.

Registered Homes Act 1984. London: HMSO.

Sexual Offences Act 1956. London: HMSO.

Youth Crime and Criminal Evidence Act 1999. London: HMSO.

REFERENCES

Brown, H. and Craft, A. (1989) *Thinking the Unthinkable: Papers on Sexual Abuse and People with Learning Difficulties*. London FPA Education Unit.

Burton, S., Reagan, L. and Kelly, L. (1998) *Supporting Women, Changing Men: Lessons From the Domestic Violence Intervention Project*. Bristol: Policy Press.

Cleveland Refuge and Aid for Women and Children (1984) *Private Violence: Public Shame*. Cleveland: CRAWC.

Department of Health, Home Office (2000) *No Secrets: Guidance on Developing and Implementing Multi-Agency Policies and Procedures to Protect Vulnerable Adults from Abuse*. London: HMSO.

Dobash, R. E., Dobash, R. P., Cavanah, K. and Lewis, R. (1996) *Research Evaluation of Programmes for Violent Men*. Edinburgh: Scottish Office Central Research Unit.

Herman, J. L. (1992) *Trauma and Recovery – From Domestic Violence to Political Terror*. London: Pandora.

Hester, M. and Pearson, C. (1998) *From Periphery to Centre*. Bristol: Policy Press.

Home Office, Department of Health, Department of Education and Employment, Northern Irish Office, National Assembly of Wales (2000) *Caring for Young People and the Vulnerable. Guidance for preventing a Breach of Trust*. London: HMSO.

Home Office (2000) *Domestic Violence. Breaking the Chain. Multi-agency Guidance for Addressing Domestic Violence*. London: HMSO. www.homeoffice.gov.uk/domesticviolence/mag.htm

Home Office Affairs Select Committee (1993) *Report on Domestic Violence 1993*. www.homeoffice.gov.uk/cpd/cpsu/domviol198.htm.

Kibblewhite, K. (1999) *Current Service Provision for Perpetrators and Victims/Survivors of Same Sex Partner Abuse in Leicestershire*. Leicester: Scarman Centre for the Study of Public Order.

Leeds Inter-Agency Project (Women and Violence) (1996) *An Overview 1990–1996. Progress Report 1996*. Leeds: LIAP.

MENCAP (1999) *Living in Fear. The Need to Combat Bullying of People with a Learning Disability*. MENCAP Campaigns Dept, London.

Women's Aid Federation England Ltd (1988) *Leaving Violent Men*. Bristol: WAFE.

USEFUL ADDRESSES

Information and advice for women living in violent relationships is available from:

Women's Aid Federation England,
PO Box 391, Bristol, BS99 7WS
Helpline number 08457 023 468
(for women experiencing domestic violence)
Administration number 0117 944 4411
Website www.womensaid.org.uk
E mail wafe@wafe.co.uk

Refuge 0990 995 443
(24-hour helpline for women experiencing domestic violence)

For men experiencing domestic violence:
Men's Advice Line and Enquiries 0181 644 9914 (Mon–Wed 9am–10pm).

CHAPTER 11

NEGLECT

NOT GRASPING THE NETTLE AND HIDING BEHIND CHOICE

JACKI PRITCHARD

I have been undertaking an experiment during the past 12 months when I have been speaking at conferences and on some of the training courses I have provided to staff in a variety of organizations. I ask the audience to raise their hand if they have heard of Mrs Lily Lilley (100 per cent no response); Jasmine Beckford (majority responded); Kimberley Carlisle (majority responded). So who is Mrs Lily Lilley? It is an unusual name so you would remember it if you had heard it. Mrs Lilley was a 71-year-old woman, who was murdered by two 15-year-old girls. They dumped her body in a wheelie bin, which they then pushed into the local canal. Mrs Lilley was a vulnerable adult, who was known to the local social services department and had been terrorized by gangs of teenagers for a considerable length of time. The adult abuse procedures had not been implemented. Mrs Lilley was neglected.

Mike Linnett commences Chapter 2 by referring to Beverley Lewis – another vulnerable adult who died. There are many more, but rarely do they hit the press in the same way as children who die. We do neglect vulnerable adults in a number of ways. In this chapter I want to focus on neglect as a form of abuse. It is an aspect of abuse which *is* frequently neglected and I believe will persist unless professionals positively seek to identify its different forms. Vulnerable adults can be neglected in a variety of ways – by carers, by staff in institutions, by bureaucratic systems, which will be discussed further below. Over the years there has been a realization that neglect is very prevalent, but it is still extremely difficult to prove in a court of law. Very often workers feel uncomfortable in dealing with this aspect of abuse and consequently it can remain well hidden.

When discussing neglect, the following problems need to be considered:

- defining neglect
- identifying neglect
- the issue of self-neglect
- gathering evidence/proving neglect
- what to do about it.

I wanted to write this chapter to highlight the importance of this category of adult abuse. I am consistently reminded in my day-to-day work that people are still not working with this aspect of abuse, that is, they are not grasping the nettle. My concerns increase when talking about neglect I hear comments like:

> 'It is only a bit of bad practice' (manager of residential home).
>
> 'She's only neglected a little bit – we don't have to worry about that' (home care manager).
>
> 'It's only neglect, so let's keep it low key' (registration and inspection officer).

It is all too easy for workers to hide behind the concept of choice, that is, they believe vulnerable adults choose to live in certain ways and this can result in them being neglected. I shall argue that some workers make judgements about adults without having undertaken a holistic assessment or in some cases, when assumptions are made, without even asking very basic questions, for example, 'Do you want to live like this?'.

Therefore, in this chapter I want to consider:

- the different types of neglect that exist
- the dilemmas facing workers in dealing with cases of neglect
- how adult abuse procedures can help to identify neglect and promote good practice in the long term.

WHAT IS NEGLECT?

In the early days of working with elder/adult abuse, neglect was usually put in the category of physical abuse. It was rarely given any substantial recognition. In 1993 the Department of Health commented on the findings of *Confronting Elder Abuse* (DOH 1992): 'An exceptionally large number of cases of physical abuse and few cases of neglect were produced' (DOH 1993, p.4). More recently, it has been acknowledged that neglect can be both physical and emotional. As in child protection work, proving neglect can be extremely difficult; this is not to deny that it exists. Any research statistics are probably a gross under-estimation of its prevalence.

In March 2000, the Department of Health launched *No Secrets: Guidance on Developing and Implementing Multi-Agency Policies and Procedures to Protect Vulnerable Adults from Abuse*, which acknowledged neglect as one of the main forms of abuse:

> **Neglect and acts of omission,** including ignoring medical or physical care needs, failure to provide access to appropriate health, social care or educational services, the withholding of the necessities of life, such as medication, adequate nutrition and heating. (DOH 2000, Section 2.7)

In the previous decade academics and researchers had started to write about both active and passive neglect. Some definitions that have been used are:

- *Active neglect*:

> ' ...the withholding of items that were necessary for daily living (food, medication, companionship, bathing), the withholding of life resources and not providing care for the physically dependent person' (Rathbone-McCuan and Voyles 1982).

> 'Intentional withholding of basic necessities or care' (British Columbia InterMinistry Committee 1992, p.6).

- *Passive neglect*:

> ' ...being left alone, isolated, or forgotten' (Hickey and Douglass 1981).

> 'refusal or failure to undertake a caretaking obligation (including a conscious and intentional attempt to inflict physical or emotional distress' (Godkin, Pillemer and Wolf 1986, 1989).

'Not providing basic necessities and care because of lack of experience, information or ability' (British Columbia InterMinistry Committee 1992, p.6).

Prior to *No Secrets* the number of policies and procedures concerned with adult abuse had increased and neglect is now usually cited as a separate category in its own right. Some typical definitions are:

The deprivation of help to perform activities of daily living and failure to intervene in behaviour which is dangerous to the individual concerned or to others. Allowing a person judged to lack capacity to make safe decisions to take unwarranted and unreasonable risks. When a manager, owner or other care provider in a position of responsibility does not ensure that appropriate care, environment or services are provided to maintain the health and safety of vulnerable people in their care then they may be open to a charge of 'wilful neglect'. (East Sussex County Council 1996, Section 3.2.8.)

Neglect may be deliberate or by default where the abuser is not able to provide the care needed and may not recognise the need for that care to be given. The abuser may also be neglecting themselves. (Hanover Housing Association and Sanctuary Housing 2000, p.15)

Physical neglect

Typical examples of physical neglect include:

- Not washing someone.
- Not dressing someone.
- Not dressing someone appropriately.
- Refusing to buy new clothes for someone.
- Not toileting someone.
- Leaving someone to sit or lie in urine/faeces/soiled clothing or bedding.
- Lack of food/drink/warmth/lighting.
- Lack of appropriate accommodation.
- Withholding medication.
- Lack of medical attention/access to medical care/treatment.
- Absence of mobility aids.

- Communal clothing, face cloths, combs and hairbrushes, bucket for false teeth.

A broad definition of physical neglect is 'lack of basic care'; but what does 'basic' mean? We all have different standards – what might be basic to one person might be totally unacceptable to another. For example, if you were living in residential care how often would you want to have a bath or shower? Once, twice, three times a day? A week? A month? How often do you wash you hair? How often do you brush your teeth? Everyone is different. What you and I take for granted, that is, the norm for ourselves, may not always be considered basic and certainly many vulnerable adults do not have the opportunity to:

- be clean – washing/bathing/cleaning teeth/cutting finger and toe nails/toiletting
- have personal items – brush, comb, face cloth, towel, toiletries, purse/wallet, handbag
- own clothes/have a variety of clothes

CASE STUDY 1

Hettie was 87 years old and slightly confused. She was physically disabled and spent most of her time in bed. She did transfer to the commode with help from her son, Roland, who lived with her and was the main carer. They had no other relatives and had nothing to do with the neighbours. They had always kept themselves to themselves. No services were going in. The practice nurse visited Hettie once a year for her annual review. However, during one week the neighbours became very concerned when they heard Roland shouting at his mother and the police were finally contacted when Hettie was heard screaming. The police contacted social services immediately when they found Hettie sitting on the commode in her nightdress. Hettie had actually been sitting on the commode for over a month. Roland had placed her there and then not transferred her back to bed. He had fed her occasionally. Her hair, which reached her bottom in length and was matted with urine and faeces, had to be cut in order to unglue her from the commode. During the adult abuse investigation, Roland was also assessed and was diagnosed as suffering with schizophrenia.

- be warm
- be fed
- be healthy
- receive medication/treatment when necessary
- feel good about themselves.

Emotional neglect

Typical examples of emotional neglect include:

- Ignoring someone.
- Lack of stimulation.
- Isolation.
- No social contact.
- Ignoring or not meeting emotional/sexual/spiritual/cultural needs.

The word 'neglect' often conjures up images of people being ignored. Many victims of neglect are literally locked away. They may be confined to one room which has few amenities (e.g. no television, radio, magazines, books) or which is poorly decorated (dark, depressing walls, old badly fitting carpet or lino, draughty/broken window, no pictures/photographs). The victim may be 'put away' because they are an embarrassment to their family/carer or maybe because it is easier to manage them in a confined space:

CASE STUDY 2

Amanda was a 24-year-old woman with severe learning disabilities. She often had violent outbursts when she would throw things around a room, causing extensive damage, but she also threw things at people. In the past she had harmed herself by holding her arm against an electric fire and cutting herself with a knife. Her mother was adamant that she did not want her daughter 'to be put away in care'. Amanda's social worker became extremely concerned when Amanda started saying she 'hated the cupboard'. When asked about this, Amanda's mother admitted that when Amanda was 'difficult' she put her in the walk-in wardrobe, which could be locked from the outside.

This was a deliberate action on the part of Amanda's mother, but sometimes neglect can be unintentional as is illustrated in the following case example.

CASE STUDY 3

Ellie was 82 years old and the main carer for her sister, Margaret (aged 80), who had severe dementia and had suffered several strokes. Ellie willingly accepted the responsibility of caring for her sister when she was discharged from hospital. Margaret could do little for herself; she needed help with washing, dressing and feeding. Home care staff came in twice a day to get Margaret out of bed and dressed and to put her to bed again in the evening. Ellie had always been very houseproud and insisted that Margaret stayed in her bedroom, which she kept spotlessly clean. Home care staff became concerned as they got to know the sisters. They felt that Margaret was being emotionally neglected because from 8.00 in the morning she sat in a chair by her bedroom window until 6.00 p.m. when she was put back to bed. Ellie came upstairs to see her sister three times during the day to give her a drink (morning and afternoon) and lunch. Ellie never sat and talked to her sister because she believed there was 'no point'.

An adult abuse investigation did take place and the case conference concluded that Margaret was being emotionally abused, but it was not deliberate. The adult abuse policy in that authority was following guidance from the Department of Health which stated abuse: '…may be intentional or unintentional, or the result of neglect. It causes harm to the older person, either temporarily or over a period of time.' (DOH 1993, p.3).

What became very clear during the course of the investigation was that the medical/nursing staff at the hospital had not spent enough time with Ellie talking about dementia and the effects of the strokes. No one had taken time to explain that Margaret could benefit from stimulation – e.g. walking with a zimmer frame, talking with her, reading to her. The protection plan that was developed organized day care for Margaret but it was also agreed that the social worker and district nurse would undertake work with Ellie to help her understand about her sister's physical and mental conditions and to teach her how to interact positively with Margaret. In this case, Ellie was seen to be the abuser, but it could also be argued that Ellie was a victim of neglect herself because the professionals had not spent time with her to explain how she could care for her sister properly.

I have come across extreme cases of isolation. For example:

- An older man was made to live in a cupboard under the stairs by his daughter-in-law. All he had was a stool to sit on and a bucket for toiletting purposes.
- A husband kept his wife, who had learning disabilities, in the garden shed for 40 years.
- A young man with mental health problems told everyone his mother had died. She was found alive 25 years later in her bedroom upstairs, where her son had kept her imprisoned.

In these cases the abuse remained hidden for years because services were not going into the homes and the victims were not known to any agencies. So even when gross neglect is taking place it can be hard to identify. Another concern is the more subtle forms of neglect which again can remain well hidden. Some examples are:

- Ezra is an older Afro-Caribbean man who goes in for respite care regularly. He is the only black person to use this residential unit. Permanent residents are extremely racist and make derogatory comments to him. Staff suggest to Ezra that he keeps out the way 'so as not to upset anybody'. Because staff do not address the issue of discrimination, Ezra spends most of the daytime playing his guitar in the entrance hall of the home where nobody talks to him and he is ignored.
- There are six male adults with learning disabilities living in supported accommodation. They all are said to have 'challenging behaviour'. The team say they need more staff to deal with these service users as they cannot cope. When they are said to 'play up', they are not allowed to have their favourite food/drink, e.g. puddings, cakes, chocolates, sweets, certain fizzy drinks, or engage in their leisure activities, e.g. watching television, going out to the shops.

Consequently, they spend a great deal of time in their own rooms.

It is all too easy to engage in certain practices that are seen to be the 'norm' because maybe they have been followed for years. Very often staff in residential settings may not question their own practice or the practice of their colleagues because the regime is well established. Some examples are:

- Hugo has Alzheimer's disease and asks to go to the toilet about every 15 minutes. A new member of staff takes him to the bathroom each time he asks her. Other members of staff tell her 'Leave him. Don't listen to him going on – he's demented.'

- Ailsa is a 36-year-old woman with learning disabilities, who lives in a supported accommodation project. She regularly makes allegations that she is being sexually abused by various people. The manager of the project tells the staff group they do not have to implement the abuse procedure because Ailsa 'has always told stories and cried wolf too many times'.

THE ISSUE OF SELF-NEGLECT

Self-neglect has rarely been included in the definitions of abuse. This is yet another example where professionals hide behind the principle of choice. If individuals are of sound mind and they choose to neglect themselves most professionals would agree that they should be allowed to live their lives as they wish. Dilemmas occur when the neglect becomes life-threatening or it affects other people in the immediate vicinity (this could be in the community or in an institution). McCreadie argues that self-neglect is often excluded from definitions of abuse because: 'Self-neglect may be an important problem, but it will almost certainly have a different set of explanations to the problem of abuse by others and require different interventions' (McCreadie 1996, p.13).

Although self-neglect is largely ignored in this country some adult abuse procedures do mention it in definitions:

> [Self-neglect] is not defined as a separate category and will not usually require the instigation of adult abuse procedures, unless involving an act of someone with responsibility for the adult's care. (Wakefield Housing and Social Care 1999, p.9)

Gloucestershire County Council include self-neglect within the definition of physical neglect:

> All adults who have been physically neglected by him/herself or others to such an extent that his/her health, well-being and/or development is significantly impaired. (Gloucestershire County Council 2000, p.19)

In the following case study of self-neglect, the adult abuse procedure was implemented.

CASE STUDY 4

Roberta was 88 years old and was said to be eccentric. Her husband had died 40 years earlier and her only daughter lived in another city but visited as often as she could. Roberta lived alone in extremely squalid conditions. Furniture and rubbish were piled up so high it was difficult to move around the rooms. She would not allow anyone to touch or move anything in the house. She kept her excrement in paper bags around the house. Maggots were found in food left in the kitchen. Roberta refused to wash and change her clothes and no one was certain whether she was eating properly. She spent long periods of time in bed; the bed sheets were never changed. The GP was often refused admission but had been concerned after previous visits about her physical deterioration. Roberta was described as being an 'eccentric', 'independent' and 'strong-willed' woman who opposed help or intervention from anyone. Her daughter said the situation was 'impossible'.

During the adult abuse investigation Roberta was assessed by an approved social worker who concluded that her level of understanding and memory were normal. The case conference recommended that the house needed to be cleaned by environmental health. It was recommended that Roberta should be offered several options for temporary accommodation but if she refused to move out whilst the house was repaired and cleaned then an application would be made to Court for admission under Section 47 of the National Assistance Act 1948.

Roberta reluctantly agreed to be admitted to hospital. When she returned home she failed to appreciate her clean surroundings, the space, the new carpets and furniture. Having been in hospital she started to eat regularly and accepted meals on wheels. Home care went in Monday to Friday, but Roberta insisted on 'having two days off from them' at weekends.

In this case, the social worker and other professionals who were involved felt very strongly that intervention was necessary, even though it was clear that Roberta was mentally sound. The work which was undertaken with Roberta was undertaken very sensitively; concerns were openly discussed with her and options put to her. The social worker in this case did grasp the nettle and tried hard to work *with* Roberta, without overriding her self-determination.

LINKING POLICIES AND WORK PRACTICES

When considering the issue of neglect, one should not only look at useful definitions of neglect but also what is required under the care management system. Adult abuse procedures cannot be used in isolation. Every adult has needs but very often when a vulnerable adult is undergoing an assessment not all of these needs are assessed thoroughly. Even if certain needs are identified, they may not been seen as a priority. The NHS and Community Care Act 1990 defines need as:

> The requirements of individuals to enable them to achieve, maintain or restore an acceptable level of social independence or quality of life, as defined by the particular care agency or authority. (DOH 1991, p.12)

The *Practitioner's Guide* (DOH/SSI 1991) states that 'the assessment should start from the applicant's own perception of their needs' (p.58) and should focus on two keys questions:

1. What is the quality of the service user's life?
2. How can the level and nature of risk be minimized?

However, at a time when resources are often stretched and budgets are constrained, needs may not be met. So in fact 'the system' could be abusing and neglecting the vulnerable adult. The NHS and Community Care Act 1990 highlights the following needs to be assessed:

- personal/social care
- health care
- accommodation
- transport/access

- financial
- education
- employment
- leisure
- carers.

It is all too easy to focus on practical resources that can be offered; sometimes it is more difficult to meet the more complex needs. Workers should be considering the following needs:

- physical
- emotional
- sexual
- spiritual
- cultural.

The following examples (Pritchard 2001) illustrate cases where spiritual and cultural needs were neglected:

CASE STUDY 5

Daniel was a Jewish man who was in his late 80s. He had been abused by a number of different people in late adulthood. The social worker focused on the physical, financial and sexual abuse he had experienced but did not address his other needs. He had been kept very isolated by his last abuser and had lost his confidence in communicating. He explained to the social worker that he had always been very religious and would like to go to the synagogue. The social worker offered him day care, but did nothing to help him make contact with the Jewish community.

CASE STUDY 6

Gregory, who came from an Eastern European country, had been financially abused and neglected by a carer. When the social worker came to interview him she bought a Russian interpreter because it was 'the nearest to his country'. This was not appropriate because Gregory had emigrated to England to escape from the Russians.

In a recent research project, the needs of older women who had been victims of elder abuse were summarized, as shown in Table 11.1:

Table 11.1: Older women's needs

- Advice
- Choice/options
- Company
- Control over own life/own affairs
- Counselling
- Feeling able to trust other people
- Food and warmth
- Health
- Hobbies/interests
- Housing
- Information
- Money/benefits/pension
- People (helpers of various kinds)
- Physical help
- Place of safety
- Practical help
- Privacy
- Religion
- Trust
- To get out and about
- To talk
- To stop the abuse/violence
- To leave the abusive situation
- To be safe
- To be believed
- To be listened to
- To protect family/abuser
- To forget about what has happened
- To reduce fear of crime
- To feel safe in the house/community
- To know who to go to for help
- To have telephone numbers

(Pritchard 2000, p. 74)

Therefore, a vulnerable adult may have a variety of needs and because of the lack of resources may consider themselves neglected.

INDICATORS

It has already been said earlier in this chapter that it can be extremely difficult to identify neglect. Workers have to acknowledge that some vulnerable adults may have different values and attitudes to those of the worker and consequently may not see themselves as a victim of neglect, because they have always lived that way:

CASE STUDY 7

Frannie, who was 22 years old, was said to have a personality disorder. She had always been cared for by her mother, who never allowed her to have new clothes. Frannie had always had to wear 'cast offs' (including underwear and shoes) from her sister and cousins. She told the new social worker that she was not allowed 'to have new things because I'm bad'.

Workers can feel uncomfortable about raising the issue of neglect; perhaps because they are frightened of being seen to be judgemental. This is where it can be easy to hide behind the principle of choice. My argument is that we must question whether someone is a victim of neglect (either physical or emotional); this has to be done by undertaking thorough assessments and continuing to monitor situations rather than shying away from situations for fear of 'opening a can of worms'. Just because neglect is difficult to prove from a legal point of view, does not mean that we should not try to work with it.

It is necessary that systems are developed so that we can monitor and record what is happening to a vulnerable adult whom we suspect is being neglected. Using checklists is a helpful tool to monitor changes in physical and medical conditions (e.g. smell of urine/faeces, weight loss, dry skin, tiredness, lethargy, dehydration) of the vulnerable adult which indicate neglect, but also changes in their mental health (e.g. depression, low self-esteem, self-harm incidents). Most adult abuse procedures will list indicators of neglect which could be developed into checklists, e.g.

East Sussex

- neglect of accommodation
- inadequate heating
- inadequate lighting
- physical condition of person poor, e.g. ulcers, bed sores etc.
- person's clothing in bad condition, e.g. unclean, wet etc.
- failure to visit or engage in social interaction
- malnutrition
- failure to give prescribed medication
- failure to access appropriate privacy and dignity
- inconsistent or reluctant contact with health or social agencies
- refusal of access to callers/visitors

(East Sussex County Council 1996, Section 4.2.7)

HIDING BEHIND CHOICE

One of the fundamental principles underpinning adult abuse work is *self-determination*. It is a basic premise that an adult can make his/her own decisions; the reality is that s/he may make a choice which other people (family, professionals, workers) find hard to understand or accept. For example, how many times do people ask *why* does a battered woman stay with her abusive partner? There is never a straightforward answer; situations and behaviours are usually very complex. Workers in whatever role they have can sometimes be over-protective; maybe they do not promote risk taking as much as they should because they fear the consequences for themselves, that is, being accused of neglecting their duties. Workers can be guilty of wanting 'to rescue' people or needing 'to be seen to be doing something'. These are just some of the reasons why people find it difficult to work with adult abuse. It can be frustrating when a victim wants to protect the abuser or chooses to remain living in the abusive situation. So we do promote *self-determination*, but do we sometimes hide behind the principle of *choice*? Are there not circumstances when professionals should intervene but do not do so because they believe it is the service user's choice to live as they are doing? There is also the danger now that many workers may become paralysed by the implementation of the Human Rights Act 1998; that is, they are scared of contravening a service user's rights. Nevertheless, there are circumstances where workers may have to consider overriding the principle of choice because it is in the best interest of that adult:

- The adult is mentally incapacitated and cannot make an informed decision:

  A person is without capacity if at the material time

  a)   he is unable by reason of mental disability, to make a decision for himself on the matter in question: or

  b)   he is unable to communicate his decision on that matter because he is unconscious or for any other reason.

  (Law Commission 1995, para 3.14)

- Other adults have been or are at risk of being harmed (that is promoting the concept of public protection).

It is very easy to make assumptions about people and maybe because of lack of time, workers undertaking assessments do not spend enough time to adopt a holistic approach. Consequently, the worker may not get enough detail about how a person has lived his/her life in the past and whether they are currently following the same lifestyles. In a recent research project, it was evident that some workers were very judgemental about male victims of abuse who were grossly neglected (Pritchard 2001). Where men were living in squalid conditions it was assumed that they had always lived like this and there was a further assumption that if a woman was not around a man could not look after himself. In several cases, home care staff had been going in to monitor the men, but none of the men had been asked if they chose to live in these conditions; it was assumed that they liked it. When the men were admitted to care, they talked about how they had felt embarrassed living in those conditions and would have welcomed help (Pritchard 2001).

Sometimes victims are neglected by one person and then, because of how they present themselves, the abuse is continued by others who make value judgements – as is shown in the case of William:

CASE STUDY 8

William was 79 years old. He had been financially and sexually abused by his wife's lover, Edmund, who was the main carer; both William and his wife were also grossly neglected by Edmund. After an emergency admission to care, William was eventually placed in permanent residential care. On admission he had few clothes, his self-esteem was very low and he was grieving for his wife, who had died of pneumonia in hospital. No work was undertaken by the residential staff to build his self-esteem. He was described as being 'scruffy', 'dirty', 'no manners' and 'a nuisance'. Many months later he started attending a survivors' group. The social worker and residential staff did not think he would agree to go or make an effort to dress up when he went out to the group. William did not present any difficult behaviours when attending the group and said that he wanted to buy some new clothes for when the group went out to Christmas dinner.

(Summarized from Pritchard 2001)

CONCLUSION

I fully acknowledge that working with neglect is very difficult and many dilemmas present themselves to workers who may be engaging with vulnerable adults who are experiencing this form of abuse. Nevertheless, it is clear that neglect, both physical and emotional, is very prevalent and it must be addressed, not swept under the carpet. Workers have to overcome their fear of asking direct questions in order to find out what is going on and to understand the values and attitudes of the services' user – that is – they have to grasp the nettle. Here are some suggestions on how to promote good practice in working with neglect:

Good Practice Tips

In order not to neglect the neglected we need to undertake the following:

1. *Consideration must be given to both the physical and emotional well-being of an adult.* In the child protection field, much attention is given to children who fail to thrive and efforts are made to closely monitor them. Vulnerable adults should be afforded the same attention, that is, their physical and emotional development should be assessed thoroughly. Workers should not adopt stereotypical attitudes; adults of all ages continue to develop and consequently will have different needs.

2. *Thorough assessment and monitoring systems must be in place.* Vulnerable adults should have *thorough* (not quick) health checks, which could be undertaken by any number of health professionals (general practitioners, practice nurses, community nurses, community psychiatric nurses, health visitors). Adults who are prescribed medication should be reviewed regularly. There is a need to monitor e.g. intake of food/drink; weight gain/loss; condition of skin.

3. *Gathering evidence/detailed recording.* When neglect is suspected workers will need to monitor situations in order to gather evidence. It is important that workers report their concerns to the line manager. Often hospital staff may have concerns because they regularly have residents from a certain residential establishment being admitted with fractures, severe pressure sores etc. It is important to keep detailed records and use body maps. If a victim of neglect dies, the investigation should not be shelved because other vulnerable adults may be at risk of the same type of abuse.

4. *Implementation of procedures and management of protection plans.* Where neglect is suspected, adult abuse procedures should be implemented. If neglect cannot be proven but there is still concern about the situation, protection plans should be developed in order to monitor situations. These protection plans should then be reviewed regularly by reconvening the case conference.

5. *Talking to other professionals.* If a worker lacks confidence in working with neglect, s/he should liaise with other professionals in order to obtain practical advice and support. This could include a wide range of individuals with expertise in different areas, e.g. health (doctor, nurse, psychologist, psychiatrist, dietician); legal (police, solicitor).

6. *Having the right attitude.* Workers should not think that neglect has less importance than other forms of abuse.

7. *Empowerment.* Many victims of neglect have low self-esteem and feel powerless to do anything about their situation. Workers must take time to empower these victims.

REFERENCES

British Columbia InterMinistry Committee on Elder Abuse and Continuing Care Division, Ministry of Health, and Ministry Responsible for Seniors (1992) *Principles, Procedures and Protocols for Elder Abuse.* Victoria: Ministry of Health and Ministry Responsible for Seniors.

Department of Health/Social Services Inspectorate (1991) *Care Management and Assessment: Practitioners' Guide.* London: HMSO.

Department of Health (1992) *Confronting Elder Abuse.* London: HMSO.

Department of Health (1993) *No Longer Afraid: The Safeguard of Older People in Domestic Settings.* London: HMSO.

Department of Health (2000) *No Secrets: Guidance on Developing and Implementing Multi-Agency Policies and Procedures to Protect Vulnerable Adults from Abuse.* London: HMSO.

East Sussex County Council (1996) *Multi-Agency Guidelines for the Protection of Vulnerable Adults.* Lewes: East Sussex County Council.

Gloucestershire County Council (2000) *Gloucestershire Adults at Risk Unit Annual Report 1999/2000.* Gloucester: Gloucestershire County Council.

Godkin, M. A., Pillemer, K. A. and Wolf, R. S. (1986) 'Maltreatment of the elderly: A comparative analysis.' *Pride Institute Journal of Long Term Home Health Care 5,* 10–14.

Godkin, M. A., Wolf, R. S. and Pillemer, K. A. (1989) 'A case-comparison analysis of elder abuse and neglect.' *International Journal of Aging and Human Development 28,* 3, 207–225.

Hanover Housing Association and Sanctuary Housing (2000) *Abuse of Vulnerable Adults Policies and Procedures.* Staines: Hanover Housing Group.

Hickey, T. and Douglass, R. L. (1981) 'Neglect and abuse of older family members: professionals' perspectives and case experiences.' *The Gerontologist 21,* 1, 171–176.

Human Rights Act 1998. London: HMSO.

Law Commission (1995) *Mental Incapacity.* No 231. London: HMSO.

McCreadie, C. (1996) *Elder Abuse: Update on Research.* London: King's College Institute of Gerontology.

NHS and Community Care Act 1990. London: HMSO.

Pritchard, J. (2000) *The Needs of Older Women: Services for Victims of Elder Abuse and Other Abuse*. Bristol: Policy Press.

Pritchard, J. (2001) *Male Victims of Elder Abuse: Their Experiences and Needs*. London: Jessica Kingsley Publishers.

Rathbone-McCuan, E. and Voyles, B. (1982) 'Case detection of abused elderly parents.' *American Journal of Psychiatry 139*, 2, 189–192.

Wakefield Housing and Social Care (1999) *Adult Abuse and Protection Policy and Procedures*. Wakefield: City of Wakefield Metropolitan District Council.

CHAPTER 12

ABUSE ISSUES RELATING TO PEOPLE WITH MENTAL HEALTH PROBLEMS

TONY RYAN

INTRODUCTION

Although the media depiction of people with mental health problems would suggest that they are more likely to be dangerous than vulnerable this perspective is far from the truth. People who experience mental health problems can be vulnerable to a wide range of abuses. In addition, abuse itself can be the cause of mental health problems in both the short and long term. This chapter addresses abuse as both a factor for developing mental ill-health and also mental illness as a reason for people being subject to a wide range of exploitation and neglect. For the purposes of this work mental illness covers the range of conditions that result in inabilities to cope, irrespective of the length of experience, with everyday living. These can range from common mental illnesses, such as depression and anxiety disorders, which may be caused by life events, through to serious and enduring illnesses such as schizophrenia, bi-polar disorders (manic depression) and organic illnesses such as Alzheimer's disease.

TYPES OF ABUSE

The categories of abuse identified by Biggs, Phillipson and Kingston (1995) are pertinent for understanding abuse in respect of people who experience mental ill-health; physical, psychological, financial, sexual and neglect and will be used throughout this chapter. The guidance developed by the Department of Health on abuse in relation to vulnerable adults builds on this work and clarifies what constitutes abuse while also adding the category of discriminatory abuse to those identified by Biggs and colleagues (see Table 12.1).

Table 12.1 Types of abuse

Physical abuse – including hitting, slapping, pushing, kicking, misuse of medication, restraint, or inappropriate sanctions.

Sexual abuse – including rape and sexual assault or sexual acts to which the vulnerable adult has not consented, or could not consent or was pressured into consenting.

Psychological abuse – including emotional abuse, threats of harm or abandonment, deprivation of contact, humiliation, blaming, controlling, intimidation, coercion, harassment, verbal abuse, isolation or withdrawal from services or supportive networks.

Financial or material abuse – including theft, fraud, exploitation, pressure in connection with wills, property or inheritance or financial transactions, or the misuse or misappropriation of property, possessions or benefits.

Neglect and acts of omission – including ignoring medical or physical care needs, failure to provide access to appropriate health, social care or educational services, the withholding of the necessities of life, such as medication, adequate nutrition and heating.

Discriminatory abuse – including racist, sexist, that based on a person's disability, and other forms of harassment, slurs or similar treatment.

(DOH 2000, p.9)

Physical abuse

People with mental health problems can be easy targets for various forms of abuse since they are often regarded as not having credible skills in providing evidence to support their claims of abuse. It may be easy to dismiss claims of abuse as being a symptom of their illness. Additionally, for people who experience forms of dementia, they may not be able to describe the abuse they have suffered because of their condition. The frustrations of staff working with people who cannot communicate effectively may lead to physical and financial abuse in particular.

Sexual abuse

From the field of neuro-physiology there is evidence to show that the effects of abuse during childhood causes trauma that in turn can have a dramatic affect upon all functions of the developing brain which can result in mental ill-health and self-harm (Perry 1993). People who have experienced childhood sexual abuse or other forms of abuse are significantly more likely to develop mental health problems in adult life than people who have not suffered such trauma during their formative years (Muenzenmaier *et al.* 1993; Mullen *et al.* 1993).

Psychological abuse

Dealing with the stigma associated with mental illness is one of the biggest challenges faced by a society that regards itself as being based upon notions of equality and fairness. Psychological abuse occurs in both direct and indirect forms through the stigmatization of people with mental health problems. At its most simple level this can occur through the verbal abuse that may people experience when living in communities that do not understand, or do not wish to understand, the nature of mental ill-health. More subtle forms of psychological abuse can be seen in the way that the media portrays mental illness, which reinforces negative stereotypes and causes distress to those with mental illnesses who then see mental illness depicted in such fashions (Philo, McLaughlin and Henderson 1993).

Financial abuse

People with serious mental health problems have been particularly vulnerable to financial abuse, especially when they are away from the public gaze in institutions of one form or another, as a long series of inquiries has shown over the past 30 years. While this has been one of the many factors behind the dismantling of the psychiatric institutions, financial abuse of this group of people is not limited to those who have lived in institutions. Many have suffered financial abuse from families, friends and neighbours (Bond *et al.* 1999; Wilson 1994).

Neglect

People with mental health problems can be abused through neglect, either through lack of awareness of their needs or through more wilful means (see for example Commission for Health Improvement 2000). At one level people may be abused through not being provided the necessary stimulus to maintain or improve their mental health. A catalogue of inquiries into mental illness institutions has shown this to be the case in the past. At another level people can easily be neglected by services and communities where they live simply through not being visible to those services or by the fact that adequate services do not exist to meet their needs. The stigma of mental illness that pervades society reinforces the need to be invisible to services.

Discriminatory abuse

People who have experienced mental ill-health, and particularly those with serious and enduring mental illness, find that they are discriminated against in a number of ways. In particular they find it difficult to enter the labour market after a period of illness, they may find themselves less able to obtain financial credit of various forms and life insurance premiums tend to increase following diagnosis. Limited challenges have been presented to the courts in the UK in respect of discrimination on the grounds of mental illness, although the new European Human Rights Act 1998 is likely to provide a basis for such challenges in the future. However, there is a 'double negative' aspect to discrimination in this area since those who tackle the discrimination they face also run the risk of being further stigmatized because of the added publicity such challenges may bring.

LOCATING ABUSE

Abuse in its various forms can run through all areas of a society. For the purpose of this work three key areas of abuse are examined as it relates to people with mental health problems: within institutions, within families and within communities.

Table 12.2 Concomitant factors as symptoms of abuse

Mental illness – Mental illness can be regarded as either a symptom or trigger for abuse. People who have never previously suffered any mental ill-health may experience a wide range of symptoms and ill-nesses following abuse. Depression and anxiety are common consequences of abuse, irrespective of its form, and may be accompanied by self-harming through poisoning or cutting. Additionally, people who experience severe and enduring mental ill-health, for example those with illnesses such as schizophrenia or bi-polar disorders (manic depression), can find that their illness triggers abuse since there are times when it leaves them particularly vulnerable.

Alcohol and substance misuse – Alcohol is often used as an initial response to trauma. Although not the best response, historically a 'stiff brandy' has been offered to people in shock. Whilst one drink is likely to have only a minimal affect on the mental health of someone abused, continued use can lead to problems of depression and anxiety as well as a range of physical health problems. People who have been abused as children make up a disproportionate number of those who develop alcohol dependency (Roy 1999).

Self-harm – A consequence of abuse of various forms can be self-harm. People who have been abused as children are over-represented among the number of people who self-harm. For example, childhood sexual abuse has been identified as a predictor of impulsive self-injury in women experiencing anorexia nervosa (Favaro and Santonastaso 2000).

Homelessness – A study by Davies-Netzley *et al.* (1996) indicated that childhood physical and sexual abuse of women who develop severe and enduring mental health problems is an indicator for homelessness in later life.

Abuse within institutions

Since psychiatry developed as a response to 'madness' those who have been admitted to its institutions have been vulnerable. Outside the walls of the institution they have been vulnerable from the public and once inside they have been defenceless against abuse from their carers. A series of investigations into the practices in psychiatric institutions has revealed that this vulnerable group can be even more vulnerable when they are away from the gaze of the public and incarcerated in hospital (DHSS 1972; DHSS 1980; HAS and DHSS 1988; DOH and SHSA 1992).

There has always been an opportunity for professionals working with mentally ill people to abuse their position of trust and mistreat those they care for in a variety of ways. Recommendations from a review of mental health nursing suggested that there is a need for a code of practice to cover issues of sexual harassment and abuse. It recognized that 'relationships of great trust and intimacy can be, and sometimes are, exploited by staff working in the field of mental health' (DOH 1994, p.34). The review also 'noted with concern the disproportionate number of disciplinary cases brought to the UKCC which involve male mental health nurses and female patients' (p.15). While nurses are the professional group who have the greatest contact with people with mental illness they are not the only group to abuse these people. In the USA Tan and McDonough (1990) found that liability claims by patients against their psychiatrists involved 7.1 per cent that allege sexual impropriety. There is also increasing acknowledgement of the existence of both sexual and psychological abuse by mental health counsellors (Russell 1993) and psychologists (Lunt 1999; The Psychologist 1998). Kumar (2000) suggests that abuse by mental health professionals can be directly attributed to client disempowerment.

It has been recognized for some time that people in hospital are vulnerable to abuse from staff and other patients. One attempt to reduce the possibility of such vulnerable people being abused when they are being treated for mental health problems in hospitals is the introduction of single-sex accommodation. Initially this policy was introduced under the Patient's Charter (DOH 1996), and the National Service Framework for Mental Health (DOH 1999) reinforces this by setting 2002 as the deadline for when '95% of health authorities should have removed mixed sex accommodation' (p.100). The actual numbers of people who are abused within mental health services can never be truly established; however, it is widely accepted that many people, particularly women although not exclusively, do not feel safe in hospitals or specialist community facilities (Copperman and McNamara 1999). In the USA, Nibert,

Cooper and Crossmaker (1989) found that 38 per cent of patients in a study of psychiatric hospitals had been sexually assaulted and that 27 per cent of these had been at the hands of staff.

Within hospital and residential services of whatever form there are a number of ways of minimizing the risk of abuse to residents. These include external scrutiny such as through the Mental Health Act Commission or, where relevant, through registration and inspection teams, staff induction, training and support (for example through supervision), robust service commissioning and contract monitoring arrangements, policy and service audit (see DOH 2000, pp.18–19) and through implementing the findings of inquiries where things have gone wrong.

Abuse within families

There has been considerable concern in recent years with the issues of paedophiles and the threat they represent to children within communities. While this is a serious and worthy concern the likelihood of someone being abused by a stranger is much less than being abused by a family member and particularly if the person is a woman with mental health problems (Steiner et al. 1998).

Abuse, of whatever form, can also be a precursor for mental ill-health. The links between domestic violence and mental illness are well established (Roberts et al. 1998). This particular study found that women who suffer domestic abuse as adults were found to experience greater mental ill-health than those who did not report such abuse. Also, those who experienced both adult and child abuse suffered greater mental ill-health than women who experienced abuse as either a child or an adult.

In relation to the possibility of a developing cycle of abuse, the needs of people with mental health problems has been examined in respect of their childrearing skills. In a study by Miller and Finnerty (1996) it was found that women with schizophrenia are more likely to have unwanted pregnancies, more abortions and suffer greater levels of abuse during pregnancy than women without mental illnesses. The authors suggest that social skills training, targeted family planning, screening for abuse of the mother and parenting skills training could impact on the levels of abuse experienced by the mother and her children.

While mental ill-health can be the result of abuse in its various forms it can also be a precursor for abuse. In a study by Coverdale and Turbott (2000) the authors identified that people with serious mental illness, such as schizophrenia and bi-polar disorder, are significantly more likely to be physically or sexually abused as adults than people without such mental health problems and that women with serious mental illness report greater levels of abuse than men with such problems. They found that among 158 patients in their study 40 per cent had been sexually abused and the same percentage had been physically abused at some point in time. A similar picture has also been identified in respect of young people with serious mental health problems (McClellan *et al.* 1997).

It should be recognized that abuse within families may be the result of lack of knowledge and as a result of stress, although in some circumstances the abuse may be wilful (Heron 1998). In respect of stress it has been shown that in relation to mental illnesses such as schizophrenia the family can be the cause of relapse in the condition due to high expressed emotion, where the stresses of living together cause negative reactions from household members towards the person with the illness (Barrowclough and Tarrier 1992; Friedmann *et al.* 1997). This creates a high level of stress within the household.

While mentally ill people may be subject to the same range of abuses that face other vulnerable people living in family settings one particular abuse that may be more likely is the inappropriate use of medications. For example, one study identified that informal carers and family members of people with serious mental illnesses employ covert strategies to administer medication as a form of risk management (Ryan 2000a).

Abuse within communities

People with mental health needs are often identified within communities and scapegoated for being different (Takahashi 1997). While many of the inquiries of the 1970s and 1980s were into the abuse suffered by people in psychiatric hospitals, most of those that have taken place since have been concerned with the danger that individuals with mental health problems have posed within the community. Interestingly, however, there have not been any inquiries into how individuals have been mistreated by communities. Health and social care service providers, and even investigative media documentaries, can provide anecdotal evidence that demonstrates the existence of nimbyism within communities and the associated physical and psychological abuse that people with mental health problems endure as a consequence (Repper and Brooker 1996).

PRACTITIONER ISSUES

There are many difficulties that practitioners face when supporting people who have been abused and who also experience mental ill-health of whatever form. Many of these issues are not unique to working with people who have mental health problems. The section that follows is not exhaustive in terms of the themes that could be covered but is intended to highlight some of the issues and stimulate the reader to further thought in this complex area.

1. *The validity of allegations of abuse made by mentally ill people.* When working with people who experience problems with their mental health there can be concerns expressed in relation to the validity of their claims of abuse. While there may be doubts expressed when people allege abuse, such doubts can be reinforced by the fact that the person has a mental health problem and that their claims are simply a feature of their illness. As professionals we have a duty to ensure that all such claims are treated with the same dignity and respect that we would expect if we had suffered abuse and were seeking help. Because a person may be suffering from a mental illness of some form this does not mean that they are imagining the abuse that they have experienced; in fact because of their illness they may be more vulnerable to abuse than many others in society.

CASE STUDY I

Rosa is a 70-year-old widow living on her own in a run-down inner-city area. She was attacked two years ago and robbed of her pension as she left the local post office. Following the attack Rosa spent three weeks in hospital with a variety of injuries. Since the attack she has become agoraphobic, suffers panic attacks and is being treated for depression by her general practitioner. A neighbour recently informed the support worker that they had seen Rosa hand money to youngsters and believed that she was being extorted.

Practitioner issues

- How might the support worker establish the truth of the situation?
- How might this be achieved without further detriment to Rosa's mental health?
- How might the support worker support Rosa if she denies the issue of extortion?
- How might the support worker help Rosa to overcome her agoraphobia and panic attacks?
- What resources might the support worker draw upon to provide a package of support to Rosa?

2.   *Recent issues.* Many people who have been abused do not feel able to disclose this until some time after the event. This can often raise difficulties that the practitioner has to struggle with in order to support the person. Practitioners often question whether it is best to explore abuse issues or leave the past where it is, particularly where exploring the issues may cause deterioration to the person's mental health. It can be very difficult for practitioners, and those abused, when faced with the 'first time' disclosure of abuse – when a person is telling someone for the very first time of their experiences. However, the very nature of abuse is such that disclosures may occur many years after the abuse. Does this make them any less important or real? Certainly it does not. However, exploring the issues with the person may clarify what they wish to see result from their disclosure. For example, if they wish to understand how the abuse has affected their life, a more satisfactory conclusion may result in exploring the issues. If however,

they wish to seek justice or retribution, this goal may be less successful even though there are numerous examples of abusers being brought to justice a very long time after the abuse has ceased. Being honest and realistic with the person in order that they may make informed decisions about the choices open to them is essential, given that exploring abuse issues will inevitably bring further trauma and may impact further on their mental health.

CASE STUDY 2

Joanne is a 38-year-old woman who has been treated for depression and alcohol misuse for over 10 years. She has just been detoxified in hospital and is undergoing a programme of rehabilitation for alcohol misuse. While undergoing detoxification, Joanne disclosed for the first time that she had been sexually abused by her stepfather for three years prior to leaving home when she was sixteen. Joanne is very ambivalent about dealing with the issue, stating that she would never have told anyone had she not felt so down when being detoxified. Joanne feels it would help her to move on in her life if she were able to work through the effects of the abuse; however, she feels that the trauma this would cause might lead her to recommence drinking.

Practitioner issues

- What should Joanne's worker do to support her decision-making?
- What benefits and dis-benefits are there for Joanne to each option she might take?
- What additional support might the worker require to support Joanne?
- If Joanne returns to drinking, what actions could be considered by her worker?
- What are the mental health issues that might present in this scenario?
- What issues does the time between the abuse and disclosure raise for how the worker supports Joanne?

3.   *Acknowledging the skills and limitations of practitioners.* All practitioners need supervision from experienced practitioners who know their own limitations and therefore are able to utilize additional support of other supervisors who are specialists in abuse work. Supervision should support the worker, utilize the expertise and experience of both supervisor and supervisee, help problem-solve and bring a degree of distance through the position of the supervisor.

4.   *The skills of users and carers.* A study by Ryan (2000a) identified that sexual, physical and financial abuse of people with mental health problems may be in part encouraged by the passive strategies they employ to manage the risk of abuse. This work also identified that both user and carers had a range of proactive risk management skills (Ryan 2000b; Ryan forthcoming). However, these were largely self-taught and improved through personal experience. Practitioners should therefore consider their role as educators in the management of abuse risk since this is an area where they can make a proactive impact.

5.   *The limitations and strengths of 'expert' practitioners.* Many practitioners feel that they are not sufficiently experienced or 'expert' at dealing with issues of abuse, particularly if they are dealing with someone who also has mental health needs. The debate as to whether or not 'specialist expertise' is better than generic practitioner skills to deal with such issues is however a largely theoretical debate. It would be an ideal world where we were able to refer on to practitioners who have expertise in abuse of people with mental health problems. Consequently, we have to rely upon the fact that good practice is often good enough, particularly in the early stages of responding to the needs of someone with mental health needs who discloses abuse for the first time. For example, many men as practitioners, who have been referred a woman who upon initial assessment appears vulnerable, would seek to pass the case to a woman or at least jointly work the case. This is simple good practice and the worker does not require 'expert' skills to recognize the inappropriateness of his continuing to work on his own with a vulnerable woman.

CASE STUDY 3

Marcus is a 55-year-old man of Afro-Caribbean descent who was diagnosed as suffering from schizophrenia when he was in his early 20s. His mother, with whom he had lived all of his life, died three years ago and he has never known his father. Although Marcus has been able to cope reasonably well since his mother died, he was recently admitted to hospital under section 2 of the Mental Health Act (1983) after his mental health deteriorated when he stopped taking his medication several months earlier. During his hospitalization Marcus told nursing staff that he had taken in a homeless man whom he 'felt sorry for'. Daryl, his 'lodger', had encouraged Marcus to use cannabis rather than his prescribed medication. Daryl has been living rent-free with Marcus and financially abusing him since he moved into the house. Marcus is fearful that Daryl might be violent towards him if he asks Daryl to leave and therefore would like to stay in hospital rather than go home.

Practitioner issues

- What action needs to be considered in order to support Marcus when he leaves hospital?
- How might workers develop confidence in Marcus in order that he might assert his wishes and ask Daryl to leave?
- How do workers ensure that Marcus does not relapse and return to hospital?
- How do workers develop a plan with Marcus that ensures he is not vulnerable to abuse again in future?

6. *Referral issues.* There are numerous issues for practitioners to consider when making referrals where people can be doubly stigmatized through having experienced abuse and mental ill health. These include ensuring that they receive sufficient support through supervision, whether this is from a line manager, peers with specialist expertise or supervision from a specialist abuse worker. Issues such as the degree of information released and gaining the informed consent of the person with the mental health problem are likely to be high on the agenda in such support sessions. Other issues to consider when making

referrals will include ethnicity, gender and sexuality issues, advocacy and the limitation of practitioners and other professionals in this role and the philosophy of the agency the person is being referred to.

CASE STUDY 4

Vicky is a 33-year-old woman who has been treated for paranoid schizophrenia for over 10 years and is being supported by a Community Mental Health Team (CMHT) and on occasions by a Crisis Resolution Team (CRT). She has been described as having a history of expressing delusional ideas about men who physically and sexually abuse her. There has never been any evidence to confirm her claims and many men who are working as practitioners refuse to work with her for fear of being accused of such abuse.

Practitioner issues

- What issues should the CMHT workers consider in their support of Vicky?
- How should the team leader or manager respond to men within the team who 'refuse' to work with Vicky?
- What issues are raised by the CMHT supporting Vicky only with women practitioners?
- How should the team ensure that they do not become complacent about Vicky's history of unproven allegations?
- Are there actions that the CMHT and CRT can undertake or agree with Vicky when she is not expressing ideas of abuse that may help her during the periods where she has such feelings?

---

7.   *Confidentiality and legal issues in abuse.* The Crime and Disorder Act 1998 established a principle for sharing information between agencies. Section 115 of the Act establishes that while the police can disclose information that may prevent, detect or reduce crime, other public bodies such as local authorities, probation committees and health authorities may also do so as long as such disclosure is necessary or expedient for the purposes of the Act. Furthermore, such organizations now have the power to

use this information. Abuse in the various forms discussed in this chapter may constitute a criminal act and therefore information gathered by agencies working with people who have been abused may be subject to disclosure under the Crime and Disorder Act 1998.

8. *Abuse and people subject to the Mental Health Act 1983.* While a dim view is taken of professionals who have sexual relations with clients or service users the sanctions that are often applied are through a professional body rather than the legal system. Often this is due to the client or service user consenting to the relationship, even though the professional may have abused their position. However, sexual relations between professionals and people being treated under the Mental Health Act 1983 are an offence, irrespective of whether or not the person consented to participate. The logic here being that people who are being treated under the Mental Health Act are not in a position to give informed consent to such relations.

A FINAL NOTE

Clearly the issue of abuse is one that will be at the heart of working with people in human services and the issues are rarely simple. This is also the case in respect of working with people who have mental health needs and particularly those who experience serious and enduring mental illnesses. Where such people have been abused in one way or another it can be one of the most challenging areas in which practitioners can work, given that abuse leads to poorer mental health that may be life-long in its impact. To truly support people who have such needs requires considerable skill, support from others and the ability to reflect on the complex issues involved.

REFERENCES

Barrowclough, C. and Tarrier, N. (1992) *Families of Schizophrenic Patients: Cognitive Behavioural Intervention.* London: Chapman and Hall.

Bond, J. B., Cuddy, R., Dixon, G. L., Duncan, K. A. and Smith, D. L. (1999) 'The financial abuse of mentally incompetent older adults: A Canadian study.' *Journal Of Elder Abuse and Neglect 11,* 4, 23–38.

Biggs, S., Phillipson, C. and Kingston, P. (1995) *Elder Abuse in Perspective.* Milton Keynes: Open University Press.

Commission for Health Improvement (2000) *Investigation into the North Lakeland NHS Trust: Report to The Secretary of State for Health.* London: Commission for Health Improvement.

Copperman, J. and McNamara, J. (1999) 'Institutional abuse in mental health settings: Survivors perspectives.' In N. Stanley, J. Manthorpe and B. Penhale (eds) *Institutional Abuse: Perspectives Across the Life Course.* pp.152–172 London: Routledge.

Coverdale, J. H. and Turbott, S. H. (2000) 'Sexual and physical abuse of chronically ill psychiatric outpatients compared with a matched sample of medical outpatients.' *Journal of Nervous and Mental Disease 188,* 7, 440–445.

Crime and Disorder Act 1998. London: HMSO.

Davies-Netzley, S., Hurlburt, M. S. and Hough, R. L. (1996) 'Childhood abuse as a precursor to homelessness for homeless women with severe mental illness.' *Violence and Victims 11,* 2, 129–142.

Department of Health (1994) *Working in Partnership: A Collaborative Approach to Care.* London: HMSO.

Department of Health (1996) *The Patient's Charter and You – Hospital Services.* London: Department of Health.

Department of Health (1999) *National Service Framework for Mental Health: Modern Standards and Service Models.* London: Department of Health.

Department of Health (2000) *No Secrets: Guidance on Developing and Implementing Multi-Agency Policies and Procedures to Protect Vulnerable Adults from Abuse.* London: HMSO.

Department of Health and Social Services (1972) *Report of the Committee of Inquiry into Whittingham Hospital.* London: HMSO.

Department of Health and Social Services (1980) *Report of the Review of Rampton Hospital.* London: HMSO.

Department of Health and the Special Hospital Service Authority (1992) *Report of the Committee of Inquiry into Complaints About Ashworth Hospital (Volume 1).* London: HMSO.

Favaro, A. and Santonastaso, P. (2000) 'Self-injurious behavior in anorexia nervosa.' *Journal of Nervous and Mental Disease 188,* 8, 537–42.

Friedmann, M. S., McDermut, W. H., Solomon, D. A., Ryan, C. E., Keitner, G. I. and Miller, I. W. (1997) 'Family functioning and mental illness: A comparison of psychiatric and nonclinical families.' *Family Process 36,* 4, 357–367.

Health Advisory Service (NHS) and DHSS Social Services Inspectorate (1988) *Report on the Services Provided by Broadmoor Hospital.* London: HAS/SSI (88)SH 1 July, 1988.

Heron, C. (1998) *Working with Carers.* London: Jessica Kingsley Publishers.

Human Rights Act 1998. London: HMSO.

Kumar, S. (2000) 'Client empowerment in psychiatry and the professional abuse of clients: Where do we stand?' *International Journal of Psychiatry in Medicine 30,* 1, 61–70.

Lunt, I. (1999) 'Disciplining psychologists.' *The Psychologist 12,* 2, 59.

McClellan, J., McCurry, C., Ronnel, M., Adams, J., Storck, M., Eisner, A. and Smith, C. (1997) 'Relationship between sexual abuse, gender and sexually inappropriate behaviours in seriously mentally ill youths.' *Journal of the American Academy of Child and Adolescent Psychiatry 36,* 7, 959–965.

Mental Health Act 1983. London: HMSO.

Miller, L. J. and Finnerty, M. (1996) 'Sexuality, pregnancy and childrearing among women with schizophrenia-spectrum disorders.' *Psychiatric Services 47,* 5, 502–506.

Muenzenmaier, K., Meyer, I., Struening, E. and Ferber, J. (1993) 'Childhood abuse and neglect among women outpatients with chronic mental illness.' *Hospital and Community Psychiatry 44*, 7, 666–670.

Mullen, P. E., Martin, J. L., Anderson, J. C., Romans, S. E. and Herbison, G. P. (1993) 'Childhood sexual abuse and mental ill health in adult life.' *British Journal of Psychiatry* 163, 721–732.

Nibert, C., Cooper, S. and Crossmaker, M. (1989) 'Assaults against residents of a psychiatric institution.' *Journal of Interpersonal Violence 4*, 342–349.

Perry, B. D. (1993) 'Neurodevelopment and neuro-physiology of trauma: Conceptual considerations for clinical work with maltreated children.' *The APSAC Advisor (The American Professional Society on the Abuse of Children) 65*, 177–193.

Philo, G., McLaughlin, G. and Henderson, L. (1993) *Mass Media Representation of Mental Health/Illness: Report for Health Education Board for Scotland.* Glasgow: University Media Group.

Repper, J. and Brooker, C. (1996) 'Public attitudes towards mental health facilities in the community.' *Health and Social Care in the Community 4*, 5, 290–299.

Roberts, G. L., Williams, G. M., Lawrence, J. M. and Raphael, B. (1998) 'How does domestic violence affect women's mental health?' *Women and Health 28*, 1, 117–129.

Roy, A. (1999) 'Childhood trauma and depression in alcoholics: Relationship to hostility.' *Journal of Affective Disorders 56*, 2–3, 215–218.

Russell, J. (1993) *Out of Bounds: Sexual Exploitation in Counselling and Therapy.* London: Sage.

Ryan, T. (2000a) 'Risk perceptions associated with mental illness and the risk management strategies of service users and informal carers.' Lancaster University: Unpublished PhD thesis.

Ryan, T. (2000b) 'Exploring the risk management strategies of mental health service users.' *Health, Risk and Society 2*, 3, 267–282.

Ryan, T. (forthcoming) 'Exploring the risk management strategies of informal carers of mental health service users.' *Journal of Mental Health.*

Steiner, J. L., Hoff, R. A., Moffett, C., Reynolds, H., Mitchell, M. and Rosenheck, R. (1998) 'Preventive health care for mentally ill women.' *Psychiatric Services 49*, 5, 696–698.

Takahashi, L. M. (1997) 'Information and attitudes toward mental health care facilities: Implications for addressing the NIMBY syndrome.' *Journal of Planning Education and Research 17*, 2, 119–130.

Tan, M. W. and McDonough, W. J. (1990) 'Risk management in psychiatry.' *Psychiatric Clinics of North America 13*, 1, 135–147.

The Psychologist (1998) 'Notices from the Disciplinary Board.' *The Psychologist 11*, 11, 555.

Wilson, G. (1994) 'Abuse of elderly men and women among clients of a community psychogeriatric service.' *British Journal Of Social Work 24*, 6, 681–700.

ACKNOWLEDGEMENTS

I would like to thank Rowan Purdy for diligently chasing many of the papers referred to in this work, Jacki Pritchard for her encouragement and support throughout writing and Janis Williamson for all of her inspiration.

USEFUL CONTACTS

Useful contacts offering a listening, information or advice service include:

Alzheimer's Society Helpline: 0845 300 0336 (www.alzheimers. org.uk)

Carers Line at Carers National Organisation: 0808 808 7777 (www.carersuk.demon.co.uk)

Childline: 0800 1111 (www.childline.org.uk)

MIND: 020 8519 2122 (ext 1) (www.mind.org.uk)

NHS Direct, a 24hr confidential helpline providing advice and information on a wide range of health issues: 0845 4647 (www.nhsdirect.nhs.uk)

Parentline: 0808 800 2222 (www.parentlintplus.org.uk)

Saneline: 0345 678 0000 (www.mkn.co.uk/help/charity/sane/index)

The Samaritans: 0845 909090 (www.samaritans.org.uk)

CHAPTER 13

AFORE YE GO! ALCOHOL
AND OLDER PEOPLE

MIKE LINNETT

BACKGROUND

I have worked as a co-ordinator in adult protection for eight and a
half years and a consistent difficulty in trying to provide a response
to the abuse, exploitation and neglect of vulnerable adults (and particularly older people) has been the hidden nature of the problem.
There are, I am sure, many reasons for this – shame, assumed guilt,
fear, denial, cultural and family standards and expectations and
perhaps a lot of 'ignore it and it will go away'. Any scan of the literature and procedures relating to abuse recognizes the difficulty of
identification and lists of indicators are generally part of any
guidance.

However, even well-established programmes in the USA
recognize that the numbers coming to the attention of services are
only the tip of the iceberg. To illustrate, the Office of Population
Census Survey survey in 1992 (OPCS 1992) concluded that
approximately five per cent of the population of older people are
subject to abuse and this seems to correlate consistently with other
research both here and in the USA. This would indicate that in the
county of Gloucestershire, there are 2700 cases of abuse or neglect
of older people. Despite a well-established service and related
training programme, 229 cases were referred to the Adult Protection Unit in the year 1999/2000 (Gloucestershire Adult Protection
Unit 2000) – the tip of the iceberg?

The government publication *No Secrets* (DOH 2000) was a
formal recognition that it is necessary to strive to identify and

respond to abuse and neglect as fully as possible but equally stated that it is also necessary to look to prevention – it being better than a cure?

But how? Models and materials have been developed in the USA with a view to prevention of financial and (to some extent) physical abuse and active neglect. Ongoing service provision tries to deal with self-neglect but it is extremely difficult to know how to devise and direct preventive action if the bulk of abuse and neglect is not identified. This makes the development of preventive schemes extremely difficult, especially as the services are still grappling with their own development. It is this background that led the unit to a growing identification of alcohol as a contributor, not only in cases of abuse but also those of self-neglect.

IDENTIFICATION

My growing awareness of the incidence of alcohol as a factor in the neglect of older people has developed as a result of being the central point for referral of adults considered to be at risk for the whole county. Between 1995 and 2000, 1755 referrals were made to the unit – of these 25 per cent were older people considered to be severely self-neglecting (Gloucestershire County Council Adults at Risk Unit Annual Reports 1995–2000).

Referrals are made by staff from all agencies, including the private sector and the public. Frequently, reference was made to the fact that the person referred used alcohol to a greater or lesser extent but this was often considered a part of the behaviour. Individual referrers often felt that this was unusual but at times it presented severe problems of management, i.e. carers having demands made that alcohol was bought as part of the shopping, then finding that the individual would become aggressive or incapable of managing body functions when the demand was complied with – a dilemma. To respect the rights and choices of the individual severely affected their health and care. It appears that most staff working with older people have one or two individuals on their caseload whose health, care and/or safety is affected by their alcohol consumption. However, most of these staff felt that it was they alone who had this particular problem but in 1997, team mangers and supervisors attending the local social services Drugs and Alcohol Steering Group were becoming increasingly concerned about the problem and its management. Alongside this, the Adult Protection Unit had noticed an inexorable rise in the number of referrals of self-neglect that involved alcohol and began recording this. Approximately *one case in four* of self-neglect had alcohol as a factor.

Although it appeared difficult to establish alcohol as the cause of the neglect or vice versa, the high incidence indicated the need for further study as the suffering of the individuals concerned was extreme, and the management and support very difficult. To illustrate, I outline below two case histories:

CASE HISTORY 1

A referral was made to the unit of Mrs A by the community psychiatric nurse (CPN), who was concerned that she may be being abused by her husband.

Mrs A, who was 79 years old, had mild/moderate dementia. She lived with her husband in a pleasant bungalow, which they had bought on his retirement (he had been a senior manager in an engineering firm). They had been married for 58 years and had three adult children, one son and two daughters.

The CPN had noticed over the preceding three months (which coincided with a deterioration in Mrs A from having mild to mild/moderate dementia) a series of bruises on Mrs A. These had been explained away by both her and Mr A as the result of falls. However, one of the daughters had recently bought a new mark to the CPN's attention and said that her mother had accused Mr A of hurting her. The incident was duly investigated and Mr A reluctantly admitted that he had grabbed his wife to stop her falling, she had become hysterical and he had slapped her to calm her down.

A case conference was called with Mr and Mrs A present as were their children. Mr A did admit hitting his wife but said it was the only way he could calm her down. The daughter raised at conference that this was not the first time and that both parents drank quite a lot and when they did they became argumentative. Mr A reluctantly agreed that they did like a drink or two when they went out and over dinner but that they had always done so and never had a problem with it.

There was some family disagreement with this statement and recent examples were quoted leading Mr A to say that it was sometimes difficult to manage his wife's behaviour and that he was torn because she asked for a drink, drank it, appeared to forget and then asked for another. If he refused she became aggressive and so he 'gave in' but argued that she did frequently become frustrated and angry and so what did a little drink matter – it at least gave her some pleasure.

Mr A was quite angry about the conference being called and saw himself as being accused of abuse but did accept that slapping his wife was inappropriate. Mrs A was registered as 'at risk'. A care and support package was offered but both Mr and Mrs A did not want personal carers in their house. She felt that she could run her house perfectly well and that carers were an intrusion. Mr A felt that it was his duty to care for his wife. However, CPN support and three days' day care per week were accepted. The psychiatrist attending also outlined what he saw as the potential dangers of high alcohol consumption alongside medication and the dementia, and Mr A agreed to try to modify Mrs A's intake. In view of the level of concern and the couple's reluctance to accept a full care package, a review was arranged in three months' time.

Unfortunately, some four weeks later, Mr A was stabbed in the arm by Mrs A over the dinner table and responded by striking out, precipitating an emergency reconvening of the case conference. It transpired that Mr A had tried to stop his wife taking her third glass of wine and she had struck out at him with her steak knife. In discussion, it became apparent that Mr A was finding it very difficult to cope with all his wife's needs – she was up frequently in the night and was extremely unpredictable during the day. Mr A was taking a drink to 'calm himself down' and was quite angry that, in following advice regarding his wife's alcohol consumption, things appeared to have got worse. In fact, observations by the staff at the day centre, the CPN and the psychiatrist all indicated that Mrs A's dementia was worsening. It was also felt that her alcohol consumption was quite high and that this was exacerbating her condition. Once again this was pointed out to Mr A and he agreed very reluctantly to try to modify her intake to one or two glasses of wine before dinner. He was not optimistic about being able to do this. Further support at home was offered and this time accepted; day care was increased and respite care offered but refused.

Over the next few months and after two reviews, Mr A struggled to manage. Despite his best efforts Mrs A continued to drink and in response to the stress so did he. Home carers confirmed the picture that Mr A had painted and despite their and Mr A's efforts, Mr A was coming close to breakdown. Despite this he still strongly wished to care for his wife and keep her at home and in doing so became a shell of himself and finally agreed to respite care.

To his and the family's surprise, Mrs A settled well in respite care, and seemed to feel that she was still at home – possibly due to Mr A's regular visits. With Mr A's agreement, the home did not give Mrs A alcohol and after some initial repetitive requests, it did not seem to bother her. Despite a deterioration in her condition, she was calmer and generally amiable.

However, after discharge home, Mrs A fell quite badly and broke her hip. The fall was observed by a home carer and was the result of a sudden lurch from her chair. Unfortunately, the fracture did not respond well to treatment and nor did Mrs A. She did not appear to be able to comprehend that she was injured and unstable on her feet and consistently and repeatedly tried to get out of her bed and chair, constantly exacerbating the injury and needing 24-hour supervision.

When discharge was being considered, all involved met to review the situation. Mr A still wanted to care for his wife at home although she was no longer able to voice her opinion. However, after long and heart-searching discussion, Mr A very reluctantly agreed with the professional assessment that the level of care and supervision his wife needed could not be provided by him. It was with tears in his eyes that he agreed to her placement in a nursing home. All those present shared great sadness as over time it had become apparent that Mr and Mrs A cared deeply for each other and now Mr A was prepared to accept separation in order to obtain the best for his wife.

CASE HISTORY 2

Mr C was referred as being 'at risk' of neglect by a private care agency. He was 79 years old – a retired chief solicitor's clerk who had worked thoroughly and efficiently until he retired at 70. His wife died two years after his retirement and the care agency had been providing a cleaning, personal care, shopping and cooking service for him since then, which he paid for himself. The service involved one midday visit of two hours per day.

He lived in a large detached town house but since the death of his wife, he had taken to living in one large downstairs room. Soon after the death of his wife he started to order a bottle or two of whisky a week. Over time, this had increased to seven bottles per week.

The agency had referred him, as over the previous year Mr C had become increasingly irritable and angry with the carers as his physical condition appeared to be deteriorating. He was now refusing to be toiletted and never left his chair. Despite pleas from the carers, he would not see his doctor or accept any help or advice regarding continence. For some months the carers had been having to remove soiled and wet clothing on a daily basis and were becoming increasingly concerned for the health and safety of both Mr C and the carers due to the severe hygiene problems. Mr C was suffering frequent gastrointestinal upsets probably as a result of the conditions and this in turn made the conditions worse. The agency had made it clear to Mr C that they would have to withdraw care unless he would accept help to try to resolve the continence problems, but he still refused to consider this. The agency, concerned for his safety, referred him to social services under the Adults at Risk procedures. He reluctantly accepted this course of action on condition that the agency continued to provide care, but he was extremely angry. His alcohol consumption at this time was at least one bottle of whisky per day.

A social worker visited to assess the situation and found the condition of Mr C and his immediate surroundings to be even worse than imagined. Mr C insisted that he had a right to live as he wished and roundly berated the social worker for trying to interfere. He again refused to consider seeing his GP or obtaining any other help or assistance and insisted that he was not at any risk, even if the agency were unable to continue to provide care. The social worker made several attempts to try to engage Mr C but to no avail, despite his contracting very severe diarrhoea and becoming extremely weak (again refusing medical input). At this stage he was informed that it was necessary to call an Adults at Risk conference to consider the risk and possible interventions/assistance. He was extremely angry about this and insisted that he would take legal advice.

In terms of Mr C's quality of life, this was a significant turning point. He contacted a partner in the practice he had worked for. The partner visited and was appalled with what he saw, so much so that he contacted the social worker to express grave concern. When at work Mr C had been almost too fastidious, both with his work and appearance, his house had been spotless and he considered 'cleanliness to be next to godliness'. The partner wanted to know what could be done in such circumstances. He realized the ethical considerations and Mr C had agreed with him that he could act as his advocate. It was explained that it was not possible to assist Mr C without his agreement unless he was considered mentally ill within the terms of the Mental Health Act 1983 or the criteria under Section 47 of the National Assistance Act 1948 were fulfilled. Mr C was not mentally ill.

A conference was duly held at Mr C's house with his advocate present and the possibility of intervention either under Section 47 or environmental health regulations identified. The implication of potential legal action had been discussed with Mr C by his advocate and had initially precipitated a hostile and negative response. However, in the meeting Mr C discussed the legalities in a rational and considered manner with the conference and his advocate (he had not been drinking that day). He concluded that rather than have his circumstances considered under Section 47, or risk the shame of environmental health intervention, he would consider alternatives.

A care and support plan was devised that addressed Mr C's care needs with an agreement from Mr C to try to address his drinking, as this was considered part of the problem. The GP, with help from the consultant psychiatrist, devised a home detoxification programme and the GP also offered the services of the practice counsellor. The agency agreed that they would provide an ongoing and increased service for three months pending review. A full clean-up of the room was also part of the plan.

Mr C responded to the detoxification programme extremely well, and by the review date he was not drinking, his physical health had improved considerably, he was walking with a stick and had made contact with extended family members. He was continent, was putting on weight and now sleeping in a downstairs bedroom. The agency, with Mr C's co-operation, was now able to keep the house and Mr C as spick and span as he wanted.

RESPONSE

It was cases like these and many others that forced me to look seriously at the effects of alcohol on the quality of care and life of older people. This was amplified by the feelings of frustration and helplessness expressed by staff working with cases where their best efforts were being negated by the effects of alcohol. This frustration was amplified by a deep-rooted ethical respect for the rights of the client – there is a right to choice, and alcohol consumption is a choice (like smoking), despite its damaging social and physical effects.

Or is it? A choice is a decision and in the field of Adult Protection it is recognized that if an individual makes an *informed* decision in relation to their situation this must be respected and it is a basic human right. But is a decision to drink and keep drinking on the part of older people an *informed* decision?

Perhaps the following information should be given to all older people who drink (and those who work with them):

- Surveys in the USA indicate alcoholism is present in 10–15% of older people (USA Seniors Health Co-operative).
- UK research indicates that between three and four per cent of older people have alcohol problems (Simpson 1993).
- Five to twelve per cent of men in their 60s have alcohol problems (Institute of Alcohol Studies 2000).
- Alcohol can have 20 per cent greater concentration (and therefore effect) in older people (Vestal *et al.* 1977; Institute of Alcohol Studies 1999).

- Alcohol is a significant factor in self-neglect (Kafetz and Cox 1982).
- Malnutrition is common in those who drink to excess (Hurt *et al.* 1981).
- The life expectancy of a practising alcoholic is shortened by 12 to 15 years (Institute of Alcohol Studies 1997).

In America, information leaflets are circulated; some good examples are included in Appendix 1.

Problems associated with alcohol consumption

Physical problems	*Behavioural problems*	*Mental emotional problems*
• Cardiovascular		• Depression
• Gastrointestinal	• Sleep problems	• Anxiety
• Unexplained fatigue	• Avoidance of old friends and activities	• Prolonged grieving
• Oedema	• Inability to make decisions or carry out simple tasks	• Confusion/dis-orientation
• Incontinence		• Memory problems
• High blood pressure		
• Diabetes	• Isolation	• Mood swings
• Pulse abnormalities	• Unkempt	• Night terrors
• Headaches	• Argumentative	• Low self-esteem
• Nausea/vomiting	• Sexual dysfunction	• Unreasonable fears
• Dry skin		• Suspiciousness
• Visual problems		• Suicidal talk
• Sweating		• Irrational anger

(Source: Breeden-Hilton 1998)

This is not a comprehensive list but it is extremely unlikely that many older drinkers are aware of many of these dangers, or for that matter, those relatives, friends and professionals involved in providing care and support for older people.

Perhaps too, some of the myths surrounding alcohol and older people also contribute to a lack of appreciation of the depth of the problem and inhibit constructive response. I outline below some of the more commonly held myths and assumptions (adapted from the Case Western Reserve University School of Medicine 1996):

Myth: Drinking may be an older person's last remaining pleasure, therefore it may not be wise to take it away.

Fact: Excess alcohol seriously impacts on physical health and quality of life and it causes more psychological pain than pleasure. People are much happier when they stop abusing alcohol.

Myth: Before you can help an older person who has a drinking problem, s/he has to want to stop drinking or must 'hit bottom' before s/he can be helped.

Fact: One of the symptoms of the disease is that the person denies s/he has a problem. Many people with an alcohol problem can be persuaded to seek treatment through a process called 'intervention' and the support of others. Recovery is more likely with early intervention and can also prevent severe physical and psychological complications.

Myth: Alcohol is good for lifting an older person's mood.

Fact: Alcohol is not an effective 'mood lifter'. As alcohol depresses the brain, a person may lose their inhibitions for a short time. However, this is soon followed by irritability. Regular use of alcohol increases depression.

Myth: A glass of wine before going to bed will help an older person to sleep better.

Fact: Alcohol is a sedative; however, the effects are short-lived and followed by periods of irritability and agitation. Alcohol leads to *increased* sleep disturbances.

Myth: Alcoholism is not a problem in older women.

Fact: Although the stigma of drinking is much harsher for women, they can and do have problems with alcohol. Women may hide their drinking more and feel greater shame and guilt. Physical differences may also lead to quicker development of problems and serious health consequences.

Myth: Older people have the lowest success rate in treatment response.

Fact: Older adults, especially those whose problem began recently, have an unusually good chance of recovery. In fact they may have a better chance of recovery than a younger person because they tend to 'stick with' treatment programmes.

Myth: Older people acquire tolerance for alcohol and eventually level off their consumption.

Fact: Tolerance for alcohol generally decreases in older people due to the reduction in body mass and fluid and the increase in body fat. This results in greater concentrations in the body and increased sensitivity to side-effects.

Myth: Many older people are too weak or frail to deal with the effects of withdrawal from alcohol dependence.

Fact: To perpetuate this myth is likely to enable the older person to continue to suffer the effects of alcohol abuse. It is more than likely that the alcohol is a contributor to the older person's frailty.

It is important to recognize all of the above in attempting to create a response and that urgency is lent to the need to respond in view of the changing patterns of alcohol consumption in older people.

Generally, alcohol consumption declines with age and the pro-portion of non-drinkers increases. The reasons for this decline are possibly connected to changes in life circumstances and attitudes and, in later middle age and older, growing ill-health. However, there is increasing evidence that the present population of older people may be relatively heavier drinkers than previous generations. This may be the result of today's older people having spent their formative years in a time of high social availability and acceptability of alcohol. Higher levels of disposable income in retirement may also be a factor. Certainly, drinking surveys suggest that since 1984 the proportions of older people exceeding 'sensible limits' of drinking have been rising steadily.

Another factor bearing on the numbers of older drinkers is that due to longer life expectancy and the ageing of the population there are more older people. In 1991 there were 10.6 million people in the UK of pensionable age (a 16 per cent rise since 1971). It is projected that there will be a further increase of 38 per cent by 2031 (14.6 million).

IDENTIFICATION AND RESPONSE

Two types of older drinkers have been identified:

1. *Early-onset drinkers*. People who have a long-standing history of alcohol consumption. There is often a family history of alcoholism. There is a higher prevalence of personality disorders and schizophrenia in this type than late-onset drinkers. However, because of the health risks connected to heavy drinking, the chances of reaching old age are reduced. They often present with malnutrition, a history of multiple injuries and a lowered socio-economic status.

2. *Late-onset drinkers*. These older drinkers are half as likely to have a family history of alcoholism as early-onset drinkers. Their early life is generally stable and well adjusted with a good positive work history. Frequently their drinking starts as a response to a traumatic event such as the death of a loved one, loneliness, pain, insomnia, retirement etc.

Depression, loneliness and social isolation are the most common antecedents in both types of alcoholism in the elderly (Schonfield and Dupree 1991). Although it is felt that late-onset drinkers have a high chance of recovery if given access to appropriate treatment such as counselling and general support, early-onset drinkers can also respond. However, to design a response, it is necessary to

Step 1

Ask about alcohol use.

? consumption – per week, occasion, history.

*

If consumption is:

greater than 14 units per week or 4 per occasion (men)

or

greater than 7 units per week or 3 per occasion (women)

*

Step 2

Assess for alcohol-related problems:

- medical
- behavioural
- alcohol dependence

*

Step 3

Advise appropriate action

Alcohol dependence   At risk of developing problems

                                                          Alcohol-related problems

Advise to abstain   Advise to cut down

Offer/refer to specialist   Set a drinking goal

support

Monitor patient progress

Figure 13.1: Alcoholism identification process

diagnose the problem. A number of screening tools have been devised in the USA, the most commonly used being the C.A.G.E., H.E.A.T and M.A.S.T. (see Appendix 2). I am not aware of particular screening tools used in the UK but a general clinical approach is outlined in Figure 13.1.

TREATMENT

Treatment and counselling of older people needs to be based on assessment and matching of each person's needs to the range of treatment and services available. Emphasis needs to be placed on non-drinking social activities such as day centres and clubs in the context of the person's life circumstance and social support network. It may be necessary to work on redefining a social or family support mechanism. It is necessary to recognize that older people have special needs and treatment programmes need to address these. Some special treatment services have been developed in the USA but outcomes compared to those involving older people in standard treatment facilities are not yet established. More specifically, certain treatments have been found to be effective in helping older people. Very briefly they are:

1. *Brief interventions.* 'There is good evidence to suggest that brief interventions work in routine clinical practice in changing the drinking habits of older adults'; 'If every physician gave a brief advice statement to every problem drinker seen, the lives of patients and their families would be significantly improved' (Fleming *et al.* 1999).

2. *Structured interventions.* Originally developed by the Johnson Institute (Blondell 1999), the treatment involves the patient's family and friends in a concerted approach.

3. *Detoxification.* If this is necessary, Thiamine must be given to prevent the Wernicke-Korsakoff syndrome. 'For individuals with mild to moderate symptoms of alcohol withdrawal, outpatient detoxification has been found to be safe, effective and a low cost alternative to hospital detoxification' (Hayashida *et al.* 1989).

CONCLUSION

The issue of alcohol and older people is there and growing. It can and should be addressed. The benefits of doing so are great, particularly in the quality of life and dignity for the individual, their families and carers, not to mention the social savings. It is vital that attempts are made to raise the awareness of all as alchohol can become everyone's problem sooner or later and we cannot afford to ignore the later.

And please be aware that the apparently kindly encouraging of a drink 'afore ye go' to an older person may actually be sending them on their way before their time.

Appendix 1

AARP
Is Drinking Becoming a Problem?
Older Women and Alcohol

Drinking Can Hurt

Drinking can be a problem at any age. But if you are a midlife or older woman – mother, grandmother, caregiver – working or retired – it can be especially harmful.

Alcohol may affect you differently than it once did because physical changes can reduce the ability to tolerate alcohol.

You may be experiencing loneliness, loss, grief, stress, or chronic pain or illness, and have turned to alcohol to help.

You may think, 'What harm will it do? It's one of the few pleasures I have left.' Unfortunately, it can do plenty of harm. Problem drinking usually gets worse. In older people, it can increase the risk of suicide. It may also impair memory, aggravate other physical ailments, and destroy relationships.

Alcoholism is a major cause of death in America.

Denial

At any age, the last person to recognize a drinking problem is often the person who has it. Denial of an alcohol problem is more common, stronger, and more predictable than any other symptom.

When something feels wrong, it probably is. And it is important to get help. Alcohol does more damage in women than in men – and it does it more quickly.

Prescriptions: Part of the Problem

The potentially dangerous combination of prescription medication and alcohol is risky and can be life-threatening. Combining alcohol with other medications, such as sleeping pills, pain relievers, or tranquilizers is always dangerous. It can be deadly. Don't do it.

The Warning Signs

How would you answer the question below? More than one positive answer may indicate that you, or a person you care about, has a drinking problem.

Do you...

- neglect physical appearance or personal hygiene?
- forget what occurred while you were drinking?
- ignore responsibilities you once took very seriously – such as feeding pets, paying bills, cleaning house, or caring for a garden?
- promise to have only one or two drinks, and then drink more?
- drink more frequently than you did before, or drink in the morning?
- experience mood swings, show super sensitivity, or fall into crying spells while drinking?
- suffer from bruises, burns, or other effects of accidents as a result of drinking?
- avoid people and places that do not include drinking?
- seek out people and places that include drinking?
- become resentful when your drinking is mentioned even jokingly?
- place alcohol ahead of family and friends?
- think more about drinking than before?

If drinking is interfering with your life and relationships, or if alcohol is more important to you than the trouble it's causing, you have a problem.

It Is Never Too Late for Recovery

If the last few months or years have not been easy, and alcohol has made you feel better – at least for a little while – it may be hard to believe that alcohol could be a problem. But you know something is wrong. You feel it inside. In fact, your life may be getting out of control.

The good news is that it doesn't have to be this way. You do not have to 'hit bottom' to be helped. You do not have to lose everything – friendships, loved ones, health, home, and work. Don't wait until everything is gone. Reach out for the help in your community. Help is available…if you ask for it.

It is a myth that older people don't change. In fact, people who develop a drinking problem late in life have a better recovery record than those who are younger. Free of alcohol, older persons often resume happy and productive lives.

Finding Help
Here are some steps to find help:

- Discuss the problem with someone you trust. Be honest about your perceptions and feelings.

- Talk to a counselor who is experienced in dealing with alcohol and addiction issues. Check with your local hospital, health center, alcohol treatment program, or clergy.

- Find a support group. Alcoholics Anonymous (A.A.) has many all-women meetings, as well as open meetings for people who are not sure if they are alcoholic. Other support groups, such as Women for Sobriety, or programs sponsored by hospital treatment centers may be available also. Support groups, such as Al-Anon, are equally important for your relatives and friends.

- Don't delay. Whether you are concerned about your own or a loved one's drinking, realize that you are dealing with a disease that will only get worse. Get help as soon as you can.

- If the problem is with a loved one, it is important to tell her how you feel … don't try to cover it up. You may want to involve the entire family or a counselor in the discussion. Sometimes problem drinkers can't stop drinking by themselves. They need help. For a woman, this help often comes from those closest to her. This may be the first step on the road to recovery.

Resources

- Call Alcoholics Anonymous (A.A.) to find local meetings. You'll find A.A. listed in the telephone book.
- Call Women for Sobriety at 1–800–333–1606 to locate a group in your area.
- Contact your local hospital or alcohol treatment center for referral to a counselor.
- Ask for books, pamphlets and other reference materials at your library.

SUBSTANCE ABUSE CASE MANAGEMENT PROGRAM FOR OLDER ADULTS

Providing support, case management and education to older adults, their families and the community

Who will benefit?

- If you have ever thought that you may have an alcohol problem,
- If others have expressed concern about your prescription drug use,
- If you use drinking or drugs to overcome feelings of anxiety, loneliness, grief or boredom,
- If you are concerned about a loved one's drinking or drug use,
- If you make excuses for their behaviour,
- If you are arguing or fighting with someone about their drinking or drug use,

...then you may benefit from the Substance Abuse Case Management Program for Older Adults.

How we can help ...

This program seeks to assist and support the older adult by providing:

- Individual Assessment and Evaluation of alcohol and drug use

- Outreach and Intervention to help break through denial and decide the next steps for treatment
- Individual Counseling with trained case managers
- Referral to Older Adult AA Groups or Other Supportive Groups to move a person toward long-term sobriety; and to support those involved with a problem drinker or drug use through a variety of methods including wellness programming
- Coordination of Services with other agencies involved with the individual
- Family Consultation for education, support and personal growth
- Community Education for community groups regarding recognition, treatment and recovery of older adults with substance abuse issues

Why participate?

Recognition of the disease, treatment and recovery can be difficult due to the uncertainty of having to learn a different way of coping without abusing a substance. Support must be given to the older adult who is faced with many changes in their life. Through this program, the participant receives assistance in facing new challenges and the changes in their roles in life.

Our services are offered in the community/neighborhood where the older adult resides and resources are available to assist the program participant. The time and location of group, individual counseling or educational sessions are set up according to the needs of the program participants.

Call 513/721–4330 today to find out how the Substance Abuse Case Management Program for Older Adults can help you or your family.

Cincinnati Area Senior Services is committed to promoting the self sufficiency and self determination of older adults.

This is especially important for older adults who may be facing an accumulation of problems and have found alcoholism to be a concern in their lives.

Our mission

The mission of Cincinnati Area Senior Services is to provide services and activities that will reinforce self-sufficiency and self-determination for older adults; to intervene to protect older adults from abuse, neglect and exploitation; and to continually respond to the needs of the community and develop new models of service to meet those needs.

Appendix 2

CHAPTER 3. ASSESSMENT

Section 2: Tools

Michigan Alcoholism Screening Test – Geriatric Version (MAST-G)

The Regents of the University of Michigan, 1991

		Yes	No
1.	After drinking have you ever noticed an increase in your heart rate or beating in your chest?	☐	☐
2.	When talking with others, do you ever underestimate how much you actually drink?	☐	☐
3.	Does alcohol make you sleepy so that you often fall asleep in your chair?	☐	☐
4.	After a few drinks, have you sometimes not eaten or been able to skip a meal because you don't feel hungry?	☐	☐
5.	Does having a few drinks help decrease your shakiness or tremors?	☐	☐
6.	Does alcohol sometimes make it hard for you to remember parts of the day or night?	☐	☐
7.	Do you have rules for yourself that you won't drink before a certain time of day?	☐	☐
8.	Have you lost interest in hobbies or activities you used to enjoy?	☐	☐
9.	When you wake up in the morning do you have trouble remembering part of the night before?	☐	☐
10.	Does having a drink help you sleep?	☐	☐
11.	Do you hide your alcohol bottles from family members?	☐	☐
12.	After a social gathering, have you ever felt embarrassed because you drank too much?	☐	☐
13.	Have you ever been concerned that drinking might be harmful to your health?	☐	☐

14.	Do you like to end an evening with a night cap?	☐ ☐
15.	Did you find your drinking increased after someone close to you died?	☐ ☐
16.	In general, would you prefer to have a few drinks at home rather than go out to social events?	☐ ☐
17.	Are you drinking more now than in the past?	☐ ☐
18.	Do you usually take a drink to relax or calm your nerves?	☐ ☐
19.	Do you drink to take your mind off your problem?	☐ ☐
20.	Have you ever increased your drinking after experiencing a loss in your life?	☐ ☐
21.	Do you sometimes drive when you have had too much to drink?	☐ ☐
22.	Has a doctor or nurse ever said they were worried or concerned about your drinking?	☐ ☐
23.	Have you ever made rules to manage your drinking?	☐ ☐
24.	When you feel lonely does having a drink help?	☐ ☐

Scoring 5 or more 'yes' responses is indicative of an alcohol problem. For further information, contact Frederic Blow, PhD, at University of Michigan Alcohol Research Center, 400 E. Eisenhower Parkway, Suite A, Ann Arbor, MI 48104, 313/988-7952.

SCREENING TOOLS

Alcohol problems in older adults

C.A.G.E. QUESTIONS

C – Have you ever felt you should *cut* down on your drinking?

A – Have people *annoyed* you by criticizing your drinking?

G – Have you ever felt bad or *guilty* about drinking?

E – Have you ever taken a drink in the morning to get rid of a hangover or steady your nerves (*eye opener*)?

Two or more 'yes' answers indicate a problem.

From Frederic C. Blow, Ph.D. presentation at National Prevention Network Prevention Research Findings and Training Conference: Middle-Aged and Older Adults, March 22, 1991.

GIVING CLIENTS THE 'HEAT'

H – *How* do you use alcohol?

E – Have you ever thought you used to *Excess*?

A – Has *Anyone* else ever thought you used too much?

T – Have you ever had any *Trouble* resulting from your use?

The 'HEAT' is a device for rapid, routine screening for alcohol use problems. A positive response to any one of the four items is reason to obtain a fuller history. Any answer that raises suspicion on the part of the interviewer constitutes a positive response. For example, defensiveness, anger, embarrassment, or discomfort provoked in the client may indicate a problem.

Any other substance may be mentioned in place of alcohol.

Excerpt from 'Evaluating Alcohol Use in Elders:, by Mark Willenbring and William D. Spring, Jr., Aging, No. 361, 1990.

REFERENCES

Blondell, R. D. (1999) 'Alcohol and self neglect in the elderly.' *Journal of Elder Abuse and Neglect 11*, 2, 55–75.

Breeden-Hilton, L. (1998) Older Adult Recovery Centre, Chelsea Community Hospital.

Case Western Reserve University of Medicine (1996) *Alcoholism and Ageing Providers Joint Training*. CWRU: Division of Geriatric Medicine.

Department of Health (2000) *No Secrets: Guidance on Developing and Implementing Multi-Agency Policies and Procedures to Protect Vulnerable Adults from Abuse*. London: HMSO.

Fleming, M. F., Manwell, L. B., Barry, K. L., Adams, W. L. and Stauffacher, E. A. (1999) 'Brief physician advice for alcohol problems in older adults: a randomized community based trial.' *Journal of Family Practice 248*, 231–234.

Gloucestershire County Council (1995–2000) *Adults at Risk Unit Annual Reports*. Gloucester: Social Services Department.

Hayashida, M., Alterman, A. T., McLellan, A. T., O'Brian, C. P., Portill, J. J., Volpicelli, J. R., Raphaelson, A. H. and Hall, C. P. (1989) 'Comparative effectiveness of inpatient and outpatient detoxification of patients with mild-moderate alcohol withdrawal syndrome.' *New England Journal of Medicine 320*, 358–365.

Hurt, R., Higgins, J. A., Nelson, R. A., Morse, R. M. and Dickson, E. R. (1981) 'Nutritional status of alcoholics before and after admission to an alcoholism treatment unit.' *American Journal of Clinical Medicine 34*, 386–393.

Institute of Alcohol Studies (1997, 1999, 2000) *Alcohol and the Elderly: Factsheet*. http:www.ias.org.uk/factsheet/elderly/htm

Kafetz, K. and Cox, M. (1982) 'Alcohol excess and senile squalor syndrome.' *Journal of the American Geriatrics Society 30*, 706.

Mental Health Act 1983. London: HMSO.

National Assistance Act 1948. London: HMSO.

Office of Population Census Survey (1992) *Omnibus Survey*. London: OPCS.

Schonfield, L. and Dupree, L. W. (1991) 'Antecedents of drinking for early and late onset drinkers.' *Journal of Studies on Alcohol 52*, 587–592.

Simpson, M. (1993) *Social Work Responses to the Misuse of Alcohol – A Literature Review*. Scottish Office: Research Unit.

Vestal, R. E., McGuire, E. A., Tobin, J. D., Andres, R., Norris, A. H. and Mezey, E. (1977) 'Aging and ethanol metabolism.' *Clinical Pharmacology and Therapeutics 21*, 343–354.

(With thanks for encouragement, information and ideas to: Sondra Britton, Director of Social Services, Cincinnatti, Ohio and Mike Ward, Surrey Social Services.)

This article is not an academic work – it has come about as a result of shared concerns and experience and the feeling that there are many others out there struggling with the problem.

CHAPTER 14

THE ROLE OF CITIZEN ADVOCACY IN ADULT ABUSE WORK

JANE LAWSON

INTRODUCTION

This chapter will consider the contribution that might be made by the involvement of an independent citizen advocate in situations involving abuse of a vulnerable adult. There are four main parts to the chapter:

1. Explanations of the terms 'vulnerable adult', 'abuse' and 'citizen advocate' are used to demonstrate how the role of citizen advocate might be well-suited to involvement in situations of abuse.

2. Case examples are used to highlight this point.

3. Consideration is given to the need for one-to-one longer-term work with victims of abuse and the way in which citizen advocacy lends itself well to making a contribution in this aspect of the work.

4. The potential role of citizen advocacy within some key aspects of work with victims of abuse is explored.

ABUSE OF VULNERABLE ADULTS: DEFINITIONS AND THEMES

What is the abuse of a vulnerable adult? What are the underlying themes in situations of abuse? A 'vulnerable adult' is:

> ...a person aged 18 or over...who is in need of community care services by reason of mental or other disability, age or illness; and who is or may be unable to take care of him or her-

self, or unable to protect him or herself against significant harm or exploitation. (DOH 2000, paras 2.2–2.3)

Abuse is also defined as follows:

> ...abuse may consist of a single act or repeated acts. It may be an act of neglect or an omission to act, or it may occur when a vulnerable person is persuaded to enter into a financial or sexual transaction to which he or she has not consented or cannot consent. Abuse can occur in any relationship and may result in significant harm to, or exploitation of, the person subjected to it. (DOH 2000, para. 2.6)

A further definition of abuse is offered by the Centre for Policy on Ageing (1996):

> Abuse is the harming of another individual usually by some-one who is in a position of power, trust or authority over that individual. The harm may be physical, psychological or emotional or it may be directed at exploiting the vulnerability of the victim in more subtle ways... Abuse may happen as a 'one-off' occurrence or it may become a regular feature of a relationship. Other people may be unaware that it is happening and for this reason it may be difficult to detect. (Centre for Policy on Ageing 1996, p.105–106)

The words 'power' and 'trust' are significant within this definition. The perpetrator is often in a position of power over the victim and is often trusted by them. Bright (1995) from Counsel and Care pursues this theme. He states: 'When the question is posed why unacceptable situations are allowed to develop, a number of words consistently appear for the defence – loyalty, fear and power are prominent among these...' (p.5). The same document concludes: 'For reasons associated with culture, power and ignorance, all of those affected by abuse find difficulty in expressing their concerns or in seeking appropriate help' (p.23).

Finally, in looking at definitions and themes within abuse situations, Clough (1988) explores the reasons why residents who are abused in care homes keep quiet. Summarising the discussion he presents, among the reasons residents keep quiet:

- they are vulnerable and need the services provided
- they have to live with the consequences if they complain
- they despair (thinking no-one will listen)

- they do not know their rights
- they fear threats
- they have feelings of ambivalence towards abusers
- residents think they will be blamed
- personal levels of confidence and self-esteem are low.

Although both Bright and Clough refer to abuse of vulnerable adults in care homes, it is clear that often the same themes and issues are present in a person's own home.

ONE-TO-ONE LONGER-TERM WORK WITH VICTIMS OF ABUSE

Some weight has been given to definitions of abuse in this discussion as the themes running through them are so pertinent in looking at the role of citizen advocacy. Themes such as consent and capacity, persuasion and power, trust, subtlety, loyalty, ignorance of remedies, despair, fear, lack of confidence/self-esteem emerge in the above definitions and discussions on abuse.

These themes reflect deeply held feelings, attitudes and self-perceptions in the abused that it will be difficult to influence. For this reason, longer-term intervention is likely to be required. Any expectation of a fast-track 'rescuing' of victims is usually unrealistic (illustrated by Nahmiash 1999).

Nahmiash talks about the importance of verbalization where:

> The facilitator encourages the person to tell their story, listening actively, asking critical questions and encouraging a process of self-reflection in the person so that the older person can weigh the pros and cons of their situation...it may take a long time for abused persons to be able to express these feelings and that certainly only happens when they are ready to share with the facilitator and when they feel they can trust them enough to confide in them. (Nahmiash 1999, pp.309–310)

The aim of this verbalization she says is that the abused individual will gain:

> ...insight and awareness about the abusive situation and is able to be critical about why s/he is in the powerlessness process and to begin to be able to move out of it. (p.305)

The kind of empowering intervention with abuse victims outlined by Nahmiash can take years rather than days or weeks.

Sometimes protocols set up by statutory agencies begin to run and investigations take place, often within a relatively short time-span (usually adult abuse procedures expect the initial investigation to be completed within 10–15 days). There is very little reference to the feelings and attitude of the victim. It is essential, however, for those feelings to be addressed before any effective action can be taken and indeed before the victim will disclose that abuse is taking place.

Often in situations of abuse the abuser is someone to whom the abused feels some degree of loyalty and who has power over them. There are often long-standing relationships and deep-seated emotions involved which prevent the vulnerable adult from feeling able to take action.

CASE STUDY I

Vera (78) lives with her son. He provides company and some feeling of personal security for her. However, every Friday night after a trip to the pub he comes home and both shouts at and hits Vera. She does not want to do anything about this because, she says, no one else will look after her if her son does not and she should therefore be grateful to him. She is, after all, physically frail due to arthritis and walks unsteadily with the help of a zimmer frame. The risk of falls is a great anxiety to her and her son's presence is therefore very reassuring.

In this example, procedures can be followed and an investigation may elicit the information in this case study. However, professionals will simply be left monitoring the situation if Vera decides that she wishes her son to remain in her house and she does not wish to press charges. Her attitude and feelings are unlikely to change without some longer-term work with Vera, along the lines suggested in Nahmiash's research. Indeed, Vera may ultimately decide to live with the risk because, for her, the positive aspects of her son's presence at home outweigh the risk he poses. Vera should be allowed time to assess the situation for herself, with support, and weigh up the positives and negatives in order to come to a conclusion.

Vera's situation illustrates the need for individuals to be empowered by someone who will facilitate access to information about all of the options and who will discuss these with the individual and ensure that the level of risk is fully understood. The role of advocate is well suited to involvement in such a situation. Many professionals will be much more inclined to rescue someone like Vera than to empower her to make the best decision *for herself.* This may be because they are 'constrained' by procedures that give definitive timescales for investigations or it may be because of their own need to give positive help in their own terms or it may be about conflicting expectations of professionals to both empower and to 'keep safe'.

This inclination to 'rescue' individuals very quickly from situations of abuse needs to be carefully analysed, questioned and often rejected in favour of a much more empowering approach, allowing the individual to arrive at their own conclusion and to be supported in their decision.

Stevenson and Allsop (1995), in their research on social workers' perceptions of risk in child protection, examine this imbalance in interventions where statutory 'systems' are not balanced by the nurturing of trust in relationships between professionals and vulnerable individuals. They state:

> The child protection system…is par excellence a system of low trust, organised around statutory and, if necessary, coercive intervention in families. What seems to us to cause the complexities for you is the following contradiction: that in order for this low trust system to function well, in terms of obtaining good information as well as effective interventions to reduce risk, it needs its front line operatives to cultivate relationships of high trust with their clients. How can such relationships be cultivated in the context of a coercive low-trust system? Nevertheless, some of the work you described with parents… [was] clearly mostly embedded within relationships which at least aimed to be facilitating and enabling and were often, as described, highly therapeutic. Such relationships are by definition high-trust and involve the mutual desire of both parties to bring about change. (p.63)

In Vera's situation, without such facilitative, enabling and empowering intervention, the very process of the investigation by powerful professionals may only serve to compound Vera's general feeling of powerlessness and render her unable to take action in part because of her feelings of inadequacy and hopelessness.

Pritchard (2000), in her recent study of the needs of older women who have been victims of abuse, stated that:

> One of the most important findings of this project is that victims have a voice – that they know and can verbalise their needs. Thus, workers *must* communicate with and engage older people in their assessment to a greater extent, so that needs can be more accurately identified and appropriate services provided. (Pritchard 2000, p.8)

It is essential that the individuality of each situation and victim is addressed and worked through *alongside* that victim, sometimes over a longer period of time, so that long-term solutions can come from within the individual and they will believe in and be committed to a course of action that they own and that becomes much more likely to succeed, both in terms of the safety and emotional integrity of the individual.

TASKS WITHIN AN EMPOWERING PARTNERSHIP WITH VICTIMS

If individuals are to be empowered they will need someone to work alongside and help them to:

- examine their initial reactions to the situation
- explore the possibilities
- find out information about alternatives
- understand the risks in their situation and the likely effects on them
- retain some sense of self-worth
- explore how they feel about themselves and their situation
- gain support if and when they take action or change the situation
- deal with the changes in their new situation.

THE ROLE OF THE CITIZEN ADVOCATE

These tasks fit well within the role of the citizen advocate:

> Citizen advocacy [is] a one-to-one ongoing partnership be-
> tween a trained volunteer citizen advocate and a person who
> is not in a strong position to exercise his or her rights and is at
> risk of being mistreated or excluded. The citizen advocate
> should be free of conflicts of interest with those providing the
> services to their partner and should represent the interests of
> their partner as if they were their own. (Dunning 1995, p.11)

In other descriptions of the role:

> Vulnerable and marginalised individuals…are linked to ordi-
> nary members of the community…on a one-to-one basis.
> They enter into a relationship with someone who will listen
> to their point of view, respect their wishes and stand with
> them to defend their rights… (Wertheimer 1998, p.7)

> The citizen advocate must constantly strive to define situa-
> tions from their partner's perspective… (Wertheimer 1998,
> p.18)

A citizen advocacy partnership is of one ordinary citizen with
another. The citizen advocate may not have specific expertise or
knowledge about the situations in which vulnerable adults find
themselves. They agree, however, to enter into a partnership in

---

DEFINITION OF THE CITIZEN ADVOCACY ROLE

Citizen advocacy:

- is a process towards empowerment
- is responsive to the expressed wishes and needs of the individual
- aims to enable individuals to exert greater influence in their lives, learn new skills and enhance self-esteem
- aims to ensure that the partner's views are listened to and taken seriously
- is an enabling and equitable partnership
- is independent and confidential.

(Lawson and Steel 2000, p.3)

which together they can explore the situation and the partner can be supported in finding alternative courses of action. The role is an enabling and empowering one, rather than advice-giving, benevolent or rescuing. The point of view of the vulnerable adult (the partner) is listened to and respected. The partner's view of the situation is the starting point.

OTHER ASPECTS OF THE CITIZEN ADVOCACY ROLE

The citizen advocacy role includes:

- lending a voice
- arming with information
- enabling informed choice
- offering support
- assisting liaison with significant agencies and people
- working alongside the partner on specific issues and goals.

(Lawson and Steel 2000, p.3)

Picking up on some terms from Clough's observations about why victims of abuse keep quiet – fear of the consequences of taking action; thinking that no one will listen, not knowing their rights; low personal levels of confidence and self-esteem – it becomes apparent that the role of citizen advocate as outlined above has the potential to make a significant contribution to the well-being of the individual.

The role of the advocate in Josie's situation (see case study on facing page) is invaluable. Although each step in the process of working with Josie is small, the issues she is working on with her advocate are significant and are likely to reap long-term benefits.

The advocate is working with Josie to:

- explore how she has come to be in this situation
- explore other interests and roles Josie might pursue now and in the future (when her father dies if she has not looked at the alternatives and made some personal choices, she may just end up caring for her sister in the same way that she became the main carer for her father)

CASE STUDY I

Josie (52) has had bouts of clinical depression over the past ten years. She has very low self-esteem and very little self-confidence. She has always lived in the north of England with her family. However, in June her mother died. She now lives with her father (who has multiple physical disabilities) and her sister. Until her death, Josie's mother had held the family together – paying bills, shopping, cleaning, cooking, caring for Josie's father and attending to the demands of her sister. Since her mother's death, Josie has automatically tried to assume her mother's role. Her sister is a loner, has few social skills and is often aggressive towards her. She shouts at her a great deal and has hit out at her on several occasions. Josie feels that she will just have to put up with this, just as she feels that there is no alternative but to assume the roles her mother fulfilled. There is a degree of concern for Josie amongst statutory agencies and an advocate has been asked to work with her.

- help confirm that Josie is a person in her own right and that she does not have to be defined by those around her and the roles she performs with them
- look at strategies for reducing the risks from her sister (by identifying the signs that an aggressive outburst is imminent and then removing herself from the situation until it has passed)
- enhance her ability to make choices
- explore her skills and strengths
- build her confidence and self-esteem.

The advocate works with Josie on issues such as making choices and building self-confidence and self-esteem via engaging together in activities that ensure that Josie begins to make choices and sees new possibilities for activities and interests opening up in her life. A key focus in this work picks up on the theme outlined by Clough that low levels of confidence and self-esteem are creating a barrier to Josie reassessing her situation, taking action, and moving on.

The advocacy partnership with Josie is of a long-term nature, exploring the general issues in Josie's life that inhibit her ability to take action to change things. In addition, the advocacy partnership explores more specifically how Josie might manage the abusive situation, and a partnership of trust is created which is likely to mean that, should the abuse worsen, Josie will confide in her advocate.

This partnership is likely to last at least two years and it is not unusual for advocacy partnerships to continue for substantially longer than this. By working on the basic issues of self-confidence and self-esteem, the advocate opens up the possibility for Josie to become capable of confronting the issue of the abuse. It is unlikely that a social worker/care manager[1] would be able to carry out this level of work in view of time constraints and work priorities and yet it is crucial to progress in Josie's situation.

There is at times a reluctance on the part of statutory agencies to afford voluntary sector workers such as advocates a formal role in protection plans drawn up at case conferences for the protection of vulnerable adults by a multi-agency team. In Josie's situation the advocate should certainly be involved at case conference stage to support Josie and then (with Josie's permission and knowledge) continue formal involvement in the monitoring and review process.

THE SIGNIFICANCE OF THE INDEPENDENCE OF ADVOCATES

One of the identifying features of citizen advocacy is its independence from statutory agencies and service providers. This is particularly important in situations such as the one outlined below in Case Study 2 where the perpetrator of abuse is a professional/paid worker.

---

1   In social services departments around the UK different job titles persist for the same role. The term 'social worker/care manager' is used in this chapter for the role of a worker who may assess and then work in the long term with a service user.

CASE STUDY 2

Miss Chester (82) lives alone. She is bed-bound and has few visitors and no surviving relatives. She owns a beach hut on the east coast of England. Her social worker gains her trust and learns of the beach hut. She makes an arrangement with Miss Chester to rent the beach hut. After 12 months no rent has been paid to Miss Chester. An independent citizen advocate becomes involved at the request of a neighbour. The advocate discusses the situation with Miss Chester and outlines possible courses of action. Together they balance the need of Miss Chester not to experience too much stress in attempting to claim money owing to her and to bring the social worker to justice. The advocate supports Miss Chester in claiming through the Small Claims Court and in pursuing a complaint with the Social Services Department. The debt is repaid in instalments.

KEY PRACTICE ISSUES AND ADVOCACY INVOLVEMENT

Some situations of abuse pose a more visible and immediate risk but still, without the permission of the vulnerable adult, professionals can be powerless in taking action. Case study 3 draws out some key issues in abuse situations that can begin to be addressed with the support of citizen advocacy.

CASE STUDY 3

Anna is 87 years old, mentally capable but physically frail. She lives in her own home with a son, Jim, and has a home carer who visits. The carer has, over a period of time, seen bruising to Anna's face and arms and notices that, when she calls one Saturday morning to help her get up and dress, Anna appears depressed. The carer has also noticed that Anna is having problems paying her bills and that there is very little food in the house. These concerns have been reported to the care manager who visits. Anna eventually divulges that her son is often very rough with her after his regular Friday night session at the pub. He sometimes punches her and shakes her. His drinking leaves him short of money and so, when he collects the pension on Anna's behalf, he keeps most of it. Anna has been willing to talk about this with the home carer and care manager but is adamant that she wishes no action to be taken. She would, she says, be silly to do anything about it, because she relies on her son both for company and for security in case she falls. The severity of the abuse means that there are very real fears that this may end in tragedy.

In helping Anna, professionals are faced with responsibilities both to empower and to protect. This dual responsibility is expressed clearly in *No Secrets*:

> ...agencies should adhere to the following guiding principles...
>
> **(ii) actively promote** the empowerment and well-being of vulnerable adults through the services they provide;
>
> **(iii) act in a way that supports the rights of the individual** to lead an independent life based on self-determination and personal choice; ...
>
> **(v) recognise that the right to self-determination can involve risk** and ensure that such risk is recognised and understood by all concerned and minimised wherever possible (there should be an open discussion between the individual and the agencies about the risks involved to him or her);
>
> **(vi) ensure the safety of vulnerable adults...**
>
> (DOH 2000, para. 4.3)

A citizen advocate can have a significant and positive contribution to make with these issues. As has been illustrated earlier, a fundamental principle of advocacy is that individuals should feel empowered and should actively take part in changing the situations in which they find themselves. Smith (1994) puts this in terms of 'helping clients to win through to the exercise of power in their own right' (p.46). There are likely to be substantial benefits in terms of the effectiveness of intervention in Anna's situation if she is empowered within it. A more passive role will nurture feelings of dependency, the very feelings that make Anna think that she cannot cope without her son. The involvement of an advocate can emphasise to Anna what she can do to change her situation. An advocate can help her re-evaluate whether she wants to take other action.

There is strong evidence to suggest that when individuals are fully involved in their own care planning and assessment they have a greater commitment to act on its outcomes and recommendations. The growth of Family Group Conferences, which originated in New Zealand and have now developed in this country, where whole families and networks are involved in child protection plans, provide evidence of this (Marsh 1998).

In Anna's situation other key issues will be:

- the need for careful assessment of risk
- the assessment of Anna's capacity to make decisions
- decisions about confidentiality.

The ongoing assessment of the level of risk to Anna will be crucial to the protection plan. Again, an advocate can contribute: developing a partnership of trust, enabling Anna to share information about the risk she is running, and allowing discussion so that Anna can fully understand the level of risk. As the situation develops, Anna can make an informed choice as to whether she continues to run that risk.

An advocate may also be necessary in the assessment of Anna's capacity to make decisions. The vulnerable person's wishes are considered critical in deciding on a course of action. But it can be difficult for statutory agencies to stop their 'duty to protect' from influencing their decision about a person's level of capacity. The advocate's role here will be to make sure that, wherever possible, vulnerable adults have a voice in decisions affecting them. They can assist too in ensuring that no one exerts undue pressure on the individual to pursue a particular course of action. Where an individual lacks capacity, there can be a key role for an advocate in ensuring that decisions are in the individual's best interests.

The assessment of a person's best interests requires some understanding of how similar situations might have been approached in the past. Familiarity with the individual helps determine how they feel about their situation. The nature of the advocacy relationship lends itself well to this.

Making Decisions (Lord Chancellor's Department 1999) also gives guidance on deciding what is in a person's best interests. It proposes that the following list of factors be considered in making an assessment of the best interests of a person without capacity:

- the ascertainable past and present wishes and feelings of the person concerned and the factors the person would consider if able to do so
- the need to permit and encourage the person to participate or improve his or her ability to participate as fully as

possible in anything done for and any decision affecting him or her

- the views of other people who it is appropriate and practical to consult about the person's wishes and feelings and what would be in his or her best interests
- whether the purpose for which any action or decision is required can be as effectively achieved in a manner less restrictive of the person's freedom of action.

(Lord Chancellor's Department 1999, p.9)

With time to get to know the individual and their circumstances, and with the emphasis on empowerment and participation, this is a very relevant role for advocates. Care managers and other professionals are often unable to fulfil this role due to competing pressures. The involvement of advocates is therefore likely to expand considerably in this area of work.

Finally, there is often a positive role for advocates around the issue of confidentiality. Advocates can help to ensure that this much misunderstood issue is discussed openly with the service user. An advocate can also help the individual to understand and assess the pros and cons of information being shared. In Anna's situation, if the care manager suggests to Anna that it might be a good idea to let the police know about Jim's behaviour, then the advocate can help Anna to weigh up what might be achieved by doing this, compared with the risk to her relationship with her son.

The Department of Health (2000) states:

> Principles of confidentiality designed to safeguard and promote the interests of service users and patients should not be confused with those designed to protect the management interests of an organisation. These have legitimate roles but must never be allowed to conflict with the interests of service users and patients. (para. 5.8)

Clearly the independent nature of citizen advocacy allows the citizen advocate to offer support in this area, free from such conflict of interest.

If statutory agencies are reluctant to share information with advocates, the issue of confidentiality can of course also impact upon the extent to which advocacy can be effective. The sharing of information is an issue which advocacy projects must confront with statutory agencies when advocacy partnerships are first established. Advocates and those they are supporting need to take the lead with statutory agencies on this issue as too often voluntary organizations can be seen as outsiders with whom information is not shared. This decision as to whether information about the service user is shared with the advocate is rightfully the decision of the vulnerable adult.

SUMMARY OF KEY ROLES FOR ADVOCATES

Through the case studies that have been outlined in this chapter a number of key roles have been identified for advocates working with victims of abuse. These are summarized in the list below.

KEY ROLES FOR ADVOCATES

- Where abuse is suspected but not proven, an advocate might be introduced to establish a relationship of trust so that the suspected victim might feel able to confide in the advocate.
- The advocate might act as a sounding-board for the vulnerable adult to consider whether they should continue to accept the abuse being suffered.
- The advocate might help the victim to communicate what is happening to a relevant professional in order to gain support.
- The advocate might ensure that professionals who are appraised of the situation by the victim listen to the victim's wishes as to how best to proceed at any particular time and engage the victim fully in the assessment.
- The advocate will facilitate access to information about all of the potential options and resources available in a particular situation.
- The advocate will discuss the level of risk involved with the vulnerable adult and ensure that this will be understood and re-evaluated.
- The advocate will explore with the victim issues such as self-esteem, self-confidence, ability to make choices, and seek to enhance these qualities in that individual.
- The advocate will be an independent person. This is especially important where abuse by a professional or paid worker is an issue.

- The advocate will ensure that issues of confidentiality are considered carefully by professionals.
- The advocate will ensure that the vulnerable adult's capacity to make decisions is properly assessed and that any actions taken are in that person's best interests.
- The advocate will support the victim of abuse in participating in case conferences and give support before and after these meetings.
- The advocate will ensure that careful consideration is given to how and where a victim is interviewed during an investigation so that anxiety and trauma are minimized and the victim's safety is not jeopardized.

CONCLUSIONS

Situations of abuse of vulnerable adults do not often lend themselves to quick solutions. In many cases work goes on over years to help the vulnerable adult assess and keep on reassessing their situation and the level of risk. Often, statutory agencies instigate a procedure to investigate a situation of abuse and this can run much too quickly to enable a victim of abuse to become personally engaged in addressing all of the very complex issues involved for them. Citizen advocates can be involved over the longer term, empowering the victim to find their own solutions and to come to terms with their situation. Sometimes it is necessary for statutory agencies to take urgent action in the short term. In many situations, however, a longer-term strategy of working alongside the victim in gaining their commitment to a course of action which, *for them*, will be the most beneficial approach will be most effective.

There is then much potential for a valuable contribution by advocates in situations of abuse. It is, however, often not easy for statutory agencies to locate an advocacy service when and where they need it. Help in locating advocacy projects might be forthcoming through local agencies such as: a Council of Community Service; a Citizens' Advice Bureau; or a local branch of Age Concern. Nationally, Citizen Advocacy Information and Training (CAIT – see references) can help to locate a local scheme.

Provision of advocacy projects across the country is inconsistent and in many areas is non-existent for certain user-groups. Many are funded to operate only part time. There is a strong argument for greater and more consistent long-term financial support of advocacy projects nationally.

REFERENCES

Bright, L. (1995) *Care Betrayed – A Discussion of the Issues Which Give Rise to Abuse in Homes*. London: Counsel and Care.

Centre for Policy on Ageing (1996) *A Better Home Life – A Code of Practice for Residential and Nursing Home Care*. Report of an advisory group convened by the Centre for Policy on Ageing, chaired by Kina, Lady Avebury. London: Centre for Policy on Ageing.

Clough, R. (1988) 'Scandals in Residential Centres.' Unpublished report to the Wagner Committee.

Department of Health (2000) *No Secrets: Guidance on Developing and Implementing Multi-Agency Policies and Procedures to Protect Vulnerable Adults from Abuse*. London: HMSO.

Dunning, A. (1995) *Citizen Advocacy with Older People*. London: Centre for Policy on Ageing.

Lawson, J. and Steel, R. (2000) *Advocacy Information Pack*. Winchester: Winchester District Advocacy and Outreach Advocacy Projects.

Lord Chancellor's Department (1999) *Making Decisions: The Government's Proposals for Making Decisions on Behalf of Mentally Incapacitated Adults*. Cm 4465. London: The Stationery Office.

Marsh, P. (1998) *Family Group Conferences in Child Welfare*. Oxford: Blackwell Science.

Nahmiash, D. (1999) 'From Powerlessness to Empowerment.' In J. Pritchard (ed) *Elder Abuse Work: Best Practice in Britain and Canada*. London and Philadelphia: Jessica Kingsley Publishers.

Pritchard, J. (2000) *The Needs of Older Women: Services for Victims of Elder Abuse and Other Abuse*. Bristol: Policy Press.

Smith, J. (1994) 'Power, Older People and Being Cared For.' In D. Hobman, R. Hollingbery, R. Means, R. Lart, and J. Smith (eds) *More Power to Our Elders: Promoting Empowerment for Older People*. London: Counsel and Care.

Stevenson, O. and Allsop, M. (1995) 'Social Workers' Perceptions of Risk in Child Protection.' Discussion paper from an ESRC-funded research project, University of Nottingham.

Wertheimer, A. (1998) *Citizen Advocacy: A Powerful Partnership*. A handbook on setting up and running citizen advocacy schemes. London: Citizen Advocacy Information and Training (CAIT)[2].

---

2   CAIT, Unit 164, Lee Valley Technopark, Ashley Road, London N17 9LN. Tel: 020 8880 4545/4546.
cait@leevalley.co.uk www.leevalley.co.uk/cait

THE CONTRIBUTORS

Janice Griffin has been an Inspection and Registration Officer within Sheffield City Council since 1991. She began her nursing career in the late 1960s. She qualified as a general nurse in the early 1970s and spent most of the next ten years as a district nurse. She joined Sheffield and Family Community Services Department in 1982 as deputy manager of a residential care home for 43 older people. Up to 1991 she held various management posts within the same social services department.

Dr Iona Heath MA, Bchir, MRCP, FRCGP, CBE has been Principal in general practice at the Caversham Group Practice in Kentish Town in the London Borough of Camden since 1977, general practice trainer since 1983 and nationally elected member of the Council of the Royal College of General Practitioners since 1989. She has been chairman of the Health Inequalities Group of the Royal College of General Practitioners since 1997 and chairman of the Committee on Medical Ethics of the Royal College of General Practitioners since 1998. She is the author of the booklet *Domestic Violence: The General Practitioner's Role* for the Royal College of General Practitioners, 1998.

Adrian Hughes is a qualified social worker and has worked in the public sector for over 20 years. He is currently employed by the Isle of Wight Council as the manager of the Joint Registration and Inspection Unit and is the Vice Chair (England) of the National Association of Registration Officers, the professional body for staff involved in statutory regulation. He is particularly interested in work around abuse and abusive regimes and settings, and considers that the role of the regulator can work in partnership and harmony with other stakeholders to establish patterns of working, policies and procedures to develop a culture which reduces the likelihood of abusive practice becoming established.

Ruth Ingram is the Adult Protection Co-ordinator in Leeds and is Chair of the Violence and Abuse Task Group of the Leeds Community Safety Partnership. Amongst other jobs she has previously worked at Leeds Inter-Agency Project (Women experiencing violence from men they know), developing good practice guidelines and training programmes with health and social service organizations. She has also worked in a hostel for young women fleeing sexual abuse and has led study and trekking tours in Bolivia and Peru.

Steve Kirkpatrick has 25 years' service with Thames Valley Police. He is currently working as Detective Inspector in the Major Crime Unit, Maidenhead. Between 1992 and 1998, as manager with the Family Protection Unit, Steve worked in partnership with the multi-agencies, directed child abuse investigations, historic abuse investigations and the maintenance of an effective response to dealing with adult victims of serious sexual assault, across Berkshire and Buckinghamshire. He also dealt with the investigations into suspicious deaths of babies. In addition, Steve was on the Berkshire working group that produced the Inter-Agency Procedures and Guidelines in January 1997.

Susan Kurrle is a staff specialist geriatrician at Hornsby Ku-ring-gai Hospital in northern Sydney where she is Director of the Rehabilitation and Aged Care Service. She works with older people both in the hospital setting and in the community. She has had a long interest in elder abuse and has researched the issue extensively in the Australian Aged Care setting. She is a professional member of the Guardianship Tribunal of New South Wales and has been a board member of the Alzheimers Association for four years, reflecting her involvement in dementia research and practice.

Jane Lawson is a qualified social worker with over ten years' practice experience in a number of local authority social services departments, mainly in the West Midlands. She currently works as Advocacy Project Co-ordinator for Winchester Area Community Action as well as undertaking freelance training in the areas of risk and of abuse of vulnerable adults. She has an interest in issues relating to abuse of vulnerable adults, having taken the lead with Hampshire County Council Social Services Department in developing adult abuse policies and policy on risk assessment and risk management. She is on the executive committee of the national organization Practitioner Alliance Against Abuse of Vulnerable Adults (PAVA).

Mike Linnett CQSW, MSR1 has been in social work service delivery since 1965. He has previously worked as a generic social worker and team manager and as an Adult Services Team Manager. He has been a long-standing approved social worker since 1973. He also ran a learning disabilities/challenging behaviour unit in the USA. He set up the Gloucestershire Adults at Risk Unit (now Adult Protection Services) and is currently the Adult Protection Co-ordinator.

Marilyn Mornington is currently District Judge, Birkenhead District Registry (LLb Sheffield). Harmsworth and Blackstone Scholar Middle Temple, Holt Shipping Scholar. She was a Barrister in Liverpool 1976–94 specializing in Family Law and became First Barrister District Judge at the age of 40. She is Chair of the Northern Circuit Domestic Violence Group; Chair of the Wirral Domestic Violence Forum; Patron of the Wirral Children and Womens' Refuge; Chair of Kids in Need and Distress; Member of Project Adhikar and lecturer and author on family law and in particular domestic violence. She is Trustee of 'missdorothy.com' and 'Dosh for Kids' and a former member of Ashworth Special Hospital Racial Discrimination Team.

Jacki Pritchard BA (Hons), MA, CQSW is a qualified social worker, who had 13 years' experience as a social worker and as a manager in both fieldwork and hospital settings. She currently works as an independent trainer, consultant and researcher focusing on abuse, risk and violence. She has written widely on the subject of adult abuse but is currently focusing on male victims of abuse and running Beyond Existing, Support Groups for Older People Who Have Been Abused.

Tony Ryan has worked in the mental health field since 1982, spending 10 years as a mental health nurse in the NHS before working for the mental health charity Turning Point for 8 years, where he developed a range of services for people with serious mental health or alcohol problems. He now works at the North West Mental Health Development Centre, where his main area of interest covers service development relating to people with severe and enduring mental health needs. His research interests have included the risk management strategies of mental health service users and informal carers and he completed his PhD in this area at Lancaster University. Tony has written considerably in these areas and edited the book *Managing Crisis and Risk in Mental Health Nursing* (1999).

Subject Index

Name Index